Sharing in God's Presence

Sharing in God's Presence

Theology for Spiritual Renewal

Roy D. Kindelberger II

WIPF & STOCK · Eugene, Oregon

SHARING IN GOD'S PRESENCE
Theology for Spiritual Renewal

Copyright © 2018 Roy D. Kindelberger II. All rights reserved. Except for brief quotations in critical publications or reviews, no part of this book may be reproduced in any manner without prior written permission from the publisher. Write: Permissions, Wipf and Stock Publishers, 199 W. 8th Ave., Suite 3, Eugene, OR 97401.

Wipf & Stock
An Imprint of Wipf and Stock Publishers
199 W. 8th Ave., Suite 3
Eugene, OR 97401

www.wipfandstock.com

PAPERBACK ISBN: 978-1-5326-3890-9
HARDCOVER ISBN: 978-1-5326-3891-6
EBOOK ISBN: 978-1-5326-3892-3

Manufactured in the U.S.A.   08/14/18

for my mom and dad

Contents

Copyright Notices | xi
Acknowledgments | xiii

Introduction: God Shares His Heart | 1

1 **Presence: God Shares His World** | 9
    God Accepts the Risk | 10
    God is Perfect Change | 13
    God Experiences Time | 16
    God Suffers Too | 19
    God Shares His Presence | 21
    Conclusion | 24

2 **Covenant: God Shares Himself** | 26
    God's Presence with Noah | 27
    God's Presence with Abram | 28
    God's Presence with Moses | 31
    God's Presence with David | 35
    God's Presence within the Heart | 37
    Conclusion | 41

3 **Salvation: God Shares His Son** | 42
    Jesus Overcame Sin and Death | 43
    God's Presence at the Cross | 46
    God Forgives Our Sins | 51
    Ritual of Entrance: Water Baptism | 54
    Ceremony of Presence: The Lord's Supper | 57
    Conclusion | 60

4   **Pentecost: God Shares His Spirit** | 62
    Introducing a Relational Kingdom | 63
    Launching His Kingdom: Spirit Baptism | 67
    Leading His Kingdom: Messiah's Presence | 70
    Manifesting His Kingdom: Word and Wonders | 76
    Conclusion | 79

5   **Prayer: God Shares His Plans** | 81
    The Best Possible Future | 82
    The Openness of Prayer | 84
    God Prays Too | 87
    God's Repentance | 91
    Faith and Prayer | 93
    Conclusion | 96

6   **Gifts: God Shares His Work (Part One)** | 97
    Introducing the Charismata | 98
    God Shares Prophecy | 100
    God Shares Languages | 109
    Conclusion | 113

7   **Gifts: God Shares His Work (Part Two)** | 115
    God's Dynamic Presence | 116
    God Shares Miracles | 118
    God Shares Exorcism | 120
    God Shares Healing | 121
    God Shares Discernment | 123
    God Shares Faith | 124
    God Shares Other Gifts | 125
    Conclusion | 127

8   **Ministry: God Shares His Power** | 129
    Introducing the Fivefold Ministry | 130
    God Shares Apostolic Ministry | 132
    God Shares Prophetic Ministry | 135
    God Shares Evangelistic Ministry | 137
    God Shares Pastoral/Teaching Ministry | 138
    Excelling in Fulltime Ministry | 142
    Conclusion | 147

9   **Revival: God Shares His Glory | 148**
    Jesus Reveals God | 149
    Jesus Reveals God's Presence | 152
    Jesus Sends His Presence | 154
    Jesus Sends Revival | 158
    Conclusion | 166

Bibliography | 169

Copyright Notices

All Scripture quotations, unless otherwise indicated, are taken from the Holy Bible, New International Version®, NIV®. Copyright ©1973, 1978, 1984, 2011 by Biblica, Inc.™ Used by permission of Zondervan. All rights reserved worldwide. www.zondervan.com

The "NIV" and "New International Version" are trademarks registered in the United States Patent and Trademark Office by Biblica, Inc.™

Scripture quotations marked NLT are taken from the Holy Bible, New Living Translation, copyright ©1996, 2004, 2007, 2013, 2015 by Tyndale House Foundation. Used by permission of Tyndale House Publishers, Inc., Carol Stream, Illinois 60188. All rights reserved.

Scripture quotations marked ESV are taken from the ESV® Bible (The Holy Bible, English Standard Version®), copyright © 2001 by Crossway, a publishing ministry of Good News Publishers. Used by permission. All rights reserved

Scripture quotations marked NASB are taken from the New American Standard Bible® (NASB), Copyright © 1960, 1962, 1963, 1968, 1971, 1972, 1973, 1975, 1977, 1995 by The Lockman Foundation. Used by permission. www.Lockman.org

Scripture quotations marked KJV are taken from the King James Version, public domain.

Scripture quotations marked NET are taken from the NET Bible® copyright ©1996–2016 by Biblical Studies Press, L.L.C. http://netbible.org All rights reserved. Scripture quoted by permission.

Scripture quotations marked NRSV are taken from the New Revised Standard Version Bible, copyright 1989, Division of Christian Education of the National Council of the Churches of Christ in the United States of America. Used by permission. All rights reserved.

Acknowledgments

I AM SO GRATEFUL for the ministries of the many pastors and theologians that I have come in contact with over the years. In the beginning of my Christian walk, I was influenced most profoundly by the preaching of pastors David Wilkerson and Carter Conlon of Times Square Church and especially by the writings of Oswald Chambers. I am indebted to Mount Zion School of Ministry for teaching me the value of prayer and opening my eyes to the beautiful reality of intimacy with Jesus Christ.

My wife has given me her endless support, grace, and kindness, and I find it impossible to imagine that the world could contain anyone sweeter or more understanding than she is. Your love, my dear, is matchless! I must also give thanks to God for the parents that he's blessed me with, Roy and Kris, who continue to be my anchor and lighthouse in this turbulent world.

Most importantly, but never quite adequately enough, thanks be to God—Father, Son, and Holy Spirit—for sharing the depths of your presence with us. Thank you, my Lord, for showing us what it means to love.

Introduction: God Shares His Heart

SHARING IN GOD'S PRESENCE means far more than "getting saved" or experiencing God's blessing in our lives. The moment we turn to God, his presence becomes a very personal part of who we are and what we do. To use the language of the Apostle Peter, we become *sharers in the divine nature* (2 Pet 1:4), becoming something new and different from what we were before. We share *in* God's presence as those who know him, but we also share God's presence *with him* as partakers of a new nature. We are so much more than a temple that houses him or a space that he fills; we are new creatures, born of God and intimately related to him! The language we use often fails to capture the significance of God's nature penetrating ours, the fullness of his Spirit permeating our hearts, and the innermost infusion of his presence in our lives! "But the person who is joined to the Lord is one spirit with him" (1 Cor 6:17).[1] Because we are "one spirit with him," we can truly experience what it means to share in God's presence.

Although God is always with us, on some momentous occasions people have actually experienced his *manifest* presence and felt him close by, or even saw or heard him. Because Scripture describes people who have seen God face to face, I'm curious who has enjoyed the privilege of spending the most time with him. Adam and his wife certainly walked and talked with their Creator. God must have spent a great deal of time interacting with them as he "raised them" and shared his heart with them, as any good father would. Yet we're never told how long or how often he walked or spoke with either of them. Of course, there were others like Enoch, Abraham, and Jacob, but what about Moses?

---

1. All Scripture quotations, unless otherwise indicated, are taken from the Holy Bible, New International Version, NIV.

Sharing in God's Presence

Moses and his forty days on Mount Sinai might be our best example. When God gave Moses the Ten Commandments, Moses "stayed on the mountain forty days and forty nights" (Exod 24:18). In fact, Scripture describes Moses as the one person in those days who God spoke to face to face, "as one speaks to a friend" (33:11). This language reflects the intimacy of fellowship and the heights of sharing in God's presence. What acceptance and privilege this man must have felt, a blessing every believer today would admire! God welcomes us into so much more than just a master/servant relationship. His yearning is for the spiritual bond of friendly fellowship that includes the give and take of a thoughtful, personal relationship, one in which each person involved can experience the freedom to share everything with each other. Indeed, the desire of God's heart is for everyone to share in his presence and experience all of him.

Moses was a man well acquainted with God's presence. On the first occasion that Moses climbed the mountain, Scripture says, "When the LORD finished speaking to Moses on Mount Sinai, he gave him the two tablets of the covenant law, the tablets of stone inscribed by the finger of God" (Exod 31:18). Inscribing the law with a touch of his finger, God had exposed his very own hands to Moses. Because no one else had entered God's presence in those days, only Moses would have known what God's touch was like, whether delicate or powerful.

To Moses' dismay, after he received the law and made his way off the mountain, he discovered the Hebrew people worshipping a golden calf! In a moment of shocking disappointment, Moses shattered both tablets of the law—not just any tablets, but the tablets that had been in God's very presence, the two tablets God himself had touched (Exod 31:19–20). At the moment, those tablets were the closest representation the people had to God's presence, and Moses destroyed them! Moses had broken the privileged link between the people and the God who sought to bring them into a special covenant commitment to himself.

So once again, Moses returned to the mountain to chisel out two more stone tablets (Exod 34:1). But then, something extraordinary happened: "Moses was there with the LORD forty days and forty nights without eating bread or drinking water. . . . When Moses came down from Mount Sinai with the two tablets of the covenant law in his hands, he was not aware that his face was radiant because he had spoken with the LORD" (Exod 34:28–29). Yes, his face was actually glowing! Moses had spent *another* forty days in God's presence, eating and drinking nothing, talking only to God, and

Introduction: God Shares His Heart

worshipping. Can you think of anyone else in all of history who has spent forty days in God's immediate presence, enjoying the supreme intimacy of face-to-face fellowship? When Moses left to visit the people, he had no idea there was a noticeable glow emanating from his countenance! For over five weeks, Moses fasted everything else but God, sustained solely by the divine presence. This example suggests that our most effective fasts will be spent doing nothing but drawing nearer to God.

Moses, Elijah (1 Kgs 19:7–8), and Jesus (Matt 4:1–2) all fasted the same amount of time. Before Elijah's forty-day fast, an angel gave him supernatural food that so strengthened him that he never once needed to eat. Led directly by the Spirit, Jesus too was sustained during his forty days in the wilderness. It's not surprising, then, that Moses' fast was also supernatural, as he feasted solely upon God's sustaining presence. Moses' nourishment came directly from the glorious face of God, radiating and even imbuing Moses' flesh! This should be a vivid reminder that anyone can draw near to God to be found in his presence, and he will reveal his glory and nourish them in a special way.

While Moses lingered in God's presence on the mountain, God gave him the law—including the Ten Commandments—which demonstrates that the significance of every divine command is found in the intimacy of communion with God. Because Moses was given the special task of receiving God's law for an entire nation, this very important calling required over five weeks of fellowship in God's immediate manifest presence, the longest anyone has ever spent—not even Adam knew fellowship like this! What Adam and his generation didn't have, the new generation under Moses would. Moses was leading his generation into the kingdom of God's presence, opening a new door of partnership for every generation to follow.[2]

When Moses came down off the mountain, he wasn't aware that "his face was radiant (*qaran*)" and generating a glow (Exod 34:29). The Hebrew word *qaran* means that his face sent out shafts or streams of light, so how could he not know? Might I suggest that he wasn't aware of it because this glorious light had become so much a part of him and his experience? It sounds quite remarkable, but there's not a single believer who should be unfamiliar with this transformative principle. To consider this in modern

---

2. The generation under Moses enjoyed glorious privileges, but ours are even better: "The Word became flesh and made his dwelling among us. We have seen his glory, the glory of the one and only Son, who came from the Father, full of grace and truth. . . . Out of his fullness we have all received grace in place of grace already given. For the law was given through Moses; grace and truth came through Jesus Christ" (John 1:14, 16–17).

terms, Moses spent so much time in the "prayer closet," the secret place of God's presence, that he took the prayer closet with him wherever he went. More importantly, Moses was becoming familiar with the incredible difference God's presence makes in one's life. As the divine presence was rubbing off on him, his soul *and body* were enriched in ways Moses could never have expected. But what do we make of Moses' glowing face? As unusual as this may sound, it seems as though Moses' flesh had somehow absorbed the physical residue of the divine presence, or perhaps it was sticking to Moses' skin! At the very least, Moses' experience indicated a special sharing in God's presence.

This whole experience is significant because there is little distinction between that glowing deposit and God's physical presence. Moses took the presence of God with him, just as you and I must take the presence of God with us. When we close our Bibles or walk out of the worship service, God is traveling with us. Moses took God's literal presence with him, and it literally imbued his face! Anyone who spends time in God's presence will know that he touches both soul and body; God changes those who draw near to him because his transformative presence has no other option. When God touches us, he leaves his mark! God is committed to transforming us because he cannot do otherwise; his presence is a transformative principle.

Moses is the rare example of a person privileged to *physically* illustrate this. What Moses experienced physically, the rest of us experience spiritually. Paul says it like this: "But we all, with unveiled faces, beholding as in a mirror the glory of the Lord, are being transformed into the same image from glory to glory, which comes from the Lord, who is the Spirit" (2 Cor 3:18). Paul is referring to the church as we gaze into God's word, while we are continually transformed by the Spirit of the Lord. Praise be to God that we are an ever-changing people, a people privileged to become like Jesus!

So far, we know that a physical display of God's presence had shone from Moses' skin, but what was so extraordinary to bring this about? It wasn't due merely to Moses talking with God, but to something more specific—God chose to share himself in the mode of personal relationship by revealing his name and character: "Then the Lord came down in the cloud and stood there with him and proclaimed his name, the Lord" (Exod 34:5). By *standing* beside Moses, the Lord (Hebrew, *Yahweh*) made the encounter even more personal: He "stood" there with Moses and proclaimed his name, Yahweh. Yahweh, the great and awesome God, stood with a man! When such a human description is ascribed to God, it emphasizes

Introduction: God Shares His Heart

the physical and relational dimension of his encounters with people. The Old Testament writers don't appear the least bit interested in reminding us that God is in fact a spirit-being without a physical body. They seem far more interested in having us reflect upon how closely God approaches people! Because God is predominantly a spirit-being, this is the picture of a personal God who approaches humanity as intimately as possible. God himself stood with Moses and announced his own name. Yahweh's actions demonstrate that the personal, even physical, manifest presence of God draws near to those who faithfully approach him.

Rather than a simple conversation, Scripture says that Yahweh animated the story of his presence and "passed in front of Moses" (Exod 34:6). We finally discover what was so exceptionally awesome about their encounter, something so significant that Moses' face began to shine! In this monumental event, Yahweh described his true character, revealing the depths of his heart: "And he passed in front of Moses, proclaiming, 'The LORD, the LORD, the compassionate and gracious God, slow to anger, abounding in love and faithfulness, maintaining love to thousands, and forgiving wickedness, rebellion and sin. Yet he does not leave the guilty unpunished; ... Moses bowed to the ground at once and worshiped" (Exod 34:6–8). Oh, the revelation of God's heart that brought this man to his knees! Yahweh is the God of compassion and long-suffering! Not easily angered! Full of covenant love! Forgiving and just! When Yahweh approached Moses on Sinai, he taught all of us that he reveals his presence so that people might learn his heart and know his character. The integrity of God was conveyed through the simple vehicle of conversational presence, inspiring Moses to respond with awe in worship.

Not only had God spoken and proclaimed his name, but Yahweh's presence had "passed in front of Moses," a sweeping visitation! In order to most fully reveal his heart to this man, God's presence moved like wind before Moses (cf. Gen 8:1). When we accept the word that God is proclaiming about himself, a word that should inspire our worship, we can be sure that God's personal presence surrounds us. When believers pray, we never speak to walls and carpet, but we speak to an ever-present God who faithfully "stands" beside us and sweeps like wind around us in order to reveal more of himself. Through God's appearance in our conversation with him, we can't help but be changed. And wherever God's name is proclaimed and his word is spoken and believed upon, he is showing up!

Sharing in God's Presence

Moses was a man who shared in God's presence and walked around with it like a mask of light. But for some observers, it was unnerving; they weren't familiar with God's intimate presence, so they were "afraid" and kept their distance as mere spectators, never getting to know his presence for themselves (Exod 34:30). For forty years, Moses lived among the people, going back and forth from his encounters with Yahweh, and every day the afterglow went with him:

> When Moses came down from Mount Sinai with the two tablets of the covenant law in his hands, he was not aware that his face was radiant because he had spoken with the Lord. . . . Afterward all the Israelites came near him, and he gave them all the commands the Lord had given him on Mount Sinai. When Moses finished speaking to them, he put a veil over his face. But whenever he entered the Lord's presence to speak with him, he removed the veil until he came out. And when he came out and told the Israelites what he had been commanded, they saw that his face was radiant. Then Moses would put the veil back over his face until he went in to speak with the Lord." (Exod 34:29, 32–35)

Curiously, there were some occasions when Moses wore a mask and other occasions when he didn't, sometimes revealing the glory and other times hiding it.[3] Throughout his life, Moses continued to return to God's intimate presence and continued to wear his mask, probably spanning the entire forty years he spent in the wilderness with God's people. He was indeed the masked man of Israel! Although Moses was just a man, he was a man who shared in God's presence.

Moses' face was glowing due to the leftover residue of God's presence, but is there another possible interpretation? Perhaps this divine encounter was actually revealing Moses' true nature. To be more specific, perhaps being face to face with God was exposing true human nature as it's *intended* to be in God's presence. If so, then Jesus' experience on the Mount of Transfiguration follows that precedent: "There he was transfigured (*metamorphoo*) before them. His face shone like the sun, and his clothes became as white as the light" (Matt 17:2). The Greek term *metamorphoo* refers to an external change in keeping with inner reality. In other words, Jesus' glowing body was manifesting the glory of his true self! It's conceivable, then, that our

---

3. By Moses taking the mask on and off, I'm reminded of Paul's word to the Corinthians: "For we are to God the pleasing aroma of Christ among those who are being saved and those who are perishing. To the one we are an aroma that brings death; to the other, an aroma that brings life" (2 Cor 2:15–16).

Introduction: God Shares His Heart

Exodus passage portrays Moses as becoming more like God, being transformed in his presence, which was the reality that Jesus already shared with God! The human race has always been destined for glory in God's presence. Although its fulfillment will be an end-times event, one day we will all be radiant in the presence of the King and his kingdom (1 John 3:2).

Let's take a final look at Exodus 34. This passage tells us that Moses "was not aware that his face was radiant because he had spoken with the Lord" (v. 29). Moses' radiance wasn't because God had spoken to him, as one might assume, but "because *he* had spoken to the Lord"! Clearly, a conversation is implied, but these words should still give us the sense that any one of us can commune with the Lord and experience supernatural results—at times, even the glory of his manifest presence! God chooses whatever degree to manifest his presence, yet it seems that we most commonly experience him through the transformative process of becoming more like Jesus through his word and Spirit (2 Cor 3:13–18). We may not see beams of light emanating from one's countenance, as with Moses, but others will inevitably notice the inner light that's creatively at work within us to make us more like Jesus.

God is calling believers into the process of becoming like him by sharing in his presence. Moses' encounter with Yahweh was unique and personal, just as God is calling every believer to experience a personalized relationship with him. We become acquainted with his heart and his ways through a daily encounter with Jesus Christ, beginning with salvation and continuing in the day-to-day experience of God's Spirit working his word into our lives. As we accept our own responsibility for prayer, ministry, and even revival, we share in the very precious dynamic of the give and response that's involved in an intimate walk with God. We share those responsibilities by receiving God's gracious presence, but he also receives from us and requires the help of our prayer and ministry to accomplish his will.[4]

Before we delve in, an important clarification is in order. The chapters that follow are an invitation to share in God's presence *by allowing God to share himself with you*. Moses was known as a great man of God because Yahweh graciously chose to share himself with him, even revealing his name and his heart to Moses. Likewise, God desires to share himself with you and me: "Come and listen to my counsel. I'll share my heart with

---

4. Does God really need our help? This rather unusual passage demonstrates that God does in fact depend upon our help: "'Let the people of Meroz be cursed,' said the angel of the Lord. 'Let them be utterly cursed, because they did not come to help the Lord—to help the Lord against the mighty warriors'" (Judg 5:23 NLT).

you and make you wise" (Prov 1:23 NLT). For the journey ahead, I pray that you'll experience the highest possible blessing through Jesus Christ our Lord by learning his heart and forever walking closely with him.

1

Presence: God Shares His World

LOOKING AROUND AT THE world, most people get the sense that God doesn't always get his way but has accepted significant risk by inviting people into his creation. Just to be clear, risk means that God doesn't always get what he wants but actually exposes himself to significant loss. If God's will was always done, then why would Jesus teach us to pray, "Your will be done on earth, as it is in heaven" (Matt 6:10)? God's singular, consistent, perfect, and pleasing will can be, and is at times, thwarted![1] God does not *will* evil and suffering in the world but actually suffers at its hands, due to the freedom that he has bestowed upon humans and angels. We can all be certain that the choices of fallen humanity do not always line up with the will of God, yet God has never stopped believing that his creation was well worth the risk. For love to even be possible, it must involve not only our freedom but also *God's* risk.

If we are to begin to understand what it means to share in God's presence, it's important to first understand the nature of the God who risks everything in order to share everything with his people. It is a profoundly freeing revelation to investigate the solid testimony of Scripture and discover in its pages a God who accepts the risk of loving and sharing himself with his creatures, what we should think of as a most profoundly *relational* theology. If we're going to benefit from a relational theology, we'll need to

---

1. The classical Calvinist defense of *two* divine wills has become untenable. The Bible nowhere teaches that God has two different and competing wills, one permissive and the other hidden and efficacious. It does teach, however, that God's perfect will is at times thwarted.

look to God's inspired word as the final source of truth and revelation and fully embrace the descriptions, experiences, thoughts, and feelings attributed to God within its pages. The magnificent God of Scripture is both almighty *and* capable of anger, jealousy, regret, frustration, surprise, desire, sorrow, suffering, hope, and risk. Exploring such intimate depths of God's open and responsive heart can revitalize the church's understanding of God's relationship to us. The God we worship is not only transcendent in power and presence but also immanent and absolutely relational. This very beautiful picture of the biblical God presents one who puts relationship first and therefore invites people to share his world!

In this chapter, we'll see that God accepts the risk of sharing himself with us, and we'll also consider how a God of perfect knowledge is even capable of risk. We'll then look briefly at God's relationship to change, time, suffering, and presence, and the role each of those play in his ability to share himself with people.

God Accepts the Risk

If I were to tell you, "God is love," would you believe me? Such a weighty question deserves serious thought. You might have second thoughts if you've only ever heard that the God of the Bible is one who stringently controls a world full of hate and violence, much of which we've personally experienced. Or that God has ordained the damnation of certain friends and family, ultimately leaving them no choice but to remain in their sins because he has chosen to save others instead. Many of us have harbored the disturbing intuition that Satan must be some kind of puppet in God's hands, while struggling to believe that God is somehow not to blame for all of the devastation caused by that demonic figure and those who abide in his kingdom of sin and death. If the world we live in exists under a God with complete and meticulous control, a God who has ordained the future in every detail, then we have no choice but to look around at all of the suffering and pain and question whether he really is the "God [of] love" that Scripture says he is (1 John 4:8, 16).

Over the years, many voices have taught me that prayers don't change God and that God doesn't actually need people in any fundamental way, along with so many other non-relational aspects of our Creator. Yet there's something about all of this that just sticks in our craw when we size up our loving Savior with a God set on damning the world and damning our

Presence: God Shares His World

loved ones for the sake of his own glory. Challenges like these leave so many people confused and questioning. Why does this strange God seem so stubborn and dogmatic, ultimately closed to our input, while selfishly seeking to uphold his own honor and reputation? Why has this peculiar being ordained all things, yet chosen to save only some of the human race? All things considered, this rather boring God doesn't take risks, prayer can't change his mind, people aren't free to accept or reject him, and ultimately, this sovereign dictator *is* responsible for all of the evil in the world. Yet the irony is that most evangelical believers live out the Christian life as if this isn't so.[2] Therefore, we can and should adopt a *relational* theology that acknowledges Scripture's emphasis on a relational God who is open to a risky love because love is at the center of his existence and all of his ways. In fact, he risks everything so that he can share everything with us.

When Yahweh gave the first humans the choice to eat the fruit of the knowledge of good and evil, he accepted the blatantly obvious risk that they might very well eat it. From the beginning, it was apparent that the risks God takes are directly tied to the freedom that he has irrevocably given to humankind, a self-determining freewill. Accepting the risk, God pursues relationships that are of a truly personal, intimate nature, in which his heart is on the line because of the possibility of rejection.

Jesus summarized the grief of being rejected as he looked out over Jerusalem and stated with sad disappointment, "How often I have longed to gather your children together, as a hen gathers her chicks under her wings, and you were not willing" (Matt 23:37). Although Jesus longed to have a close relationship with God's people, that desire went unfulfilled. Such grief is largely due to the costly risk that allows the kind of freedom that can reject God's love in the first place. Yet God continues to risk so much because he aims so high and lovingly longs for more from us.

Although God wills and yearns for a loving relationship with every single person, that future prospect is not guaranteed. God hasn't ordained every detail of the future but allows true freedom for the sake of relationship. For instance, there have been times when Yahweh remained undecided about Israel's judgment because he was hopeful for their repentance. On one occasion, the LORD said to Jeremiah, "*Perhaps* they will listen and

---

2. The exception to this picture of a domineering God has often been with liberal theologians who present a God of love and acceptance, but they do so at great cost to the authority of Scripture and the testimony of the gospel of the cross and resurrection. The cost might be a Jesus of history who's not God-in-flesh, a morality without repentance, a religion without divine relationship, or some other defamation of God's sacred word.

each will turn from their evil ways. *Then I will relent* and not inflict on them the disaster I was planning because of the evil they have done.... *Perhaps* when the people of Judah hear about every disaster I plan to inflict on them, they will each turn from their wicked ways" (Jer 26:3; 36:3, emphasis added).³ Passages like this imply a great deal of uncertainty from God—*perhaps* my children will do this or that! Although God hopes that they will change their wicked ways, he doesn't know for certain! Such passages support the contention that the future is not set in stone but is full of possibilities.⁴

Prayer makes the most sense if the future is full of possibility. In one well-known Old Testament story, when King Hezekiah became ill and was about to die, a prophet came to him and in no uncertain terms declared, "You are going to die." To avoid any confusion on the matter, the prophet added, "You will not recover" (2 Kgs 20:1; cf. Isa 38:1–6)! But the king cried out to God anyway, hoping that Yahweh wasn't stubbornly set in his ways, and in a surprising turn of events, the prophet returned with quite a different message from the LORD: "I have heard your prayer and seen your tears; I will heal you.... I will add fifteen years to your life" (2 Kgs 20:5, 6). And yet he had been promised death, beyond recovery, which leaves readers to draw no other conclusion than the obvious—King Hezekiah's prayer *changed God's mind!* This is just one example of how prayer changes not only you and me but also God's plans. Surely it would have been disingenuous for God to predict a death that wasn't a real, or even likely, possibility. This king was doomed to die, yet the LORD regards a believer's prayers to such a degree that the future can be changed.

Along with Hezekiah, most believers feel confident to approach God. We feel confident that he is a God who hears us and assures us of his love, because we've actually come to know him through worship, morning devotions, or by just spending time to seek him. We believe that our God really does *want all people to be saved* and to choose his love and salvation (1 Tim 2:4). We serve those in need as if God really does in some way depend upon us as his hands and feet, and we pray as if God really will change his mind because we asked. So we conclude that God must be vulnerable because he

---

3. If language means anything at all, the term *perhaps* conveys uncertainty. Regarding the divine *perhaps*, see Jer 36:7; 51:8; Isa 47:12; Ezek 12:3. Also cf. Luke 20:13.

4. Numerous books have been written on the openness of the future. See, e.g., Sanders, *God Who Risks*; Pinnock, *Most Moved Mover*; Boyd, *God of the Possible*; Pinnock et al., *Openness of God*; Basinger, *Case for Freewill Theism*; Hasker et al., *God in an Open Universe*.

chooses to use *us* to love the world, despite the fact that we are so irreparably flawed. Every day we very much live as if God accepts the risk of using imperfect people to accomplish his will, even to the extent that if we fail in our sphere of influence, there might not be a backup plan.

God is Perfect Change

If God is perfect, then how is he even capable of risk? Because even with a perfect God who has perfect knowledge, much of the future is still *uncertain*. The openness of the future is a good introduction to the idea that God is able to change. If God is going to extend a real invitation for us to share in his presence, change is a necessary prerequisite, and the changeability of God's experience is most notably related to his dynamic knowledge of the future. God's perfect knowledge of the future includes knowing what is certain *and* what is possible. God knows reality in terms of its correspondence to truth, so the truth of the matter is that the future doesn't yet exist except mostly in terms of infinite possibilities, each of which are perfectly known to God. This is due primarily to the nearly infinite choices open to freewill creatures at any given moment. God knows what free people will *possibly* do, even though what they will actually do remains largely unknowable. Hence, God changes in his experience because he experiences our freedom in new ways when we finally act upon our choices and live out the consequences of our decisions.

As farfetched as all of this may sound, let me illustrate from Scripture. God's unique knowledge of the future is demonstrated in such passages as Abraham's great test of faith when God asked him to sacrifice his son Isaac.[5] At the moment of Abraham's obedience, when the knife was grasped tightly in hand and suspended over his child, Yahweh's Angel abruptly interrupted: "'Do not lay a hand on the boy,' he said. 'Do not do anything to him. *Now I know* that you fear God, because you have not withheld from me your son, your only son'" (Gen 22:12, emphasis added).[6] Talk about a close call! The

---

5. Samuel Terrien identifies the element of risk involved in Yahweh's test for Abraham: "In the context of the Hebraic theology of presence, with the absurdity of its demands, religion no longer means the ritual exchange of sacrality with a static cosmos through which man attunes himself to the life of nature but, on the contrary, the courage to face the abyss of being, even the abyss of the being of God, and to affirm, at the risk of assuming all risks, the will to gamble away not only one's ego but even one's hope in the future of mankind" (*Elusive Presence*, 83–84).

6. This wasn't the only time that God tested his people to learn what they would

Hebrew indicates that God's knowledge here is inchoative or ingressive, meaning *God has come to learn something new*: "Now I have come to know that you fear God." That God has received new information implies that the future is not settled; rather, God changes in his knowledge and experience with people.

God's changeability and the divine desire to engage humanity and share in human experience all lead to the conclusion that our God has opened himself up to a unique vulnerability, which includes the capacity to experience loss. One poignant example is found in the book of Exodus when Yahweh was preparing Moses to confront Pharaoh. Because God chooses not to use sheer power to engage the world, his plans are often at the disposal of frail human messengers. This was evident in his use of such an apprehensive and imperfect messenger as Moses. After God described to Moses the great wonders that he would perform to persuade Pharaoh to let the people go, Moses' response was essentially, "Okay God, but what if . . ." (Exod 4:1). What if Pharaoh doesn't listen? What if your plan doesn't succeed? What if they call me a liar? Then what?

The Lord's response was nothing like one might expect from a God believed to maintain both meticulous control and comprehensive foresight. Instead of rebuking Moses—how dare you question my knowledge and power!—the Lord humbled himself, acquiesced to Moses' concerns, and offered a solution to the potential problems he had proposed. God basically told Moses, "If plan A fails, we'll move on to plan B and show them a miraculous sign—your staff will turn into a snake. But if plan B fails, then we'll consider plan C, and your hand will turn leprous." The Lord was not merely acquiescing for the sake of valuing an active dialogue or a give-and-take with his chosen leader, although that was surely part of it; instead, Yahweh believed that Moses' concern was legitimate and agreed with the possibility of Moses' conclusions. If Pharaoh doesn't listen, we need other options!

The Lord did not predict a definite response from Pharaoh but agreed with Moses that they should be prepared with alternative actions: "Then the Lord said, 'If they do not believe you or pay attention to the first sign, they may believe the second. But if they do not believe these two signs or listen to you, take some water from the Nile and pour it on the dry ground. The water you take from the river will become blood on the ground'" (Exod 4:8–9). Readers should be confident in the reliability of ancient Scripture

---

ultimately do; see Exod 16:4; 20:20; Deut 8:2; 13:3; 2 Chr 32:31.

Presence: God Shares His World

and rest assured that God is not certain whether Pharaoh will believe the first or second signs. The possibilities denoted in the Lord's use of such language as "if" and "may" should be understood as truly representative of the divine perspective; otherwise, the very integrity of his communications is suspect (cf. 33:3, 5)![7] Although Yahweh knows every possible outcome, Pharaoh will still need to choose.

In an almost humorous interchange, Moses has second thoughts and begins to plead with God to send someone else—anybody else! Even after the Lord patiently assures Moses that he is more than capable to help, Moses still isn't satisfied but continues to plead with God to "please send someone else." Finally, the Lord *gives in* and agrees to send Moses' brother Aaron (Exod 4:10–13). This is a supreme example of how God humbles himself and changes his plans at the request of an imperfect servant. If the plans of God change, then God necessarily changes as his knowledge considers alternatives and his heart responds to the needs of his people. Because the God of Moses is a God of relationship who is willing to share real experiences with him, we can be confident that God has made a way for each of us to share in his presence.

In response to any naysayers, God's openness to the future certainly doesn't imply that he's ever unprepared for any imminent possibility or that he doesn't possess the wise resourcefulness to effortlessly handle any future contingencies, because he is and he does. Exodus 4 is a microcosmic example, on a human level, that God does in fact plan ahead and have effective alternatives in place for accomplishing his overarching goals. Yahweh used Moses to accomplish his goal, despite Pharaoh's stubbornness and Moses' reluctance. This passage can be superimposed upon the full revelation of Scripture, such that we can remain confident that God will one day fully establish his kingdom by using imperfect human beings to bring it about, whether by plan A, B, C, or Z.[8]

Without pressing the matter too far, one could look as far back as the garden of Eden to see that God has always been a resourceful plan B kind of Creator: "Now the Lord God had formed out of the ground all the wild animals and all the birds in the sky. He brought them to the man to see what he would name them; . . . But for Adam no suitable helper was found" (Gen

---

7. Regarding the divine *if*, see 1 Kgs 9:4–7; Ps 132:12; Isa 1:19–20; Jer 4:1–2; 7:5–7; 17:24–27; 22:4–5; 26:4–6; 38:17–18; 42:9–16.

8. What happens after plan Z, if plan Z should fail? The believer should have utmost confidence in the wisdom and power of God that history would never move anywhere near plan Z.

2:19–20).[9] The LORD not only granted Adam the responsibility of choosing a helpmate but also allowed him to reject God's numerous creative proposals. This was after Yahweh described the very situation he had brought the man into as "not good" (v. 18). Regarding that *not so good* situation, literary scholar Lee Humphreys remarks, "Apparently Yahweh God judges his creative effort as not yet quite right. He has second thoughts about the human condition."[10] This is quite a provocative statement, yet it rings true that God did say that what he himself had made was not good.[11] It seems that God has accepted the necessity of his own vulnerability in his new relationship to a freethinking, foreign being, so much so that he has invited this new creature's critiques into his once independent existence. Yahweh was now experiencing what it means to bring another volitional, freethinking, wise, and even critical being into his own world. God truly does share his world with us.

God Experiences Time

Because God is working with freewill creatures, people who daily make decisions that involve real alternatives, the LORD has freely and voluntarily entered into a God-world relationship that involves risk. He created the framework of the world by his design and choosing. The same world that depends on him for its existence and maintenance—it is this world that God has made himself dependent upon as the meeting ground for him and his creatures. Because the divine nature is faithful love, he honors his relationship with the world by experiencing the world and humanity as they truly are, a world construed of time and space. If God is going to share himself with people who exist *in time*, then it's important for us to understand that he is not absolutely *timeless*.

Every narrative of Scripture implies that God has created a world that he is intimately involved in, one in which he moves about in time and space

---

9. Bonhoeffer makes an interesting observation about Adam's search for a potential helpmate. He says, "God first of all forms animals out of the ground from which God has taken humankind. According to the Bible human beings and animals have the same kind of body! Perhaps the human being would find a helper who is a suitable partner among these brothers and sisters—for that is what they are, the animals who have the same origin as humankind does" (*Creation and Fall*, 96).

10. Humphreys, *Character of God*, 39.

11. Granted, the connotation may be something more like, not *yet* good, but that is not what the text explicitly says.

Presence: God Shares His World

in some sense comparable to the creature's pace: "This is what the Lord says: 'About midnight I will go throughout Egypt'" (Exod 11:4). Yahweh experiences the sequence of human lives, conversations, prayers, and cause and effect relationships. This means that God is in some sense related to time, and therefore, *temporal*. Temporal means exactly that: God is *related to time*. God is not eternal timelessness, as if he has no duration or no before and after. Timelessness implies that God somehow stands outside of time and all at once observes past, present, and future, which necessarily entails that the future is entirely ordained.[12] Nonetheless, such a theory is more philosophical than biblical and should be reconsidered.

Although God is eternal because he has always existed, he is not eternal in the sense of timelessness. The Greek philosopher Permenides (sixth century BC) was the first to introduce the definition of eternity as timelessness, something later avowed by both Plato (fifth century) and Aristotle (fourth century). Such a theory, however, is nowhere suggested in sacred Scripture. Throughout the Bible, every description of God is related to time and devoid of any notion of timelessness. God is "from everlasting to everlasting," "the First and the Last," "the Beginning and the End" (Neh 9:5; Rev 2:8; 21:6).[13] He is the "eternal God," which could also be translated "God of old" from the Hebrew term *qedem*, a temporal word meaning ancient time (Deut 33:27). Among other things, *qedem* is also used of mountains (Deut 33:15), days (2 Kgs 19:25), sayings (Ps 78:2), and human kings (Isa 19:11), none of which provide an example of eternal timelessness. Truly, the Lord is the *everlasting* God; he is not the God of timelessness but literally the "God of the age" (Isa 40:28), the "Ancient of days" (Dan 7:13), and the "King of the ages" (1 Tim 1:17).

Paul Fiddes, author of *Participating in God*, is one of many theologians today who affirm divine temporality. Fiddes comments, "It seems doubtful whether we can speak of God's 'acting' at all unless there is some temporality in God, some movement from one state of being to another."[14] Just as God experiences a future full of possibilities as just that, future possibilities, so he also experiences this temporal world as it is, temporal. Do the narratives of Scripture portray a God whose home is timeless or whose home is

---

12. Although God's presence may extend into the past, it cannot extend into the future because the future doesn't exist.

13. The phrase "from everlasting to everlasting" occurs multiple times in Scripture to describe God and his attributes; see 1 Chr 16:36; 29:10; Pss 41:13; 103:17; 106:48; Neh 9:5.

14. Fiddes, *Participating in God*, 122. See also Swinburne, *Coherence of Theism*, 225.

a heaven and earth that belong to time and space? The prophet Amos records, "He builds his lofty palace in the heavens and sets its foundation on the earth" (Amos 9:6; cf. Mic 1:3). Considering passages like this, it's difficult to maintain the claim that God's home is a timeless eternity outside of the created order. Most Bible passages point to God's temporal movement within time and space: "When he had finished speaking with Abraham, God went up from him" (Gen 17:22; cf. 35:13).

Throughout Scripture, God's movements parallel the movements and pace of his creatures, making it apparent that God honors his relationship to our temporal reality. We should assume that he honors that relationship without stepping outside of our existence to look at a panoramic view of time, what some describe as an *eternal now*, which nowhere appears in Scripture. For God to do that would imply timelessness. God knows us and we know him in terms of the created space in which he encounters us. We could not possibly grasp any revelation of inspired Scripture apart from the space we live in—God's temporal world—so God wants us to know him on the basis of what he has revealed in Scripture.[15]

If we're to understand God's relationship to time, our most dependable source is Scripture. Scripture presents God as one who experiences duration and time; he is never portrayed as distant and static but always creative, dynamic, and interacting with humanity within our world.[16] Far from existing in some state of an eternal now, God experiences time with all the necessary nuance involved in interacting with freewill creatures. He experiences grief, surprise, regret, celebration, and dialogue, while answering prayers, loving people, and receiving love. None of this would be genuine if God sits in timelessness! The word of God reveals an infinite being whose eternal nature now exists primarily in sequence with people and their world. The LORD moves beside us, dialogues with us, awaits the future with us, experiences the hurts and ravages of time with us, and faces obstacles and challenges beside us. I would suggest that only this kind of God can genuinely invite people to share in his presence.

---

15. Theologian Karl Barth summarizes his view on God's space, saying, "He possesses and He is Himself space" (*CD* 2/1:471). If there is a *timeless* space that is only God and of God, such as an eternally timeless throne room, humanity cannot understand it apart from the creation we are born into. But more importantly, if God is occupying a timeless space, our theology cannot grasp it, nor does the Bible affirm it.

16. See Gen 4:16; 11:5; 17:22; 18:21; Exod 11:4; 20:24; 25:8; Num 23:15; Deut 33:2; 2 Sam 7:6; 1 Kgs 19:11–12; Job 1:12; 2:7; Pss 9:11; 10:1; 74:2; 76:2; Isa 24:23; 37:14; Hos 11:9; Joel 3:17; Jonah 1:3, 10; Hab 3:3; Zech 8:3.

Presence: God Shares His World

To be clear, I am not suggesting that God is ravaged by time or is in any sense worn down by it—the second law of thermodynamics need not apply with God!—but he does personally experience the pain and suffering of his creatures and our world, as people live out and experience the ruining effects of time. Although philosophers and theologians alike debate whether God is one of eternal timelessness or everlasting temporality, one thing is clear: The God we encounter in the narratives of Scripture appears, for all intents and purposes, to be involved in current, causal, relational conversations and interactions with humanity. Our spiritual life and worship depend on this!

This temporal world is as much God's world as it is ours, so he shares his world with us. Scripture nowhere describes an eternally distant God who at once observes past, present, and future, while standing outside of our temporality. As Fiddes observes, "It has become clear, in much recent discussion, that the notion of an absolutely timeless God is a concept of Greek philosophy, replacing the biblical picture of the 'everlasting God' for whom time has meaning, but who is not trapped within it as we are."[17] Even though God relates to us in time, his relationship to time is nonetheless unique. Although every human encounter with him appears as if he lives within history, he is not flesh and blood but is spirit. He experiences this temporal world from a most unique perspective, not as a human being but as one who is divine perfection, all-powerful, and ever-present. Although God is in some sense related to time, he enjoys a vantage point that we cannot conceive of, all the while inviting us to share in his timely presence.

God Suffers Too

God has assumed certain limitations in order to share himself with people, and he can do this because he is nothing less than perfect freedom. Any vulnerability, limitation, or risk with God is one that he has *voluntarily* assumed and freely entered into throughout this age. In the words of philosopher Jeff Pool, "Unless God also possesses the capacity to limit the divine self in the operation of any attribute, then God cannot be unlimited in any of those respects."[18] The story of Jesus' life and death affirms this truth from beginning to end: God has demonstrated in the person of Christ that he is capable of limiting himself. Philippians 2:7 says that Jesus "emptied

17. Fiddes, *Participating in God*, 122.
18. Pool, *God's Wounds*, 158.

himself" or "made himself nothing" (Greek, *kenoo*) by becoming human, which theologians refer to as the *kenosis* of Christ. This means that Jesus became the vehicle for a new addition to the everlasting Godhead, the *humanity* of God. For eons, the second person of the Trinity had existed in one divine nature, but now he forever exists in two—divine *and* human. Thus, change itself must be intrinsic to the essence of God and who he is.

There is profound revelation and interpretive value in the *kenosis* of Jesus Christ, that self-emptying, self-limiting experience of the second person of the Trinity. The vulnerabilities of this human God become immediately apparent in the virgin birth. Jesus' birth highlights divine self-limitation but also the risk and vulnerability of becoming human under the political conditions of the first-century world. The Mediterranean world was a hostile, hateful environment under the political reign of King Herod who sought immediately to kill this vulnerable messianic figure (Matt 2:1–18).

Yet even from the divine perspective, Jesus' life was always intended to be an obedience unto death (Phil 2:8), never demanding his personal rights but always opening himself to loss. How much more vulnerable could we expect God to become than to experience a mortal's birth and death? This vulgar idea of death has always been a strange and hostile element in God's creation. Because death can only be considered a foreign element to the "good" that God spent six days creating (Gen 1:3–31), Jesus' death would have been an experience that took the divine life into unchartered territory. God truly is the risk-taking, vulnerable Lord of history.

Fiddes rightly comments, "When we think at all carefully about it, suffering must involve being changed by something or someone outside oneself. It means being affected, conditioned and even afflicted by another. A suffering God must be 'vulnerable' in the strict sense of 'open to being wounded.'"[19] Because the human Jesus was truly open to being wounded, so was God. If God suffers, and he does, then God changes; and if God changes, then he would be less than perfect if change was not internal to him. Scripture itself lays the foundation for the perfection and changeableness of God, so it is Scripture which leads us to conclude that God's essential nature involves perfect changeability. Jesus, Son of God, who once existed in one nature, now exists in two. This human God died a physical death and then added yet another addition to the triune identity, an immortalized resurrection body. Because these changes were extraordinarily radical and

---

19. Fiddes, *Participating in God*, 170.

involved God's very nature, we can arrive at only one satisfying conclusion: God is perfectly changeable.

When God's perfect changeability finds expression in the creation, the result is vulnerability, risk, and even suffering.[20] God suffers because he chooses to open his perfect changeableness to the free experience of human beings, both as the God-human and by sharing our pain to the degree that it becomes his own. It is internal to God to suffer with those who suffer, "for we do not have a high priest who is unable to empathize with our weaknesses" (Heb 4:15). Yet even before Jesus became high priest and "empathize[d] with our weaknesses," God's experience had always been to bear our suffering. The moment Yahweh introduced free creatures into his world, he embraced their suffering, and even rebellion, as the "bearing" principal of an everlasting God of *long-suffering* love.[21] Because long-suffering is one of God's eternal attributes, by his very nature he bears the sin and suffering of the many: "Surely he took up our pain and bore our suffering" (Isa 53:4). And because God's suffering is real, he can never be the same again, so we should praise him for who he is: perfect changeability.

God Shares His Presence

Because God freely chooses to share himself with us, we can share in his spiritual presence. Swiss Reformed theologian Karl Barth remarks that God "is everywhere completely and undividedly the One He always is, even if in virtue of the freedom of His love He is this in continually differing and special ways."[22] Regarding the divine presence, Barth's thoughts are helpful to emphasize the idea of God's freedom. God freely and sovereignly moves in the world as his nature deems appropriate, though I'd like to expand on

---

20. The constraint of personal power was God's decision regarding his relationship to the world, but changeability itself is not God's decision because it is intrinsic to him.

21. Prior to the creation, we simply do not know what kind of suffering God might have experienced. Beyond the suffering of the cross, among the greatest risks God took was opening himself up to the vulnerability of his own personal suffering from those who would reject him. But is it possible that in a universe with an open future, prior to creation, God was not suffering? If the future is not preordained, and therefore, the fall is not certain but only possible, perhaps God was not anticipating the fall and was therefore not suffering. The eventual entrance of sin and death could have been a rather unexpected anomaly, rearing its ugly head in God's good creation.

22. Barth, *CD* 2/1:470. For a summary of Barth's view on omnipresence, see Gabriel, *Lord is the Spirit*, 152–55.

this. The freedom of God means that he is perfectly within his rights to limit, change, enhance, or remove his presence in the world and is certainly powerful enough to do so.

We creatures certainly benefit from experiencing God's presence in "continually differing and special ways," as Barth puts it. Anyone reading the Hebrew Bible can see that there are times throughout Israel's history that Yahweh manifests himself in special and unusual ways in order to share himself with people. The Spirit is the prominent representation of God's presence as far back as Genesis 1:2, where he is described as "hovering over the waters." But it didn't take long for that ancient presence to move from brooding over waters to brooding over people. At one point, the LORD told Moses,

> Gather for Me seventy men from the elders of Israel, . . . and bring them to the tent of meeting, and let them take their stand there with you. Then I will come down and speak with you there, and I will take of the Spirit who is upon you, and will put Him upon them; and they shall bear the burden of the people with you, so that you will not bear it all alone. (Num 11:16–17 NASB)

The Spirit-presence of God had rested upon Moses as an anointing for leadership over the people and to "bear" their burdens, not unlike the God who bears our suffering. Although others would join Moses in "bear[ing] the burden of the people," the Hebrew doesn't read that Yahweh will *take the power of* the Spirit from Moses. Instead, it says more simply that Yahweh will *take of* the Spirit. This uniquely changeable presence of God was able to be taken in portion from Moses and transferred—even multiplied—to the 70 elders![23]

More than the unique presence that rested upon Moses and the elders, the humanity of Christ is possibly the most explicit example of how God's presence is manifested and experienced in a special way. German theologian Wolfhart Pannenberg makes this very point when he says that "there is room for becoming in God himself" and then gives the example that God "became something that he previously was not when he became man in

---

23. The Israelites experienced just how portable and mobile the divine presence was. Yahweh moved along with the camp in a fire by day and a cloud by night, hovering over a golden ark, meeting with Moses in a tent that was repeatedly set up and torn back down. The Old Testament doesn't contain a simple category for the presence of Yahweh but recognizes God's dynamic involvement in the events of human history and in the experience of his people. God was a moving God, an elusive and even wandering presence.

Presence: God Shares His World

his Son."[24] As goes the Son of God, so goes the Spirit in the world. Andrew Gabriel notes, "Similar to how the presence of God changes through the Son in the incarnation, the presence of God also appears to change in the person of the Holy Spirit."[25] The Holy Spirit is naturally movement. The Spirit is dynamic breath and wind. The Spirit can be given, removed, and poured out. In fact, don't we intuitively get the sense that the Spirit's presence is changeable and dynamic? We conceive mental images of the Father and Son, but the Spirit remains ambiguous, like wind between our fingers.

Gabriel boldly asserts that "as the Spirit intensifies, the Spirit changes,"[26] leaving room for God's presence to change by more than mere appearance. If it's not merely our perception of his presence that changes, then perhaps his presence can actually change on the level of something "physical" or internal to God. Is it too much to consider that the Spirit's involvement in the world may include real, dynamic, and personal change? Jesus knew firsthand the perfect changeability of the Holy Spirit in his own life and ministry when the Spirit "descended on him in bodily form like a dove" (Luke 3:22), a beautiful illustration that combines the perfect changeableness of both the Son and the Spirit. Scripture doesn't say that the Spirit *was* a dove but that he was "like" a dove, possibly in movement only, as he descended through the air. But quite significantly, the Spirit took on "bodily form," a translation of the Greek word *somatiko*, which means bodily or corporeal—so the Spirit became physical and tangible! Thus, Jesus' meeting with the Spirit at his baptism suggests a change in God and his presence.[27]

As remarkable as divine change is, it is also inexplicable; we cannot possibly know to what degree God actually changes from day to day, as he interacts with us and our world. Nevertheless, the perfect changeability of God's presence is necessary and useful for meeting believers in certain places and at certain times and filling those spaces with new life and

---

24. Pannenberg, *Systematic Theology*, 1:438.

25. Gabriel, *Lord is the Spirit*, 156. Incarnation is a theological term that refers to God becoming a human being. God did not merely become human, however, but he added humanity to the divine existence. Jesus Christ is both completely God and completely human perfectly united in one person.

26. Ibid., 176. After criticizing the interpretation that only our perception of God's presence changes, Gabriel goes on to state that the language of intensifications of the Spirit's presence is merely metaphorical: God cannot be more or less in any given place but is "fully present everywhere" though in "different and changing ways in different places" (ibid., 157, 176).

27. Ibid., 159.

renewed mission. God's changeability guarantees that he is able to truly share himself with his people. After Jesus rose from the dead, he poured out the divine presence and "all of them were filled with the Holy Spirit" (Acts 2:4). That pentecostal event meant that everyone would share a unique experience of God's presence, even the Spirit himself! For the Holy Spirit, Pentecost was a personal experience of his own changing presence when he connected with the church.

Pentecost ushered in the special presence of God in a most vivid and extraordinary way, with signs confirming. Because the divine presence changes, people can truly experience God. Otherwise, an eternally static God might write on dead scrolls, but we would never be able to experience his power at work through us. The written word depends upon the perfect changeability of the Living Word who dynamically works through it and through us! Almost immediately after the pentecostal outpouring and the Spirit's occupation of the church, our mission began. Where the Spirit of the LORD is, there is liberty, mission, and liberation (2 Cor 3:17). The early church went out with miraculous displays of God's presence, a presence demonstrated in perfect changeability. They went out in the power of the *charismata* ("gifts" from God) and changed the world.

Conclusion

We worship an everlasting God of change who suffers with us and invites us to share in his presence. We saw in this chapter that God accepted the risk of creating creatures capable of sharing in his presence or rejecting it. In fact, one of God's perfections is his changeability and his natural experience to change in relation to people. This is particularly the case because the future is open to the degree that God knows some things as certain and some things as possible and remains eager to experience what freewill creatures will ultimately choose. Being the personal God he is, Yahweh cares about our thoughts and feelings and will even change his plans in light of our prayerful input.

Yahweh is a God who remains close, not eternally timeless, but *everlasting* and related in some sense to time. This temporal world is God's world too, so he shares his world with us. Because he experiences before and after, he is able to share himself and engage in relationships with people who exist in time and space. Hence, he experiences a full range of divinely expressive emotions such as: anger, jealousy, regret, frustration, surprise, desire, sorrow, hope, risk, and of course, suffering. Because Jesus suffers, God suffers. Just as Jesus' humanity adamantly demonstrates God's perfect changeability, so we know that the divine presence is capable of change. Therefore, the Spirit's pentecostal presence is able to permeate the church body and make us new creations on mission for prayer and ministry!

Now that we've introduced God's willingness to risk and the perfect changeability of God's Spirit in the world, we're ready to review God's presence at work throughout the Old Testament covenants leading up to the promise of a new covenant for the heart.

2

Covenant: God Shares Himself

IF WE'RE TO UNDERSTAND how vast God's desire has been to share his presence with the world, we should start with the Old Testament to see just how involved he's been. The Hebrew Scriptures tell the story of Yahweh seeking to keep the nations close to him through the commitment of covenant relationship. Most often, God has chosen to share himself with people through the mode of covenant. But despite God's best efforts, the Hebrew people were still human and thus rebellious, so the entire nation experienced the consequences of rejecting God's law when they were conquered by the Assyrians in 722 BC and later exiled to Babylon in 587 BC. Needless to say, countless people were enslaved and many even died, as a result. Through Israel's entry into exile, we observe an unparalleled illustration of the distance caused by sin and death in the Old Testament—a distance that separated people from family, land, and God.

The conditions of exile were dreadfully grim and, in many ways, reversed the blessing of the divine presence that God sought to share with the world through his chosen people. Because the Israelites were covenanted to Yahweh to enjoy the land of promise under the personal care of his presence, as a covenant people they were also meant to be a light to the world to overcome its darkness, rather than being defeated by it. In constant reminder to the Israelites of their *raison d'être*, Yahweh often and graciously warned his people, saying such things as, "Take warning, Jerusalem, or I will turn away from you and make your land desolate so no one can live in it" (Jer 6:8). In the Hebrew, the phrase "I will turn away from you" literally reads, *lest my soul departs from you*, attributing to God a soul that can abandon the people! Despite the constant failures of the Israelite people, they were nonetheless given the covenants to keep them close to the heart and purpose of God.

As we consider what it means to share in God's presence, we will look at the covenants of the Old Testament which reveal God's vigorous attempts to guard his presence among a worldly people. First, we will review God's commitments to Noah, Abram (later Abraham), Moses, and David. We will then see the promise of a new covenant that surpasses them all, a covenant of the heart.

God's Presence with Noah

The worldwide devastation of the flood brought about the finality of death's distance to every wicked person in the world (Gen 7:20–23). After the flood, even though humanity didn't change, God certainly changed in the way he dealt with them, because he was determined to raise up a faithful remnant to share himself with. Perhaps Yahweh reflected upon the expectations he had for the human race back in the garden of Eden and considered the downturn of wickedness and the utter devastation caused by *his* worldwide flood. Because the cost was far too great, the Lord refused to go down that path again. It seems, however, that the greatest influence upon his decision was the hope that he found in one faithful man named Noah. Faithful Noah had become God's sole representative remnant on the earth:

> Then Noah built an altar to the Lord and, taking some of all the clean animals and clean birds, he sacrificed burnt offerings on it. The Lord smelled the pleasing aroma and said in his heart: "Never again will I curse the ground because of humans, even though every inclination of the human heart is evil from childhood. And never again will I destroy all living creatures, as I have done. . . . I establish my covenant with you: Never again will all life be destroyed by the waters of a flood; never again will there be a flood to destroy the earth." (Gen 8:20–21; 9:11)

Because of one man's faithfulness, a singular remnant voice, Yahweh looked down on mortal humanity and concluded that he would not give up on us, despite the distance caused by every human thought being "evil from childhood." This was the first of many commitments God made in the form of a covenant.

An important nuance of the covenants is the reality that God holds himself accountable. Yahweh sought to reduce sin's worldwide distance by holding himself accountable to people, calling Noah out of the world and inviting him into a future full of hope and promise. Because the earth's entire population would come through Noah's lineage, he represented the whole human race before God. Unique to the Noahic covenant, God made himself accountable to humankind by placing a visual reminder in the sky—the warfare *bow* of cascading colors: "I have set my rainbow in the clouds, and it will be the sign of the covenant between me and the earth" (Gen 9:13). The rainbow is forever a sign that Yahweh will not bring a similar warring devastation upon people again; he is not at war with creation but at war with the distance of sin and death. The formality of God's oath grants humanity the privilege to hold him accountable.

In light of the flood, is it possible that Yahweh's experiment with free-will creatures proved more devastating than he first imagined? Rather than allowing the distance to once again grow *ad infinitum*, he made a covenant with Noah and then later with Abram and his descendants. Because God would continue to share himself with the human race, the covenants made with Noah, Abram, Moses, and David were all promissory oaths, depending largely upon God's faithfulness rather than people. God would not destroy the earth but would remain committed to the betterment of human beings and their world.

God's Presence with Abram

The first five books of the Old Testament introduce the story of God's faithfulness to reduce the distance, presenting him in terms of Creator and Covenant-keeper, while highlighting his relationship to Abram and, later on, to Moses. After making his promise to Noah, Yahweh also "cut a covenant" with Abram the Semite, promising salvation and blessing to the nations through this man's descendants (Gen 15:18).[1] Instead of giving up on the nations, God sought to display his faithful intentions toward an undeserving nation, Israel, the children of Abram. Yahweh would exhibit divine justice and faithfulness by destroying the distance caused by the sinfulness of his chosen nation.

---

1. In Genesis 15:18, the Hebrew literally reads, "On that day the Lord cut a covenant with Abram." Regarding Yahweh's covenant with Abram and his descendants, see Gen 3:15; 12:1–3; 13:14–17; 15:4–5; 17:4–8, 19; 18:18–19; 22:17–18; 26:3–4; 28:14–15; 35:12.

Covenant: God Shares Himself

"The Lord had said to Abram, 'Go from your country, your people and your father's household to the land I will show you. I will make you into a great nation, and I will bless you; I will make your name great, and you will be a blessing. I will bless those who bless you, and whoever curses you I will curse; and all peoples on earth will be blessed through you'" (Gen 12:1–3). "You will be a blessing" can also be translated from the Hebrew as an imperative—*Be a blessing!* In other words: *Abram, follow me, represent my presence, and be a blessing!*

Yahweh later reiterated those promises in Genesis 15 and assured Abram that he would indeed bless him by giving him a land. In response, we could say that Abram had the audacity to question Yahweh's faithfulness: "Sovereign Lord, how can I know that I will gain possession of it?" (Gen 15:8). This early Genesis account should impress upon the reader just how approachable Yahweh really is; only an open-minded God would expect his creatures to engage him so candidly! In response, Yahweh condescended to Abram's concerns by reassuring Abram through a ritual of animal sacrifice and a powerful dreamlike vision.

While Abram was sacrificing to the Lord, "birds of prey came down on the carcasses, but Abram drove them away," signifying that God would defeat Abram's enemies (Gen 15:11). Afterward, Abram fell into a deep sleep of "dreadful darkness" that likely represented the Hebrews' imminent slavery in Egypt. Despite such a miserable prediction, Yahweh then declared to Abram the deliverance of his people and the punishment of their enemies (vv. 12–16). Finally, God's presence was dramatically represented by a "smoking firepot with a blazing torch" that passed through the animal carcasses in order to reassure Abram that none other than God's presence would go with his people as they fought for the promised land (v. 17). So it was that "on that day the Lord cut a covenant with Abram" (v. 18).

The essence of that covenant was Yahweh's promise to be *present* with Abram and his people; they were promised to share in God's presence! This was the first time in history that God made a promise of his presence, linking his presence to a people and a land. Any distance felt by this people in this land would also be felt by God in the most profound of ways. Yahweh volunteered to enter into solidarity with Abram's descendants, which meant his own vulnerability as a heavenly Father to his new children. That new relationship was fleshed out throughout the prophetic books: "For the Lord has spoken: 'I reared children and brought them up, but they have rebelled against me'" (Isa 1:2). God himself had raised those children, so he had lofty aspirations for them. Yet even with the best intentions and the very best efforts of a divine Father, the children were still prone to rebel. Thankfully, God had covenanted to be their father *and ours*; he had committed to sharing his presence with his children.

As Yahweh reared a rebellious household, he made their suffering his own, as any good father would. The prophet Isaiah draws attention to a divine empathy that motivated Israel's heavenly Father to deliver his people from their suffering: "In all their distress he too was distressed, and the angel of his presence saved them" (Isa 63:9). In this summary of the divine response, Yahweh *shared* Israel's distress as his own, and it was quite literally God's own presence—the "angel of his presence"—that brought the deliverance they needed. And why was this so? Zechariah tells us, "This is what the LORD Almighty says: 'I am very jealous for Zion; I am burning with jealousy for her'" (Zech 8:2). Because of God's heart as Creator and Covenant-keeper, he would not give up on his children but continued to pursue their affections like a jealous lover.

Notice the language Hosea uses to express the LORD's commitment to his people: "How can I give you up, Ephraim? How can I hand you over, Israel? How can I treat you like Admah? How can I make you like Zeboyim? My heart is changed within me; all my compassion is aroused" (Hos 11:8). With a heart that responds with passionate fervor, the Covenant-keeper fully embraced the profoundly intimate depths of his covenant relationship and therefore chose not to neglect or abandon Israel. Hosea goes so far as to say that the LORD's "heart is changed" and his emotions stirred, demonstrating that this prophet was given insight into the very heart of God—a God of perfect change! Hosea can therefore conclude on behalf of Yahweh, "I will not carry out my fierce anger, nor will I devastate Ephraim again. For I am God, and not a man—the Holy One among you" (Hos 11:9). The prophet assures them that God would remain "among" them, committed to his covenant family.

Until Yahweh called and covenanted with Abram, the divine presence had never before been so intimately involved with any other group of people. Old Testament scholar Lawrence Boadt observes, "Israel recognized that the covenant was a gift from Yahweh and an honor for them and not the other way around. God freely chose to bind himself to this people, but not blindly no matter what they did in return." Boadt continues, "Most of all, he will be present whether it is a time of prosperity or of failure, for he has laid claim to this people as his own."[2] Readers should detect in Boadt's language a *partiality* of the divine presence. Although God is no respecter of persons, a certain partiality has always been at the heart of Yahweh's covenant with the patriarchs: "He has revealed his word to Jacob, his laws and decrees to Israel. He has done this for no other nation; they do not know his laws" (Ps 147:19–20; cf. Deut 4:7–8).

But even with God's undivided attention, the people would never comprehend the reality of the divine presence as much as the reality of God's absence.[3] We observe this very early in Israel's worship, even before a tabernacle was erected. For instance, we see it in the travels and worship of Abram's grandson Jacob. Jacob dreamed of a stairway to heaven that revealed the angelic presence that would accompany him along his journey, a presence that represented God's own. Scripture says, "When Jacob awoke from his sleep, he thought, 'Surely the Lord is in this place, and I was not aware of it.' He was afraid and said, 'How awesome is this place! This is none other than the house of God; this is the gate of heaven'" (Gen 28:16–17).

Jacob was completely caught off guard by God's elusive presence! Not only was Jacob ignorant that Yahweh was at Bethel, but he also lacked a general awareness of an omnipresent deity; Scripture says that he wasn't aware of it! One could say that Jacob, whose name was later changed to Israel (Gen 35:10), represented a common ignorance of the divine presence among the Israelites. Such ignorance would be perpetuated as long as God's presence was restricted to places and structures, whether altars, tents, temples, or Mount Zion.

God's Presence with Moses

Even though Yahweh constantly sought to minimize sin's distance through his covenant relationship to Israel, that relationship was often tested.[4] Stephen, the first martyr of the New Testament church, recounts God's history with the Hebrew man, Moses, when his covenant was tested time and again:

2. Boadt, *Reading the Old Testament*, 175.

3. Samuel Terrien says as much: "For fifteen centuries the recurrent motif of divine nearness is historically limited to a few men. The sense of presence is persistently compounded with an awareness of absence" (*Elusive Presence*, 28–29).

4. Yahweh had brought about worldwide devastation through the flood (Genesis 7) and then a lesser devastation when he destroyed Sodom and Gomorrah (19:1–29). Moving from worldwide to individual cities, God clearly reduced the destruction of his judgments.

> "I have indeed seen the oppression of my people in Egypt. I have heard their groaning and have come down to set them free. Now come, I will send [Moses] back to Egypt." . . . He was sent to be their ruler and deliverer by God himself, through the angel who appeared to him in the bush. . . . But our ancestors refused to obey him. Instead, they rejected him and in their hearts turned back to Egypt. They told Aaron, "Make us gods who will go before us. As for this fellow Moses who led us out of Egypt—we don't know what has happened to him!" . . . But God turned away from them and gave them over to the worship of the sun, moon and stars. (Acts 7:34, 35, 39–40, 42)

After 400 years of enslavement to Egypt, the groaning of Yahweh's covenant people captured his attention, so Stephen tells us that God looked down and *saw* and *heard* their outcry. He decided to *come down*, first to appear to Moses and then to rescue his people. Then on Mount Sinai, there was an immediate test of the covenant renewal which Yahweh had initiated when he presented Moses with the Ten Commandments: The people had begun to worship a golden calf (Exod 32:1–8)! Through that test, the significant role of a covenant mediator was brought to the forefront. When Moses their mediator was absent, the people assumed the absence of God and created their own gods to replace him.

Covenant holds God accountable but not without the help of a mediator who is acquainted with God's heart and understands the necessity of covenant faithfulness. In response to the golden calf, Yahweh fully intended to destroy all the people and fulfill his covenant promises through Moses alone: "Now leave me alone so that my anger may burn against them and that I may destroy them. Then I will make you into a great nation" (Exod 32:10). God went so far as to ask Moses to "leave me alone" so that his injured wrath could "destroy them," knowing full well that if Moses failed to intervene, God would surely eliminate them! But instead of eradicating the people, Moses was able to *persuade* God to keep them alive: "Then the Lord relented and did not bring on his people the disaster he had threatened" (Exod 32:14). This was certainly not the last time Yahweh changed his mind about destroying his people solely in response to a covenant mediator. Although it would be an exaggeration to call this a common occurrence, the Lord's threats were squelched on a number of occasions.[5]

Under Moses, God gave the people an elaborate system of law and priesthood in order to safeguard his presence within the nation. The

---

5. See Num 14:1–20; 16:16–27, 41–50; Deut 9:18–21.

Covenant: God Shares Himself

priesthood was intended to subdue the distance through atoning sacrifice. This truth was symbolically transferred to temple worship and brought out especially in the categories of cleanness and uncleanness, particularly in the book of Leviticus (see Leviticus 1–7). Regarding the concept of uncleanness under Moses' law, T. D. Alexander writes that "people who willfully ignore God's commands, decrees, or laws are a source of uncleanness and defile all that they touch. Their actions both distance them from God and bring them further under the domain of death."[6] In order to diminish such distance, the law was given, in addition to the priesthood, to outline God's expectations for his people and to provide descriptive warning of the consequences of disobedience, which was ultimately death and exile away from the divine presence (Lev 26:14–46; Deut 28:15–68).[7]

In keeping covenant with an earthly people, Yahweh condescended to a non-ideal situation, specifically tabernacle worship. Not only was this context restrictive of God's presence, but it also reeked of the stain of animal blood with its overtones of slaughter, death, and distance. In one sense, the heart of God was misrepresented by a violent context, while the presence of God was closed off to a select few from among the priests and Levites. Although Yahweh accepted the mutilated sacrifices of the tabernacle, his presence there was fleeting and obscure.[8] As long as the Israelites worshiped in portable tents or even in the temple that Solomon later erected, God's presence would remain elusive and largely ambiguous.[9]

The law and priesthood were means to help ensure that the divine presence would remain within the nation. Moses maintained the firm

---

6. Alexander, *From Paradise to Promised Land*, 212.

7. Seeing that Israel's unfaithfulness could result in exile or even death, it was obvious that God's temporal covenant faithfulness was not something to be taken for granted: "The LORD will also bring on you every kind of sickness and disaster not recorded in this Book of the Law, until you are destroyed.... Then the LORD will scatter you among all nations, from one end of the earth to the other" (Deut 28:61, 64). Despite God's desire to be their Healer, the chosen people always had the choice to distance him and bring disease and death upon themselves.

8. Michael Hundley comments, "The nature of his presence in his dwelling remains a mystery. His true form and location remain hidden. Although he presumably rests between the cherubim, his whereabouts between appearances are unclear. The ambulatory nature of the theophanic elements hints that he may come and go" (*Keeping Heaven on Earth*, 50).

9. Regarding this transitory period in Israel's history, Terrien remarks, "The nomadic motif of movement through space emerges as a symbol of openness to the future" (*Elusive Presence*, 73).

conviction that Yahweh's presence must abide with the people for his promises to be fulfilled and for the Israelites to possess the land. Even though God had historically revealed himself in the form of an angel or messenger,[10] with Moses he distinguished between himself and the angel, saying, "I will send an angel before you and drive out the Canaanites, Amorites, Hittites, Perizzites, Hivites and Jebusites. Go up to the land flowing with milk and honey. But I will not go with you, because you are a stiff-necked people and I might destroy you on the way" (Exod 33:2-3). God's uncertainty about the future becomes blatantly transparent in this passage. Yahweh voices genuine concern over the real possibility that he might become provoked and terminate the people along the way! We mustn't conclude that God's attitude is in any way impure or unjust, but there is clearly a negative dimension of feeling and emotion to the openness of God's heart.

Notice Israel's response: "When the people heard these distressing words, they began to mourn and no one put on any ornaments. For the LORD had said to Moses, 'Tell the Israelites, "You are a stiff-necked people. If I were to go with you even for a moment, I might destroy you"'" (Exod 33:4-5). They grieved over the possibility that God would send with them someone other than his own presence. Moreover, their response implied the possibility for a messenger other than God to accomplish a mission on his behalf, while God himself remained absent from the process altogether—an assumption Yahweh never once challenged! But finally, albeit grudgingly, the LORD yielded to Moses' request and reassured him with these words: "My presence will go with you, and I will give you rest" (Exod 33:14). Yet even after such a confident reassurance, Moses still wasn't

---

10. It is possible that many, if not most, appearances of Yahweh in the Old Testament are actually the mediatory appearance of an angel or other created vehicle, such as a cloud or flaming bush. We are told that it was the angel or "messenger (*malak*) of Yahweh" who appears to Moses in the fiery bush (Exod 3:2-4) and interrupts Abraham from sacrificing Isaac (Gen 22:11-15). It is this same *malak* of Yahweh who appears to Gideon, the judge. Yet Gideon became fearful because he found himself in the very presence of God (Judg 6:11-23)! In Judges 13:9 and other places, this *malak* is also called the "angel of God" (Gen 31:11; Exod 14:19). In the Hebrew Bible, we are told that Moses received the covenant law as "inscribed by the finger of God" (Exod 31:18; Deut 9:10), but in the New Testament, Paul informs us that "the law was given through angels and entrusted to a mediator" (Gal 3:19; cf. Heb 12:2). In the book of Acts, Stephen mentions the "angel who appeared to [Moses] in the bush" and "the angel who spoke to [Moses] on Mount Sinai" (Acts 7:35, 38). Stephen is consistent in crediting angels with activities we'd more naturally ascribe to Yahweh in the Old Testament, and he is quite comfortable doing so. Stephen also reports that the Israelites "received the law that was given through angels" (Acts 7:53). See also Exod 33:2; Num 20:16; 1 Chr 21:15; 2 Chr 32:21.

satisfied but continued to express his concern: "Then Moses said to him, 'If your presence does not go with us, do not send us up from here'" (v. 15).

Through covenant, Yahweh took his stand in human history to reduce the distance between himself and the people of the earth. That distance involved more than sin and death, but included even the Hebrew notion of sickness and disease as encroaching forms of death: "He said, 'If you listen carefully to the LORD your God and do what is right in his eyes, if you pay attention to his commands and keep all his decrees, I will not bring on you any of the diseases I brought on the Egyptians, for I am the LORD, who heals you'" (Exod 15:26). In Boadt's discussion on covenant, he captures this same sense: "God pledges himself to be Israel's personal protector and helper, not only against foreign enemies, but against sickness, disease, and chaos as well."[11]

Yahweh sought to eliminate distance from *every* facet of life, promising to share his presence with a chosen people. If they would choose obedience to his commands and decrees, then he could be the LORD who heals and keeps them in perfect health and safety.

God's Presence with David

This brings us to the Deuteronomist history and Israel's descent into exile. Scholars commonly recognize that the book of Deuteronomy and the Former Prophets (Joshua, Judges, Samuel, Kings) "stood as a *single literary piece* written from a *single interpretive angle* as a commentary upon the destruction of Jerusalem in 587 and as a meditation upon the ensuing crisis of exile."[12] Those five books are of utmost importance because they present a reliable theological interpretation of history. They relay the story of Israel's deliverance from Egypt, along with the rise of priest, prophet, and king, only to show Israel on a self-destructive path into exile.

From the outset, the Deuteronomist identifies the crisis of presence and makes explicit Israel's choice between divine presence or absence: "See, I set before you today life and prosperity, death and destruction.... But if your heart turns away and you are not obedient, and if you are drawn away to bow down to other gods and worship them, I declare to you this day that you will certainly be destroyed. You will not live long in the land you are crossing the Jordan to enter and possess" (Deut 30:15, 17–18). It becomes

11. Boadt, *Reading the Old Testament*, 175.
12. Brueggemann, *Introduction to the Old Testament*, 104, emphasis original.

apparent here that the intensity of God's warning has changed drastically since the garden of Eden. The "certainly die" for Adam's disobedience has been replaced with the more hostile, you will "certainly be destroyed," which implies that there is something inherently wrong with the objects of wrath (Gen 2:17).

Before Israel came to have a king, the primary point of contact for the divine presence had been the offices of priest and prophet. Unfortunately, those offices had become morally corrupt (e.g., 1 Sam 2:12–17, 22–25). The resultant situation is reflected in 1 Samuel 3:1, which says, "In those days the word of the LORD was rare; there were not many visions." Although there were still a few people who remained obedient to Yahweh and pursued the promise of his presence, like Hannah and her son Samuel (1 Samuel 1–3), the corruption of those offices displayed a failed relationship with God that dramatically affected the nation as a whole. Israel's priests and prophets had stifled the divine presence and muffled any prophetic evidence of it.

During that time period, one of the most dramatic analogies of God's absence came when the Philistines captured "the ark of the covenant of the LORD Almighty, who is enthroned between the cherubim" (1 Sam 4:4). Since the days of Moses, the golden ark was kept hidden behind the curtain in the Most Holy Place of the tabernacle where God's immediate presence was known to visit (Lev 16:2). If the ark was in some sense the location of God's enthronement, then it could be said that the vulgar Philistine army had captured God! The evidence was that "the Israelites were defeated and every man fled to his tent" (I Sam 4:10). By analogy, the sinful condition of Israel resulted in the loss of God's presence. In this way, his presence could be "captured" and taken away from the nation when her sin welcomed defeat from physical or spiritual enemies, who, in this case, were the Philistines.[13]

Within the corpus of Deuteronomist history, Yahweh introduced a further development to his everlasting covenant with Israel, the addition of a king forever enthroned. This was accomplished through God's everlasting covenant with King David and his descendants, otherwise known as the Davidic covenant (2 Sam 7:10–16). Unlike the defeat that the Israelites had experienced at the hands of the Philistines and the loss of the Ark-presence of God, under this renewed covenant "wicked people will not oppress them anymore, . . . I will also give you rest from all your enemies" (2 Sam 7:10,

---

13. This scenario is reminiscent of Moses' concern that without the divine presence the Israelites could only suffer defeat (Exod 33:12–17).

11). That promised kingdom would be the royal sphere of the divine presence and a kingdom of rest for the king's people, the children of Israel. Contained within this covenant renewal was the promise of an eternal kingdom and the assurance of the king's presence with his people (v. 16); hence, God was sharing his throne!

Once the Abrahamic, Sinaitic (or Mosaic), and Davidic covenants were in place, God was covenanted to a people in a promissory relationship of long-suffering, faithful love. Even so, we mustn't misunderstand and think that Yahweh hadn't always possessed the virtue of such persevering love. The difference was that the nations would now see God's long-suffering on unique display through the Hebrew people. God's presence in the world became known through a particular people and connected to a particular place: first the patriarchal prophets, then his priests and judges, then his kings and the tabernacle of Zion, and finally through all the prophets of Israel. Although it's strange to think that the divine presence could be restricted to a temple or land (2 Sam 7:6), Yahweh nonetheless limited his presence by making Israel his primary point of contact to the world (1 Kgs 8:59–60). In a particular place among a particular people, God made his name known and manifested his glory.

The Old Testament books of Deuteronomy and the Former Prophets provide a detailed explanation of Israel's exile, demonstrating that the reason for exile was Israel's sin and her failure to maintain covenant faithfulness as outlined in God's law (Deut 28:15–68). Yet despite her failings, the covenants were at work to reduce the distance: "But the LORD was gracious to them and had compassion and showed concern for them because of his covenant with Abraham, Isaac and Jacob. To this day he has been unwilling to destroy them or banish them from his presence" (2 Kgs 13:23).

God's Presence Within the Heart

As part of their personal history, the prophets experienced the nation's rebellion while they delivered a two-sided message of warning and hope for restoration and renewal. The prophet Isaiah once said, "No one calls on your name or strives to lay hold of you; for you have hidden your face from us and have given us over to our sins" (Isa 64:7). But as covenant mediator, Isaiah also beseeched the LORD on behalf of the nation, saying, "Do not be angry beyond measure, LORD; do not remember our sins forever. Oh, look on us, we pray, for we are all your people" (v. 9). Isaiah's response to God's warnings was the only responsible action for Israel—a prayer of repentance that begs for mercy! In the same breath, Isaiah exhorts the Lord to eliminate the distance by looking upon his people. Because once again, perhaps the Lord will relent.

Besides warning Israel of the tragic consequence of exile, the writings of the prophets also present the hope of restoration and the return of God's presence. The return of the divine presence would coincide with the return of the exiles. Distance for the nation of Israel was just for a season so that the chaff could be separated from the wheat. Zechariah attested to this when he declared God's word to the sixth-century people of Judah, saying, "Though I scatter them among the peoples, yet in distant lands they will remember me. They and their children will survive, and they will return" (Zech 10:9). Although many would continue in their rebellion to their own destruction, there was always a remnant of those who would "remember" and repent. That remnant would eventually return to the land of God's promise and presence.

While the prophets remained hopeful that a repentant remnant would ultimately prevail, there was nonetheless an encroaching concern that the Israelites could bring about their final destruction. Ezekiel was another sixth-century prophet whose cry reflected that concern: "While they were killing and I was left alone, I fell facedown, crying out, 'Alas, Sovereign Lord! Are you going to destroy the entire remnant of Israel in this outpouring of your wrath on Jerusalem?'" (Ezek 9:8). Speaking two centuries before Zechariah and Ezekiel, the prophet Hosea said of the people of Israel, "But the more they were called, the more they went away from me. They sacrificed to the Baals and they burned incense to images.... Will they not return to Egypt and will not Assyria rule over them because they refuse to repent?" (Hos 11:2, 5). Because of such recurring trends of rebellion and refusal to change their ways, it remained a real concern for the prophets that Yahweh would once and for all destroy this rebellious people.

Time and again the Lord had argued for the utter annihilation of his people, just as in the days of Moses, so the prophets were concerned because they believed him. In fact, the prophet Zephaniah spoke such a devastating word from Yahweh that it resembled the judgment of Noah's day, using language indicative of destroying both Israel and Judah and all the wicked nations of the world: "'I will sweep away everything from the face of the earth, when I destroy all mankind on the face of the earth,' declares the Lord. 'I will sweep away both man and beast; I will sweep away the birds in the sky and the fish in the sea—and the idols that cause the wicked to stumble'" (Zeph 1:2–3). Now that's a word that would make anyone tremble! Yahweh wanted to destroy every wicked person as well as the source ("cause") of their temptation! Nonetheless, among others, the prophet of Lamentations maintained the assurance that "no one is cast off by the Lord forever" (Lam 3:31; cf. Lev 26:44).

The prophets spoke doom, but they also understood that Yahweh's greatest burden was to return to his land and temple so that the people could share in his presence. Among the greatest promises of Scripture, Yahweh told Ezekiel,

> I dealt with them according to their uncleanness and their offenses, and I hid my face (*panim*) from them. Therefore this is what the Sovereign LORD says: I will now restore the fortunes of Jacob and will have compassion on all the people of Israel, and I will be zealous for my holy name.... I will no longer hide my face (*panim*) from them, for I will pour out my Spirit (*ruach*) on the people of Israel, declares the Sovereign LORD. (Ezek 39:24–25, 29)

Ezekiel refers to the face (*panim*) of God, which is used here and in other Old Testament passages as the Hebrew equivalent for God's overall *presence* (e.g., Gen 3:8; 4:16). Through the eloquence of Hebrew parallelism, Ezekiel described the restoration of the divine presence in terms of a dynamic, personal metaphor—namely, a renewed outpouring of God's Spirit (*ruach*). Ezekiel was saying that it would be through an outpouring of the Spirit that the people would share in God's presence in an unparalleled fashion.

Ezekiel anticipated not only a renewal of God's Spirit but also a return of God's glory. After God's glorious presence departed from the temple in Ezekiel 11, the prophet predicted his certain return: "Suddenly, the glory of the God of Israel appeared from the east. The sound of his coming was like the roar of rushing waters, and the whole landscape shone with his glory.... And the glory of the LORD came into the Temple through the east gateway. Then the Spirit took me up and brought me into the inner courtyard, and the glory of the LORD filled the Temple" (Ezek 43:2, 4–5 NLT).[14]

---

14. Brueggemann summarizes this return of God's glorious presence, contrasting it with the ultimate punishment of divine absence: "The dramatic return of YHWH's glory in 43:1–5, a glory now permanently secured for the temple in 44:1–3, is the decisive antidote to the departure of YHWH's glory in chapters 9 and 10. Thus, the supreme punishment of YHWH, in priestly purview, is *absence*; the supreme resolution of crisis in priestly purview is restored cultic *presence*" (*Introduction to the Old Testament*, 203, emphasis original). Even though God's presence was secured in the temple, it was also

Although Ezekiel described God's restored presence in terms of glory, he was hopeful for the more relational dimension of a personal encounter with the Spirit: "Therefore prophesy and say to them: 'This is what the Sovereign Lord says: My people, I am going to open your graves [of exile] and bring you up from them; I will bring you back to the land of Israel.... I will put my Spirit in you and you will live, and I will settle you in your own land'" (37:12, 14). Ezekiel emphatically predicted such a future hope, but he wasn't the only one talking about restoration. Centuries earlier, Isaiah and others were speaking the same promises.

More than a century before Ezekiel, the prophet Isaiah also spoke a positive message from Yahweh, saying, "'In a surge of anger I hid my face from you for a moment, but with everlasting kindness I will have compassion on you,' says the Lord your Redeemer" (Isa 54:8). A contemporary of Isaiah, Amos also declared from the Lord, "I will bring my exiled people of Israel back from distant lands, and they will rebuild their ruined cities and live in them again. They will plant vineyards and gardens; they will eat their crops and drink their wine" (Amos 9:14 NLT). Hosea, another eighth-century prophet, echoed similar thoughts: "After two days he will revive us; on the third day he will restore us, that we may live in his presence" (Hos 6:2).

Within the hopeful message of the prophets was a nuance of expectation, not for another covenant altogether, but for a new kind of covenant that involved the renewal of the human heart. Ezekiel referred to this when he said, "I will give them an undivided heart and put a new spirit in them; I will remove from them their heart of stone and give them a heart of flesh" (Ezek 11:19; cf. 36:26). The Lord gave the prophet Jeremiah a similar message, saying, "'The days are coming,' declares the Lord, 'when I will make a new covenant with the people of Israel and with the people of Judah.... This is the covenant I will make with the people of Israel after that time,' declares the Lord. 'I will put my law in their minds and write it on their hearts. I will be their God, and they will be my people'" (Jer 31:31, 33).

As you can see, the prophets looked forward to a dramatic resolution to the problem of humanity's distance from God, a "new" covenant that dealt intrinsically with the rebellious and sinful heart. This fresh renewal would become the unique occasion for people to truly possess God's

---

secured away from the people (Ezek 44:1–2). Until the future outpouring of God's Spirit, his presence would continue to be restricted solely to the prince: "Only the prince himself may sit inside this gateway to feast in the Lord's presence" (44:3 NLT).

presence and for God to know and possess them. Jeremiah added, "'No longer will they teach their neighbor, or say to one another, "Know the LORD," because they will all know me, from the least of them to the greatest,' declares the LORD. 'For I will forgive their wickedness and will remember their sins no more'" (Jer 31:34). In other words, Yahweh looked forward to a time when he would share himself with *everyone*, "from the least of them to the greatest"!

Promises were made and hope was being restored within the nation, but by the end of the fifth century BC, the prophets stopped speaking altogether. A cold silence settled upon the land for four hundred years while the Mediterranean world warily awaited the covenant that would be established upon the blood of the unique Son of God, the Lord Jesus Christ. Four centuries was plenty of time for Israel to question her distance from Yahweh and entertain the unsettling thought that he might not return to his people.

Conclusion

Yahweh made certain covenant commitments to safeguard his presence among the nations. Both sides of the covenant, God and people, are equally privileged to hold each other accountable to its terms. The Noahic covenant protected the entire human race from another worldwide exile into the flood of death. Yahweh's covenant with Abram committed the divine presence to a specific people and land. God's covenant with Moses sought to protect the Hebrew people from the abyss of national exile through law and atonement. Lastly, the Davidic covenant was the promise of an eternal kingdom where the people of God would dwell in the presence of a Davidic king forever.

Despite the LORD's long-suffering and gracious promises, Scripture asserts the utter failure of the Israelites to remain faithful to his covenants, ultimately resulting in their exile both in the eighth and sixth centuries BC. Even so, God was always looking for a repentant remnant to return to the land to usher the return of his glorious presence. His prophets continued to warn against covenant unfaithfulness, while they also eagerly anticipated a widespread renewal from God's Spirit.

Within the message of the prophets was the promise of a renewed covenant of the heart, the new covenant that we'll see worked out in chapters three and four.

3

Salvation: God Shares His Son

ONCE THE ERA OF the Old Testament prophets had ended, God allowed 400 years to pass before he revealed his ultimate plan to share his Son with the world. Jesus Christ is God's gift to everyone, the perfecter of a new covenant inscribed by the blood of his sacrifice, a covenant that touches the heart through forgiveness and the gift of God's presence. Because "the Father has sent his Son to be the Savior of the world," our Lord Jesus Christ truly is the hero of the Christian faith *and* the whole world (1 John 4:14).

After God's presence came to earth in a most dramatic fashion through the virgin birth, Jesus ultimately yielded himself to the epitome of human violence so that he could share the divine presence with anyone who trusts in his resurrection. The resurrection is literally a renewed presence of God in indestructible fashion: "For the perishable must clothe itself with the imperishable, and the mortal with immortality" (1 Cor 15:53). Now that God has made his own flesh-and-blood humanity incorruptible, we can begin to see the boundless depths that his awesome presence is capable of!

The resurrection of Jesus Christ is not only the central tenant of the Christian faith but also the basis for sharing God's saving presence with the world. The Apostle Paul declares that the essence of his preaching is "Christ and him crucified" (1 Cor 2:2). Although the brutal murder of God's Son sounds like an awful and abhorrent message, the crucifixion of an imperishable being just happens to be the best news to share with the world. Because sin and death create a nearly impossible problem for every human being, we have nowhere else to turn but the cross! As scandalous as the cross was, it is overshadowed *ad infinitum* by the glory of Jesus' resurrection, the testimony of an eternal God conquering the distance of death so that he could draw all people into his presence by sharing his Son with the world.

In this chapter, we'll focus on the gift of God's Son through new covenant salvation. We'll look at Jesus' victory over sin and death, the presence of the triune God at the cross, the believer's complete forgiveness, and the two sacraments of water baptism and the Lord's Supper. While this chapter will highlight the new covenant emphasis of forgiveness, the next chapter will feature the other major aspect of the new covenant, the gift of God's Spirit.

Jesus Overcame Sin and Death

Because mortality and decay have an uncompromising agreement with sin and death, they sought to devour even God's own presence when he became a man, no doubt bewildered by what occurred *after* Jesus died. When we consider our salvation and the array of metaphors attached to it (sacrifice, substitute, redemption, etc.), ultimately it comes down to this: Through resurrection, Jesus Christ defeated death in order to deliver humankind from the power of sin, death, and the devil.[1] Through Jesus' mortal experience of birth, life, and death, he repeated the history of every human being. But he then accomplished what no human ever could when he rose from the grave, immortalizing God's presence within the human race. Indeed, death has been overthrown and replaced with incorruption through "Christ Jesus, who has destroyed death and has brought life and immortality to light through the gospel" (2 Tim 1:10).

The cross has no merit or meaning apart from resurrection, the powerful display of divine presence in action. By rising out from the midst of an historical record of dead mortals, Jesus alone broke death's record of

---

1. This position has been described as the Christus Victor ("Christ is Victor") model of atonement, which interprets the cross primarily as Jesus' victorious display of love against every form of opposition. Through the power of love and the victory of resurrection, Jesus conquered sin, death, Satan, the cosmic powers, and even the fallen creation. The author of Hebrews describes it this way: "Since the children have flesh and blood, he too shared in their humanity so that by his death he might break the power of him who holds the power of death—that is, the devil" (Heb 2:14). Other prominent models of atonement include penal substitution, satisfaction, moral government, moral influence, and the ransom theory.

hopeless defeat. Our hope is lost apart from God raising Jesus out from among the dead ones, which is what the cross represents (1 Cor 15:14). Salvation is nothing less than resurrection! Jesus' resurrection stands as the decisive victory over sin and death, not merely as a demonstration of the Father's approval over a great accomplishment.[2] Resurrection is the game changer! Because resurrection is God's incorruptible display of his glorious presence, the divine presence is now the presence of resurrection glory! After death reared its ugly head in the garden of Eden, people now need life more than anything else—specifically, resurrection life. Truly Jesus is "the resurrection and the life" for all who believe in him (John 11:25).

At the cross, Jesus overcame death and the Demon who holds the power of death (Heb 2:14), but not because he was brutally punished by his Father, a popular belief held since the Reformation.[3] A largely misunderstood passage, Isaiah 53:4 says, "Surely he took up our pain and bore our suffering, yet we considered him punished by God, stricken by him, and afflicted." In the context of Isaiah 53, this so-called punishment from God is the misunderstanding of those looking upon the suffering servant: "*we* considered him punished by God." The New Living Translation adds some clarity: "And we thought his troubles were a punishment from God, a punishment for his own sins!" The idea here is that those looking upon the suffering servant were wrong, not only that the servant was being punished for his sins, but that he was experiencing punishment at all. What they perceived as punishment was actually for their deliverance! "But he was pierced for our transgressions, he was crushed for our iniquities; the [so-called] punishment that brought us peace was on him, and by his wounds

---

2. Andrew Louth summarizes the importance of resurrection for every believer: "This belief that Christ did not succumb to death, but overcame death: something manifest in the resurrection, when he demonstrates that death has not taken him, but he has overthrown death—it is this that is the fundamental Christian belief" (*Introducing Eastern Orthodox Theology*, 55).

3. The widespread view of the cross as divine punishment is commonly described as the penal substitutionary atonement. This theory was developed by the Reformers in the 1500s based on the satisfaction theory that was articulated by Anselm in AD 1098 (*Cur Deus Homo*). The debate over the nature of the atonement includes numerous viewpoints. "To mention just a few spikes in the controversy, we have Abelard's 'moral theory' versus Anselm's 'satisfaction theory' (11th century), the Socinians's attempt to rebuff the Reformers (16th century), John Owen's answer to Hugo Grotius's 'governmental theory' (17th century) and a host of alternatives that arise in the 20th century (most notably Gustaf Aulen's "*Christus Victor*" and René Girard's mimetic theory)" (Jersak, "Nonviolent Identification," 24). For response and rebuttal to the penal theory, see Jersak and Hardin, *Stricken by God?*; and Beilby and Eddy, *Nature of the Atonement*, 99–116.

Salvation: God Shares His Son

we are healed" (Isa 53:5). Divorced from any notion of torture from his Father, Jesus suffered at the hands of violent *people*: "And you, with the help of wicked men, put him to death by nailing him to the cross" (Acts 2:23).[4]

Jesus' *suffering* for our sin should by no means be equated with *punishment* for sin. In fact, the prophet Ezekiel teaches that a person cannot be punished and put to death for someone else: "The one who sins is the one who will die. The child will not share the guilt of the parent, nor will the parent share the guilt of the child. The righteousness of the righteous will be credited to them, and the wickedness of the wicked will be charged against them" (Ezek 18:20; cf. Num 35:31; Deut 24:16). The cross is not an expression of divine brutality, but on the contrary, it remains the most profound display of the long-suffering, vulnerable love of God. Jesus experienced God's wrath not by punishment, but by death, so that he could destroy death through resurrection power.

The resurrection is not alone in its effects on salvation. It empowers such wonderful graces as forgiveness of sin, removal of guilt, pardon from God's wrath, and justifying righteousness, along with all the other special gifts associated with salvation. Yet the essence of our redemption is ultimately resurrection *through and with* Jesus Christ: "He who raised Christ from the dead will also give life to your mortal bodies because of his Spirit who lives in you" (Rom 8:11). Resurrection incited Jesus' death for the benefit of us all; he died for everyone so that anyone could share in his resurrection. No other religion answers the problem of death because anything short of bodily resurrection capitulates to death, leaving the glory of Jesus' resurrection without comparison in all of salvation history.

Every human being before Jesus—except perhaps Elijah, Enoch, and possibly others we're not aware of—ended up in the ground, "for dust you are and to dust you will return" (Gen 3:19). But resurrection reverses the death sentence through Christ Jesus, guaranteeing that those who stand with him will share in the same resurrection. According to James Payton, "Christ became the guarantee of the fulfillment of God's original creative purpose for all of creation—namely, life with God forever."[5] Jesus' resurrection assures us that we can share in God's presence because it provides the basis for us to possess the very same internal Spirit that raised Jesus from the dead. The Spirit's perfect changeability guarantees that he can infuse

---

4. See Matt 20:18–19; 26:2–4; 27:20, 35; Mark 15:24; Luke 22:22; 23:21, 33; 24:20; John 11:53; 19:18; Acts 2:36.

5. Payton, *Light from the Christian East*, 125.

the unique contours of every mortal spirit, filling believers with the same presence of God that will one day raise us from the dead. So the psalmist can confidently declare, "The upright will live in your presence" (Ps 140:13).

Despite death's power over everyone else, it had no sway over Jesus because he didn't follow in the first Adam's rebellious footsteps but always yielded to his Father's authority (cf. 1 Cor 5:12–21). Because of this, Satan's kingdom is powerless against the second Adam! Jesus told his disciples, "The prince of this world is coming. He has no hold over me" (John 14:30; cf. Matt 4:8–10). Because sin could not hold the power of death over Jesus, it's a theological possibility that he could have lived on indefinitely; but instead, he freely chose to lay down his life to overcome sin and death once and for all (John 10:18). Now that Jesus stands as victor in the face of our greatest enemy, he becomes victor over *all* our enemies and can be trusted with our very lives. Andrew Louth says it this way: "Because it is death that Christ has overthrown—death that reduces all our efforts to nothing—Christ is shown to be beyond the reach of any power that could threaten us."[6] Because Jesus truly is our Hero and Savior, well beyond the reach of Satan, sin, and death, he saves us from every possible enemy.

God's Presence at the Cross

As Christ hung on the cross, he shocked the universe with that terrible outcry, "My God, my God, why have you forsaken me?" (Matt 27:46; Mark 15:34). But what could he have possibly meant by this? Was he suggesting that his Father had abandoned him and left him alone when he needed him the most? It begs the question: If God would forsake his own Son in his darkest hour and at the moment of his greatest need, could his presence also abandon me? Because sharing in God's presence is meant to provide us with a secure relationship with God, we should consider whether the Father literally abandoned his Son at the cross.[7]

---

6. Louth, *Introducing Eastern Orthodox Theology*, 55. See Rom 8:38–39. Louth adds that "Christ's love for human kind is able to overcome death, for it does not succumb to death, but seeks it out" (ibid.).

7. Dean Harvey remarks on what is arguably the most common understanding of this event: "*[Jesus] was now sinful,* and since God cannot look upon sin, God had to turn his back on Jesus . . . for a moment in eternity, never to be repeated again, the Father *withdrew His presence and turned His back*; He couldn't look any more" (*Ransom: High Cost of Sin*, 93, 99, emphasis added). You heard him right—according to Harvey, Jesus became sinful!

Salvation: God Shares His Son

In what sense was Jesus *forsaken* by his Father? Thankfully, it is highly unlikely such words even remotely convey a removal of the Father's presence. Just moments after Jesus uttered those terrible words, he spoke to his Father in a manner conducive to familiarity and utmost trust: "Jesus called out with a loud voice, 'Father, into your hands I commit my spirit.' When he had said this, he breathed his last" (Luke 23:46). Jesus knew that in the moments leading up to his death, the Father was close enough to take hold of him, hence his godforsaken outcry can only be understood within that context. Far from being a cry of abandonment, perhaps Jesus' outburst represents some aspect of the special rapport that exists between him and his Father: Jesus was crying out to the only one who would hear him in that dreadful hour (cf. Job 13:16).[8] No one else but the Father remained close enough to receive his Son's cries and respond to his pain. Jesus even told his disciples, "Do you think I cannot call on my Father, and he will at once put at my disposal more than twelve legions of angels?" (Matt 26:53).

Even in the context of Psalm 22:1, which Jesus quotes nearly verbatim ("Why have you forsaken me?"), the conclusion is one of God's supportive presence and not of separation: "For he has not despised or scorned the suffering of the afflicted one; he has not hidden his face from him but has listened to his cry for help" (Ps 22:24). Although Jesus remained helpless to change what was happening to him, he knew that if everyone else had abandoned him entirely, he could still look to his Father and share his grief with God in the midst of extreme agony. According to Paul Fiddes, "It is a cry of protest, . . . but even in that cry he is beginning to relate his experience of death to God."[9] In the midst of a nightmare, Jesus' raw outcry appears to be his final attempt to feel the embrace of his Father's relationship.

Jesus' outcry is often identified with a "spiritual death" on the cross, as if the Father had abandoned him because he literally became sin. But the Father did not turn his back on Jesus because Jesus did not in any real sense "be[come] sin for us" (2 Cor 5:21). He only *became sin* in the sense that Isaiah 53:10 asserts, that his life was made an "offering for sin," which points to his death. Because Jesus did not literally become sin, he qualified

---

8. In that moment of personally experiencing humanity's violent hatred, Jesus questioned the Father but knew full well why he hung in anticipation of death, having directly questioned the Father in Gethsemane on that very subject just hours before the cross. It was there at Gethsemane that Jesus resolved to surrender himself to the Father's plan, determining, "Father, if you are willing, take this cup from me; yet not my will, but yours be done" (Luke 22:42).

9. Fiddes, *Participating in God*, 158.

as the perfect, stainless Lamb of God who takes away the sin of the world by dying for everyone.[10]

Far from the notion of a "spiritual death" occurring on the cross, Jesus did not experience the full brunt and consequence of sin until the moment he took his last breath and physically *died*.[11] This truth could not be more evident throughout the New Testament: "Christ died for our sins, just as the Scriptures said" (1 Cor 15:3 NLT; cf. 1 Pet 3:18; Heb 9:28). At the moment Jesus *died*, he confronted the most ruthless enemy of every human being—death itself (1 Cor 15:26). This is why the New Testament so often refers to the "blood" of Christ to evoke the significance of the cross, because it is a metonym of spilt blood which represents Jesus' physical death.[12] On the cross, it was not some mystical spiritual death that was needed to secure our salvation but a physical death that needed to be overcome through a physical resurrection.

The judgment of Almighty God against sin was fulfilled through Jesus' physical death on the cross, the *tetelestai* moment. Just before Jesus died, in John 19:30 he cried out *tetelestai*—"It is finished!"—in imminent *anticipation* of ultimate victory over sin and death. Jesus knew the time had come to surrender his spirit to the Father, which would bring his mission to completion. If we can identify a moment in time when God would abandon his Son because of sin, it would be that moment of physical death, "for the wages of sin is death" (Rom 6:23). Yet in that very moment Jesus cried out in dependence and utter confidence in his relationship to the Father,

---

10. Jesus has always been entirely free from sin in nature, thought, temptation, and deed; see Matt 7:11; 11:29; John 4:34; 8:29, 46; 15:10; Acts 3:14; 2 Cor 5:21; Heb 4:15; 7:26; 1 Pet 1:19; 2:22; 1 John 2:1; 3:5.

11. Sin is not *quantitative* as satisfaction and penal substitution theories have suggested, as if sin can be counted up and quantified so that a restitution or punishment equal to or greater than the offense is required. Scripture never teaches that all of humanity's (or the elect's) individual sins were somehow imputed to Jesus on the cross, what some think of as a spiritual death, so that he could pay for, be punished for, or make restitution for trillions of specific sins. At the cross, the "imputation" of sin was rather the *qualitative* reality of death itself. When Christ suffered physical death, the judgment of God was final and sin was overcome.

12. The "blood" of Christ is a figure of speech known as a metonym of cause for effect. Blood is a metonym for death, the cause representing the effect. In other words, the spilling of blood leads to death. For passages that refer to Jesus' blood, see Matt 26:27–28; Mark 14:23–24; Luke 22:20; John 6:53–57; 19:33–34; Acts 20:28; Rom 3:25; 1 Cor 10:16; 11:25–27; Eph 1:7; 2:13; Col 1:19–20; Heb 9:12–14; 10:3–14, 19–22, 28–31; 12:24; 13:11–12, 20; 1 Pet 1:1–2; 1 John 1:6–9; 5:6; Rev 1:5–6; 5:9–10; 7:14–17; 12:10–11.

Salvation: God Shares His Son

saying, "I commit my spirit" into your hands, into your care and personal presence (Luke 23:46).

Ultimately, Jesus' godforsakenness points to the Father's refusal to intervene in his Son's death, leaving him helpless and without rescue, though only temporarily.[13] In the truest possible sense, Jesus was experiencing death *and the fear of death* because he was helpless to stop it (Heb 2:15). This is what death does; in fact, this is what death is. Death is significant because it is the fearful and absolute end to life, when all living ceases.[14] But this experience was cut short by resurrection as the Father's conclusive answer to Jesus' helplessness. With resurrection looming on the horizon, Jesus was able to finally express thoughts of total safety and assurance, saying, *Father, I commit my spirit into the care of your strong hands.* Far from being driven apart, the Trinity accomplished its assault on the kingdom of darkness as a united, organized cohort. On the cross at Calvary, it was "*Christ*, who through the eternal *Spirit* offered himself unblemished to *God*" (Heb 9:14, emphasis added).[15]

Finally, in addition to being an expression of helplessness rather than abandonment, Jesus' cry reflects two central truths. First, Jesus experienced a mortal's death. By specifically associating with humankind's mortality, Jesus joined himself in solidarity with humanity's experience of distance

---

13. Although it's not immediately apparent in the lexicons, a nuance of the term *egkataleipo* ("forsake") in the New Testament and other early literature means *to remain or leave helpless*, not merely to forsake and cause separation. See BDAG, "ἐγκαταλείπω," 909. BDAG provides only two definitions. The first is to cause something to remain in a positive sense, *leave behind progeny*. The second is to separate connection with, *forsake, abandon, desert*. An undetected nuance is a third definition, which involves leaving alone but not necessarily separating connection; i.e., *to leave helpless or uncared for*. For instance, Hebrews 13:5 says, "Never will I leave you; never will I forsake (*egkataleipo*) you." The first term means to separate connection ("leave"), hence the latter term would likely contain a different nuance, such as to leave someone uncared for, *helpless*. Also cf. Matt 27:46; Mark 15:34; Acts 2:27, 31; 2 Cor 4:9.

14. Jesus' solidarity with mortal nature was complete once death eclipsed any hope beyond the grave. Job summed up this perspective of mortality when he lost all hope: "What strength do I have, that I should still hope? What prospects, that I should be patient? Do I have the strength of stone? Is my flesh bronze? Do I have any power to help myself, now that success has been driven from me?" (Job 6:11–13).

15. Doesn't basic theology inform us that the triune God is one, not many, and without division or distinction in essential nature? Along with the Spirit, the Father and Son are coexistent, coequal, and coeternal, one in essence and therefore indivisible in their shared essence. Isn't it, therefore, an absurd impossibility to suggest that the Father could literally abandon his Son! The Trinity cannot cease to be the Trinity or God would cease to be God.

from God in all of its animosity, confusion, and heartbreak. Jesus' words reflect the godforsakenness of the mortal human condition. Because Jesus repeated the life-experience of all humanity from birth through every stage of life into death, he identified with human nature in its experience of death along with death's cruel sense of distance from God.

Jesus' outcry was an expression of empathy characteristic of a shared human nature as it experiences the most disturbing distance in life, our *death* due to sin, with emphasis on dying. This truth becomes more apparent when we reduce the difficulty of Jesus' words down to the simple truth that only mortal human nature is capable of uttering words even closely resembling a godforsaken state. Those are human words, not divine! Jesus not only experienced the death of a mortal but also all the turmoil and agony leading up to it, a total cross-death experience. God died as a human being! Such an outcry could only come from a human nature that was actually "tast[ing] death for everyone" (Heb 2:9). The godforsakenness expressed in Jesus' words does not befit the experience of an everlasting God, yet God uttered those exact words, words reflecting the vulnerable human condition.

Second, Jesus was speaking on behalf of humanity with words that express our reproach toward God for allowing death in the first place.[16] God abandons the entire human race to death and leaves us helplessly in its clutches; he doesn't intervene but allows each one of us to die, just as he did with Jesus. So we revolt against him for following through with his promise that we would "certainly die" if we ever ate that cursed fruit (Gen 2:17)! Yet the irony is that Jesus' words affirm that the dying God was taking his mission to its ultimate conclusion—namely, death: "My God, my God, why are you letting me die? Why won't you help me out of this deathly experience?" Although the Father could not intervene to help his Son escape death, he nonetheless remained his God while maintaining their relationship beyond the possibility of any real distance or separation. Falling short of patripassianism, the "death of the Father," the Father nonetheless experienced the agony of the cross along with his Son.[17] How could he not, for on that day

---

16. This reproach is summed up by Job: "If the only home I hope for is the grave, if I spread out my bed in the realm of darkness, if I say to corruption, 'You are my father,' and to the worm, 'My mother' or 'My sister,' where then is my hope—who can see any hope for me? Will it go down to the gates of death? Will we descend together into the dust?" (Job 17:13–16; cf. Isa 26:14).

17. My mother once shared a very thoughtful revelation with me that she had experienced during a time of prayer. She was upset with Father God over the suffering that

Salvation: God Shares His Son

God died on the cross at Golgotha? Any separation we might detect in Jesus' words is practical and empathetic, an emotional and spiritual solidarity with mortal humanity.

Believers can now rejoice because we are free from sin and death, not because Jesus hung on a tree or was somehow spiritually pummeled with our sins, but because he underwent the full experience of *death* on our behalf (Heb 2:9). In selfless love, Jesus surrendered to a world full of hate as it wrapped its ugly arms around him, tortured him, and the world abandoned him, while the Father would not, and in fact could not, neglect his Son. Jesus experienced the torment and agony of the cross and finally died a physical death in the arms of his heavenly Father. As sharers in God's presence, we need never fear that he might abandon us in our darkest hour.[18]

God Forgives Our Sins

Because divine love is stronger than death, the cross was able to solve the sin problem once and for all by boldly displaying God's radical love for all the world to see (cf. Song 8:6). Scripture declares that at just the right time, God sent his one and only Son to die a bloody death on a tree in order to manifest perfect love in the face of the vilest evil, confronting and conquering Satan's kingdom of sin and death for all time (Rom 5:6–8). The powerful loving influence of the cross is designed to draw all humankind into God's saving presence (John 12:32). When anyone responds to the good news of God's grace and forgiveness through Jesus Christ, their sins are washed away! In other words, not a single obstacle remains between them and God.

Jesus had to endure to save us. As she described it to me, she was angry because the cross was the Father's plan: he made us, we sinned and needed reconciled to him, yet it was Jesus who suffered horribly. She cried to the Father: "Jesus had to do all this suffering, but you didn't. You didn't have to suffer at all to save us!" It was evident that her anger was directed at the Father because of her tremendous love for Jesus. But then, in the midst of her aching prayer, the Father answered and spoke very clearly to her heart: "My daughter, how deeply would you suffer if you had to give up your son, as I gave up mine?" Instantly, a strong impression entered her mind of her firstborn son, my brother Brad, and she immediately broke down and bawled. In that moment, she knew that the Father's suffering was extreme. She knew that the price the Father had paid was just as severe as Jesus' suffering.

18. Derek Flood understands this point well: "This image of the suffering God revealed in the weakness of the cross means that no matter how helpless and alone we may feel, God is with us" ("A Relational Understanding of Atonement," 42).

But even without a sacrifice, God can still forgive sin. Before and after the cross, God's extravagant love has offered forgiveness in unexpected ways. We expect God to forgive when someone repents, but he also forgives those who are stubborn and rebellious (Exod 34:9; Mic 7:18). He forgives when someone else intercedes (Num 14:19–20), but he also forgives others who commit the most wicked acts (Luke 23:34)! The basis for such generous forgiveness has always been the merciful *love* of God (Ps 51:1). When Jesus forgave sin even before the resurrection, he demonstrated that God chooses forgiveness whenever possible: "But I want you to know that the Son of Man has authority on earth to forgive sins" (Mark 2:10).

Even though God forgives sin because he's merciful, people can only be assured of such forgiveness when they personally choose to place their trust in God. Everyone who believes in Christ is *totally* forgiven in their standing before God, absolved of all guilt and thoroughly washed "white as snow" (Isa 1:18). Whenever the believer begs the LORD not to look upon his sin—"Hide your face from my sins and blot out all my iniquity" (Ps 51:9)—God's response is always the same: "I, even I, am he who blots out your transgressions, for my own sake, and remembers your sins no more" (Isa 43:25). *God is desperate to forgive us for his own sake!* Because sin has fundamentally broken God's relationship with people, he suffers terribly and wants nothing less than to forgive and erase those sins from his memory. Once anyone enters a saving relationship with God through Jesus Christ, sin can no longer cast its shadow between them.

When sin and death no longer darken the believer's path to God, it is because of the gracious gift of his compassionate forgiveness. Understanding God's attitude toward him, the psalmist says, "Because of your great compassion, blot out the stain of my sins" (Ps 51:1 NLT). With a forgiveness full of compassion, God does that very thing; he welcomes us into the healing depths of his salvation. The psalmist later describes salvation as a rescue from death into a walk of newness in God's presence—no distance whatsoever! "For you have rescued me from death; you have kept my feet from slipping. So now I can walk in your presence, O God, in your life-giving light" (Ps 56:13 NLT; cf. 1 John 1:7). Just as this psalm declares, the forgiveness of sin is also the entrance of life-giving, transformative light. When we're forgiven, we receive God's light and life! And because a tremendous potential for righteous living is deeply rooted in forgiveness, this newfound life in God's presence actually *keeps my feet from slipping*! Even though believers can never live entirely sinless lives, our pardon is complete, and we can never be anything less than absolutely forgiven. Hence, we have no excuse but to live righteously before our God and Savior! He will never again hold our sins against us but draws us near to himself in newness of life.

Even after salvation, confession and the Christian's struggle with sin can never change a person's status as once-and-for-all forgiven. The first Johannine epistle is largely misunderstood as teaching that believers must continually "confess" sin in order to remain in fellowship with God, which has often been equated with a post-salvation need for forgiveness: "If we confess our sins, he is faithful and just and will forgive us our sins" (1 John 1:9). However, the author is contrasting a certain kind of person—the confessing believer—with the nonbeliever who claims to be "without sin" or to "have not sinned" in the first place (vv. 8, 10). Throughout this epistle, the author is writing about salvation from a rather strict perspective: Either you abide with Jesus in the light of salvation or you abide in darkness among the unsaved. You're either in or you're out, forgiven or not, but there's no in between!

According to the theology of First John, the believer is forgiven and the nonbeliever is not. The believer need not confess his sins to remain forgiven, but the believer will always confess his sins *because* he is forgiven! And because no true believer would ever shy away from confessing his sins, the following is also true of him: "If we are living in the light, as God is in the light, then . . . the blood of Jesus, his Son, cleanses us from all sin" (1 John 1:7 NLT). The fact that we remain forgiven and this purification is an ongoing reality is brought out in the Greek present tense that's found in this passage: The blood of Jesus *keeps on continually cleansing us* from all sin.

When believers sin, we are not somehow unpurified or unforgiven until we get around to confessing that thing to God. In 1 John 1:9, the Greek term *homologeo* translates to *confess* and means to speak the same thing or to *agree*. We remain cleansed because we are characteristically a people who maintain transparency before God and always *agree* with him that our flesh is sinfully weak. Claiming that one is sinless and without guilt before God is the position of the nonbeliever (vv. 8, 10), but acknowledging that my own sin has kept me from God's presence is the confession of every true saint (v. 9). Confession is the attitude of a new life that remains in God's forgiveness because that person is now "living in the light, as God is in the light."

When believers confess sin, they don't become any more forgiven. Rather, confession and repentance are as much an emotional exercise as a spiritual one, designed to open up the confessing heart to God's healing presence (cf. Matt 6:12). Confession makes the heart and conscience transparent to God's presence in a manner that welcomes divine healing, deliverance, and holiness to replace the deceitfulness of sin. Even though confession can't add a crumb of forgiveness to my life, it does work to apply the gentle cleansing ointment of God's renewing presence: "Against you, you only, have I sinned and done what is evil in your sight; . . . Cleanse me with hyssop, and I will be clean; wash me, and I will be whiter than snow. . . . Create in me a pure heart, O God, and renew a steadfast spirit within me" (Ps 51:4, 7, 10).[19] By confessing our sins regularly, we keep our hearts from deceit, our thoughts pure, and our lives steadfast in the presence of God our Savior.

Because this chapter addresses matters of salvation, we will turn our attention to the two sacraments of the church, water baptism and the Lord's Supper. When faith is applied to each of these sacraments, believers become partakers of forgiveness and the divine presence.

Ritual of Entrance: Water Baptism

Entrance into the community of faith has always been open to everyone, even under the old covenant, because God wants the whole world to share in his presence (e.g., Isa 51:4–5; 66:18–19). The call to follow and serve him, however, was not always connected to *water baptism* as it is today under the new covenant. Since the moment that John the Baptist announced the arrival of "the Lamb of God who takes away the sin of the world" (John 1:29), the church's message has been uniquely tied to repentance and water immersion as a public rite of passage. In nearly every case, the earliest records of the call to repent in the book of Acts include instruction to be

---

19. Complete forgiveness is not the same as *forever* forgiveness: "We have come to share in Christ, *if* indeed we hold our original conviction firmly to the very end" (Heb 3:14, emphasis added). Although forgiveness is the enduring possession of every believer and should belong to us forever, the warnings of Scripture are numerous that any believer can potentially lose their salvation; see Matt 10:22; John 15:6; 1 Cor 15:2; 2 Tim 2:12; Heb 6:4–6; 10:26; 2 Pet 2:20–21. We should, however, share the attitude of the writer of Hebrews, who says, "Even though we speak like this, dear friends, we are convinced of better things in your case—the things that have to do with salvation" (Heb 6:9).

immediately submerged in water:[20] "Repent and be baptized, every one of you" (Acts 2:38).[21]

There should be no doubt that any person in Acts who believed in Jesus was baptized without delay. Regarding the Philippian jailer, Scripture attests that "immediately (*parachrema*) he and all his household were baptized," *parachrema* meaning at once or without delay (Acts 16:33). This passage is by no means exceptional, as even a cursory review of Acts demonstrates that this urgency was the norm.[22] When anyone expresses faith in Jesus, they should be asking the same question posed by the Ethiopian eunuch: "What can stand in the way of my being baptized?" (8:36). The answer: Nothing at all! By all means, you should be baptized. This was exactly Philip's response: to baptize without delay (8:37–38). This resonates with Ananias's urgency toward Paul's baptism: "And now what are you waiting for? Get up, be baptized and wash your sins away" (22:16). When the Gentiles received the good news, the Apostle Peter "ordered (*prostasso*) that they be baptized in the name of Jesus Christ" (10:48). Because the term *prostasso* is emphatic, used even of the "appointed times" marked out by God (17:26), it indicates that this is something that *must* occur: Peter ordered the Gentile converts to be baptized! Based on the Acts passages alone, we can deduce that the first-century church knew nothing of an acceptance of salvation in Christ that did not include water baptism.

If baptism should regularly accompany faith, why the urgency? Because baptism offers a unique look at the believer's initial immersion into God's saving presence, a drama of spiritual significance that's acted out right in front of us! The immediate faith-accompanying act of water baptism is important because of what it represents. Baptism is the promise that God's presence abides with his people through the Spirit. Although a passage like Romans 6:3–4 interprets Christian baptism as being "baptized into [Jesus']

---

20. See Acts 2:41; 8:12–13, 16, 36, 38; 9:18; 10:47–48; 16:15, 33; 18:8; 19:3–5; 22:16.

21. Some would object to interpreting baptism as a command in this passage, arguing that only the imperative to *repent* holds the force of a command. Robert Stein responds, "No great weight should be put on the fact that the dual command in 2:38 involves a second person plural imperative ('you repent') and a third person singular imperative ('each one of you be baptized'). The latter simply seeks to underscore emphatically the command to each one addressed. Examples of the use of a second person plural imperative and a third person singular imperative side by side can be found in Exod 16:29; Josh 6:10; 2 Kgs 10:19; Zech 7:10; 1 Macc 10:63 in the LXX and in *Did.* 15:3" ("Baptism in Luke-Acts," 37 n. 10).

22. Where faith and baptism are closely linked, see Acts 8:12–13, 35–39; 10:43–48; 16:14–15, 31–34; 18:8; 19:4–5.

death," which is clearly the case, the book of Acts opens up the dimension of baptism that's related to the Spirit's presence. In Acts, Christian baptism is a rite of passage to be acted out, an initiatory ceremony into the new covenant promise of the Spirit. Whereas Paul highlights the negative, that a death has taken place, Acts focuses on the positive and illustrates submersion into a new experience of God's saving presence that makes every believer part of a new family of faith.

The waters of baptism anticipate the flood of the Spirit's presence: "For John baptized with water, but in a few days you will be baptized with the Holy Spirit" (Acts 1:5). Here Jesus contrasts John the baptizer's water baptism with the newness of the Spirit's work, which finds its fulfillment in Acts 2: "When the day of Pentecost came, . . . All of them were filled with the Holy Spirit" (vv. 1, 4). Shortly after that occurs, Peter announces, "Repent and be baptized, every one of you, in the name of Jesus Christ for the forgiveness of your sins. And you will receive the gift of the Holy Spirit" (vv. 38-39). Although the Spirit was initially poured out in a manner apparently unrelated to water baptism (vv. 1-4), Peter clarifies the connection between baptism and the Spirit's reception for those who would hear the message from that day forward. Throughout Acts, baptism is closely related to the believer's initial reception of the divine presence and entrance into the new life of the Spirit.[23]

This unity of both water and Spirit Baptism becomes evident in Paul, "one Spirit, . . . one baptism" (Eph 4:4-5; cf. 1 Cor. 12:13), and through Jesus' words to Nicodemus. Jesus says, "Very truly I tell you, no one can enter the kingdom of God unless they are born of (*ek*) water and the Spirit" (John 3:5). Regarding Jesus' statement, Frederick Bruner comments that "Jesus is describing *one* event, signaled by the *single* preposition *ek* (literally, 'up out of') connecting the two nouns, 'water and spirit.'"[24] Bruner also says that the use of the Greek preposition *ek* ("out from") rather than *en* ("in") suggests immersion into and up out of the waters of baptism.[25] In other words, anyone who wants to enter God's kingdom must be birthed out from the baptism that is *both water and Spirit*, again indicating the close connection between baptism and God's holy presence.

---

23. There are a few passages, however, that mention baptism without any explicit event of the Spirit; see Acts 8:36-39; 16:14-15, 31-34; 18:8.

24. Bruner, *Gospel of John*, 175, emphasis original.

25. Ibid., 176.

Water baptism is the public rite of passage recognized by the community and thus an acknowledgment of the Spirit's preparatory work in a person's life. Baptismal waters accompany the sovereign work of the Spirit that graciously guides a person into salvation. Apart from the Spirit, no one would approach God to begin with (John 3:8), so the climax of the Spirit's work of grace is experienced as the waters wash over us and guarantee our new position in a spiritual family here on earth, the *visible* kingdom of God. Those same waters provide entrance into God's *hidden* kingdom through the all-consuming presence of God's Spirit, joining us to a family of believers both alive and dead, and bringing us under the kingship of the Lord Jesus Christ who reigns from a heavenly throne. Hence, the waters of baptism serve to illustrate entrance into the hidden and visible spheres of the kingdom of God. The moment the flood pours over us is the moment we're meant to become aware of the new reality of sharing most dramatically in God's presence with God's family.

Initial reception of the Spirit is likened to total submersion into waters that fully cover and encompass. Believers are thus introduced to God's kingdom through immersion into the fullness of his presence, a baptism of water and Spirit.[26] But that's not the only ritual the Christian church participates in. Every week, by participating in the Lord's Supper, we're meant to feast upon the presence of Jesus Christ in a most vivid and memorable way.

Ceremony of Presence: The Lord's Supper

The Lord's Supper, Eucharist, Communion, the Table is, by its very nature, a dynamic ritual of presence involving both word and action while the gathered community observes the eating of broken "flesh" (bread) and the drinking of spilt "blood" (wine). In dramatic fashion, by faith believers see Christ's sacrifice in front of them and personally appropriate the elements

---

26. Who may *administer* Christian baptism, and *how* should one be baptized? Baptizing new Christians is open to any believer who is willing to do dunk them. Scripture never restricts this open aspect to ordained clergy, deacons, or anyone else. Scripture, however, does restrict those who may be baptized. Those who are baptized must readily and consciously express the decision to accept God's way as revealed in the person of Christ. This is, therefore, a denial of infant baptism, which has been adequately addressed elsewhere; see Aland, *Did the Early Church Baptize Infants?* For very early sources, see Lewis, "Baptismal Practices," 1–17. Finally, full bodily immersion is the ideal means for baptism. A full dunk best illustrates both burial with Christ and complete immersion in the Spirit.

while receiving Christ to themselves with all the benefits of his salvation: "Is not the cup of thanksgiving for which we give thanks a participation (*koinonia*) in the blood of Christ? And is not the bread that we break a participation (*koinonia*) in the body of Christ?" (1 Cor 10:16). The Greek term *koinonia* can be translated participation or fellowship. Consequently, we experience the *fellowship* of his body and blood by mysteriously *participating* in his loving sacrifice. This participation implies our own transformation, as we vividly encounter the truth behind the elements and begin to grasp that we too must lay down our lives following Jesus' example.

Besides the fellowship of Jesus' body and blood, believers also enjoy the *koinonia* of the church as the body of Christ, one loaf rather than many: "Because there is one loaf, we, who are many, are one body, for we all share the one loaf" (1 Cor 10:17). As one body partaking of one loaf, the church is brought to terms with the reality that new covenant election and participation includes every believer who has placed trust in Jesus Christ for salvation. Through the Communion celebration, we therefore *renew* the terms of that covenant—the new covenant of the heart, the covenant of God's presence. That renewal includes both our responsibility and God's. We renew our obligation to faith and obedience, while God renews his obligation to make the benefits of his presence fully known in order to lead us into the fullness of salvation. Because the ultimate fullness of our redemption awaits the end of the age, we also feast together with God's community to look forward to the day when we'll all be reunited with our King in a restored paradise (Matt 26:29; Mark 14:25). Only in that paradise will we experience God in an even greater way than the presence our ancestors enjoyed in Eden.

The Reformers believed that it was fundamental to the experience of salvation for the gathered church to locate the presence of Christ in the sacrament in one manner or another. Because God now had a body, they differed on their opinions of how the resurrected presence of Christ was revealed in the Supper. They were generally in agreement, however, that the elements did not literally transform into Christ's physical body as in Roman Catholicism's doctrine of transubstantiation.[27] Although Martin Luther and the Lutherans rejected the Catholic view, they have held that Jesus'

---

27. Transubstantiation teaches that the physical elements of bread and wine are changed, though not in appearance, into the physical, *substantial* body and blood of Jesus Christ. This is historically what Roman Catholicism has intended by the language of real presence.

Salvation: God Shares His Son

physical presence is invisible but nonetheless real and intermingled with the elements, somehow located "in, under, or beside" the bread and wine.

John Calvin and the Reformed tradition promoted the doctrine of virtualism, which teaches that "although Christ's body ascended to heaven, the Supper of the Lord, when received with true faith, conveys a unique spiritual power [virtue]."[28] Calvin reasoned that because Jesus' physical body was limited to the right hand of God, it was necessary for the Holy Spirit to spiritually unite our souls with Christ in heaven.[29] Beyond Luther and Calvin, others have maintained that the Lord's Supper presents Christ purely in terms of a memorial or reminder. This view has been held primarily by Ulrich Zwingli and his followers as well as the Anabaptists. They would say that Christ is present in the Meal, just as he is present throughout the Christian life, but not in any way unique to the elements.

Although debate will no doubt continue over the nature of Christ's presence in the Eucharist, believers can unite over the truth that we do indeed share in the divine presence through the Supper. Whether that presence is somehow real and invisible, or a symbolic reminder that Jesus is always with us, the presence of the one who died and rose again is received in an exceptional way by partaking of bread and wine in the context of the community of faith. By the experience of both word and deed, we receive the body and blood of Christ!

The church is the body of Christ because we have all equally entered God's presence through repentance and Christian baptism. As the church, we also enjoy the privilege of experientially feasting upon that presence in a most spiritually profound way. We feast beside brothers and sisters in Christ, observing in the words and actions of the community a drama that is lived out before our very eyes. Not only is our separation from God eliminated, but so is any distance between one another as believers unite to renew God's covenant as *one body* in unity of *one faith*.[30]

---

28. Campbell, *Methodist Doctrine*, 75. John Wesley and the Methodists have also held to a form of virtualism.

29. Calvin, *Institutes*, 104–7. The idea behind Calvin's virtualism is that Jesus' humanity now consists of a resurrected human body that can only be in one place at any given time. His physical body remains at the right hand of the Father in heaven, making it impossible for him to be physically united with the elements while the Eucharist is being observed in many places throughout the world.

30. Who may *administer* the Lord's Supper, and who may *participate*? Any willing believer is able to administer the Supper. As with baptism, Scripture nowhere restricts this open aspect or requires ordained clergy to reside over it. There is strong evidence that the earliest practices of the Lord's Supper took place in the context of a meal known as the

Conclusion

This chapter set forth a climactic tone in the dramatic reversal and defeat of sin and death through God's most glorious display of presence in resurrection. But before Christ Jesus could enjoy such a victory, he experienced the fact of mortality—everyone dies. From the cross, the raw honesty of Jesus' outcry reveals the shock and dread of the mortal condition in the face of death: *Oh my God, why have you left me for dead?* This was not a cry of abandonment but of helplessness, expressing the backlash of mortality as well as Jesus' solidarity with every human being.

Jesus' sacrifice demonstrates that salvation is secured through a physical death on the cross as blood was spilt, having nothing whatsoever to do with any distance between Jesus and his Father. God the Father did not punish his Son but stood by him while the world rejected him, demonstrating their resolute love in the face of hatred and grotesque violence. Jesus remained sinless and voluntarily surrendered his life in order to defeat death as the greatest expression of cruel evil. Although God's experience with death was real, it was strikingly disappointed by its reversal in resurrection. Jesus showed humans and demons the immense power of God's presence to become immortalized among the human race. The resurrection of Jesus Christ is literally an indestructible presence of God expressed through humanity!

When people embrace the profoundly simple message of knowing God through resurrection life (John 17:3), they submit to the waters of baptism and thereby become immersed into God's presence for the first time. God so thoroughly cleanses them from sin that no more forgiveness is ever needed. Nonetheless, believers will regularly confess their sins because it leads them into God's healing arms where they are continually changed by

---

agape feast (Acts 2:42, 46; Jude 12; 2 Pet 2:13). In most cases throughout Christian history, however, the church has deviated from the meal and serves only a minimal amount of wine (or juice) and a morsel of bread. It would be ideal to partake from a single cup of wine and a single loaf of bread.

The other question of who may *partake* of the Meal is also quite open. Although not ideal, Jesus' acceptance of Judas at the Last Supper ultimately leaves open the possibility for nonbelievers to participate. John Wesley apparently permitted nonbelievers to the Table if they came with *trust* ("faith") that God would act. Wesley's consent may resemble the Puritans who believed that committed, church-going "nonbelievers" were not justified until they had a special experience. According to Wesley, the Eucharist was ordained by the Lord as "a means of conveying to men either preventing, or justifying, or sanctifying grace, according to their several necessities" (Outler, *Works of John Wesley*, 1:381). See also Curnock, *Journal of Rev. John Wesley*, 2:361.

Salvation: God Shares His Son

his presence. This new life is dramatized often through the Lord's Supper, a renewal of the new covenant that celebrates our closeness with God and each other.

4

Pentecost: God Shares His Spirit

IN THE LAST CHAPTER, we introduced new covenant salvation in terms of the resurrection of Jesus Christ, that momentous occasion when God's presence became indestructible among humanity. When Jesus introduced resurrection into a world of mortality, the whole spiritual landscape changed. From his throne in the heavenlies, divine life could now touch a dead world; the portal was opened! In Scripture, God's heavenly throne is largely symbolic of the untouchable immortality of the fullness of his presence. But the heavens were rent! Jesus' death tore a hole in the fabric of a mortal universe to make room for immortality and the presence of God (cf. Matt 27:51). The division between corruption and incorruption was forever mended, creating a free-flowing channel between the two. As a result, mortals who are now touched with the gift of eternal life become the immortal children of God!

The cataclysm of the cross was followed by the world-changing event of the resurrection, when Jesus was crowned Victor and exalted to the right hand of the throne of God, where he now reigns over sin and death. Jesus' ascension to his throne ushered in the glory of Pentecost when the Holy Spirit flowed freely into people's lives, God's most splendid and sustained expression of divine presence in society. Thus, the re-creation of the universe in God's presence begins with his people, a new community for a new era under the newness of the Spirit.

In this chapter, we will review the impact that the resurrection has on the church in her sustained encounter with God's presence. We will look closely at Jesus' spiritual reign and the initial impact of resurrection on the

Pentecost: God Shares His Spirit

kingdom of saints—the arrival of the pentecostal presence of God. We'll see how Christ is Lord over an open and expanding kingdom in a spiritual reign that is both relational and dynamic.[1] Most importantly, we'll see that Jesus oversees every believers' experience of sharing in God's presence, because he is the one who personally shares God's Spirit with us.

Introducing a Relational Kingdom

When God approached Abram to covenant with him, he promised to bless the whole world through this man and his descendants. Even though that promise was being carried out through the Mosaic and Davidic covenants, the prophets still expected more. Thomas Schreiner summarizes their perspective: "The prophets looked forward to a day when God's saving promises would be fulfilled, his kingdom would come, the New Covenant would be inaugurated, a new exodus from Babylon would be realized, the Spirit would be poured out on Israel, and Israel would keep God's law. The prophets promised a new creation, a new temple, a new covenant, and a new king."[2]

Throughout the book of Acts, we see those expectations being fulfilled under the designation of a *new* covenant, which provides the framework for a new spiritual kingdom in the dawning of a new age under God's rule. We can summarize the new covenant as God's commitment to forgive and indwell people, the covenant inaugurated by Christ in his death (Mark 14:24; 1 Cor 11:25). The reality of covenant joins the people of God to the presence of God, while the kingdom is the sphere for living out life in relation to his presence. That new covenant kingdom is God's way of comprehensively satisfying the expectations of Israel and her prophets, those who were looking forward to the forgiveness of sin, the arrival of an ultimate deliverer, and a special relationship to God's Spirit—the very presence of God.[3] This doesn't at all imply that the Hebrews had never experienced forgiveness, or a work of the Spirit, or even divine deliverance under the old covenant (or Moses' law). But the sense behind the promise of newness was something

---

1. Amos Yong uses the designation "God's relational kingdom" in his article "Relational Theology and the Holy Spirit," 20.

2. Schreiner, *New Testament Theology*, 44.

3. Regarding a unique deliverer's anointing with the Spirit, see Isa 11:2; *1 En.* 49:3; 62:2; *Pss. Sol.* 17:37; 18:7; *T. Levi* 18:6–8; *T. Jud.* 24:2. On the forgiveness and cleansing from sin that are wrought by the Spirit, see Ezek 36:25–26; 1QS 4:20–21; 1QH 16:11–12.

permanent and decisively victorious for Israel. The new covenant meant the final acceptance of God's people to himself and a final rebuke to the dark forces of sin and death constantly at work against them.

The new covenant would satisfy those and other hopes, bringing victory over sin, victory by a new activity of God's Spirit-presence, and an anointed Deliverer who would bring the decisive victory blow against God's enemies. That new Deliverer would be the messianic finale to trump all of Israel's previous deliverers, a Savior *par excellence*.

From Covenant to Kingdom

Before the cross, believing *and* nonbelieving Israelites were called out from the world to live under Moses' law, the distinguishing legislation of a nation privileged to live under God's rule. Morally speaking, some people abided in the spiritual sphere of God's kingdom, while others intentionally or unwittingly dwelt in the kingdom of Satan. The former lived close to God, the latter at a distance. Nonetheless, Yahweh had given birth to Israel to eliminate the distance and to keep the world close to him through a chosen race of mediators who would intercede between God and the kingdoms of this world. Although Moses' law functioned as a tutor to point both believer and nonbeliever to God (Gal 3:24), the warnings of that law, including death, were often met with resistance, resulting in even greater distance (Rom 7:5).

Because the old covenant law defined sin and, at times, produced death (Rom 7:7–13), it's not surprising that the people were anxiously awaiting its revision. God's chosen people continued to fail miserably, on an individual and national level. Their ongoing inability to live up to the law's standards pointed to the need for something better, something intrinsic and empowering, something the prophets were calling a *new* covenant (Jer 31:31). Although there were hints of Gentile inclusion, deliverance under the law had always belonged primarily to Israel (Matt 10:6; 15:24), so they could not have known that the change that was coming would mean a radical move away from a national law to an international spiritual law for the whole world.[4]

The new covenant would mean the law of God written on people's hearts by the Spirit (2 Cor 3:3)—God's Holy Presence—who fills *and frees* the believer (2 Cor 3:17; cf. Rom 8:21). That covenant would reach so deep

---

4. See Jer 32:40; 50:5; Isa 24:5; 55:3; 61:8; Ezek 16:60; 37:26.

Pentecost: God Shares His Spirit

as to cleanse the conscience (Heb 9:14) and would extend so far as to bring about a new community of followers indwelt with the God-presence (2 Cor 3:6), a new community in a new era designed to highlight a unique fellowship with the triune God and the dawning of his relational kingdom. Covenant is all about relationship with God, and so is the coming kingdom. The new covenant would inaugurate a *relational* kingdom, one in which the former distance is mocked by the uniquely close fellowship that believers would experience in union with Israel's Messiah, a King from the lineage of David, who possesses and gives away "the Spirit without measure" (John 3:34 ESV).

Under the old covenant, God poured his spiritual presence into a few individuals for important service, such as priests, prophets, and kings. But with Jesus' own blood as the basis for the new covenant, by the removal of sin's distance through forgiveness and the removal of death's distance through resurrection, God brings every member of the church into harmony for ministry through a living source of unity, the gracious gift of God's Spirit. Once a person's eyes are opened by the light of the glory of the gospel of Jesus Christ, they can escape their slavery in Satan's kingdom and surrender to the reign of a new King. By placing faith in the God of a new covenant made up of many members, believers enjoy entrance into the present spiritual kingdom of God and of his Christ (Col 1:13).

In this spiritual kingdom, God's presence within his people has made true unity and a united mission possible, creating a new movement characterized by "one body and one Spirit, ... one Lord, one faith, one baptism" (Eph 4:4, 5). This new, highly relational sphere of existence, entered into by a mutual faith and surrender to Jesus Christ, is designed to display the kingdom of Christ on earth.

King of a Relational Kingdom

Jesus' life was an unparalleled display of God's presence on earth, not to mention the impact of his ministry of signs and wonders—signs that displayed God's presence and miracles that evoked wonder from everyone who saw them. Jesus personified the in-breaking of God's kingdom on earth and manifested the power of that reign through his own person. The kingdom of God was present in and through Jesus' personal presence (Luke 11:20; 17:21),[5] the very one who now reigns at the right hand of the throne

---

5. In Luke 17:21, "the kingdom of God *is in your midst*" can also be translated *is*

of God! From the highest position of power and authority, Jesus' presence extends to his church through the medium of the third person of the Trinity, the Holy Spirit. As the Spirit remains actively involved in the church, the reign of Christ's kingdom is made known.

At the opening of Acts, Jesus alludes to a substantially spiritual kingdom when the disciples ask him if Messiah would now restore the sociopolitical kingdom to Israel. They expected a manifest kingdom to conquer the Roman world! In response, Jesus contrasts their notion of a visible, conquering kingdom with the current spiritual one that was still awaiting empowerment from God's Spirit: "[Jesus] said to them: 'It is not for you to know the times or dates the Father has set (*etheto*) by his own authority. But you will receive power when the Holy Spirit comes on you; and you will be my witnesses in Jerusalem, and in all Judea and Samaria, and to the ends of the earth'" (Acts 1:7–8). The Greek term *etheto* indicates that the kingdom they were anticipating is "set" or fixed for a future time that only God the Father has the prerogative over. At least for now, the permanent establishment of Christ's kingdom over the entire world remains open-ended.

What was not open to debate was Jesus' prediction that the disciples would "receive power when the Holy Spirit comes on you," a prediction of an unparalleled sharing in God's presence that would occur in the very near future at Pentecost, the harvest festival that the Hebrews celebrated each year. In the book of Acts, the event of Pentecost presents the climax of God's relational kingdom in this age. Although Jesus inaugurates such a kingdom, it won't see its full establishment until the end of the age (1 Cor 15:24–27). His kingdom's formation remains open, so that it can continue to grow. In fact, Jesus had assured his disciples that the presence of the Spirit would cause his kingdom reign to expand from Jerusalem all the way to "the ends of the earth" (Acts 1:8).[6] And even though the kingdom would

---

within you (KJV).

6. Jesus' summary of the kingdom's advance was Luke's way of introducing the outline to the book of Acts, allowing readers to experience the journey of this encroaching kingdom mission from Jerusalem to the Roman world in chapters 1–28: "You will be my witnesses in Jerusalem, and in all Judea and Samaria, and to the ends of the earth" (Acts 1:8). Craig Keener encourages readers that "Acts does not conclude with the completion of the mission but offers a model for its continuance and completion: the good news to the ends of the earth, including parts of the world that Luke's audience could not have known about" (Keener, "Power of Pentecost," 54).

continue to advance in Acts, the story is ultimately left open for believers today to continue the mission.[7]

When the Spirit was poured out at Pentecost, Christ's kingdom became the shared reality of the church and, in one sense, a new invisible reality, though a reality nonetheless (cf. Luke 17:20–21). Jesus' kingdom is invisible only in the sense that we do not yet see all enemies subdued under him (Acts 2:34–35). But we do see his kingdom manifest through the presence of the Spirit, through signs and wonders, and through a kingdom of priests and the prophethood of all believers who obey their Lord's marching orders.[8]

Launching His Kingdom: Spirit Baptism

The first-century Jews had no idea when or how God's kingdom plan was going to come together, so they forcefully sought to make Jesus their king (John 6:15). It wasn't until the kingdom story began to play out in Acts that anyone could begin to see a clearer image of God's kingdom in this age. It would not be an abrupt and dominating kingdom but an open-ended reign that slowly progressed through the kingdom message.[9] In a conversation surrounding that kingdom in Acts 1, Jesus entreats his disciples to wait for *the promise of the Father*, which we immediately learn is the Holy Spirit (vv. 4–5). This prediction would have been significant not only to the disciples but to all Israel. We might simplify the matter of first-century Jewish expectation by the three fundamental ways in which the Israelites viewed God's Spirit. They understood the Spirit as: an end-times outpouring, a special empowerment for prophetic utterance, and characteristically resting upon the Messiah who was to come.[10]

Because the new covenant is characterized by a new experience of God's Spirit, which is also characteristic of the coming Messiah, Jesus

---

7. On the open-endedness of Acts, see Dunn, *Acts of the Apostles*, 278; and Marguerat, *First Christian Historian*, 152–54, 230.

8. On the church as a kingdom of priests, even a royal *priesthood*, see Rev 1:6; 5:10; Exod 19:6. But we are also a *prophethood* of believers because we have each received the Holy Spirit who inspires us to know God's word and confidently proclaim it; see Stronstad, *Prophethood of All Believers*. Being prophetic means that every believer is Spirit-influenced, but in chapter six, we will look at the gift of prophecy as distinct from the general prophethood of all believers.

9. See Matt 13:31–32; Mark 4:30–32; Luke 3:18–19.

10. Menzies, *Empowered for Witness*, 102.

stepped into his role as the new Prophet of God and succinctly brought these many thoughts together when he announced his own ministry of Spirit Baptism, albeit a waterless spiritual baptism: "Do not leave Jerusalem, but wait for the gift my Father promised, which you have heard me speak about. For John baptized with water, but in a few days you will be baptized with the Holy Spirit" (Acts 1:4–5). Indeed, Jesus' baptism of the Spirit is the promise of the Father, a promise stated and restated throughout the Old Testament prophets for centuries beforehand.[11] At last, God's presence would be sustained among his people.

The movement of the Spirit specifically as a *baptism* is mentioned in only six places in the Gospels and Acts. In each occurrence, it follows immediately after mention of John's water baptism.[12] In two of those places it is called the baptism of "the Holy Spirit and fire" (Matt 3:11; Luke 3:16). In one instance, John the Baptist says that Messiah "will baptize you with the Holy Spirit and fire. His winnowing fork is in his hand, to clear his threshing floor and to gather the wheat into his barn, but the chaff he will burn with unquenchable fire" (Luke 3:16–17 ESV). Here, John declares that the Messiah would indeed mediate the Spirit, paralleling predictions of the old covenant prophets (e.g., Isa 44:3).

Such an outpouring was long anticipated throughout the prophets of old. Among others, Ezekiel writes, "I will no longer hide my face from them, for I will pour out my Spirit on the people of Israel, declares the Sovereign LORD" (Ezek 39:29). In poetic parallel fashion, Ezekiel implies that the *presence* of God's "face" is revealed through the *Spirit* itself. Another prophet, Isaiah, expected a divine Deliverer to one day operate "by a spirit of judgment and a spirit of fire," which imagines an end-time outpouring of both blessing *and* judgment (Isa 4:4). Numerous Old Testament prophecies point to a future outpouring of God's Spirit as a ministry consisting of both purification and punishment, depending on whether the message was accepted or rejected.[13] John's language of Spirit and fire was no different, anticipating both blessing and judgment.

Similar to Isaiah's promise of a Spirit-and-fire baptism, when John spoke of Jesus' ministry, he also used language reminiscent of the end of

---

11. See Jer 32:39; Isa 42:6; 49:8; 59:21; 54:10; Ezek 11:19; 18:31; 34:25; 36:26; 37:26; Hos 2:18–20.

12. The language of Spirit Baptism is found in Matt 3:11; Mark 1:8; Luke 3:16; John 1:33; Acts 1:4–5; 11:16.

13. Larry Hart conveys these thoughts in "Spirit Baptism," 111. See Joel 2:28–32; Ezek 36:25–27; Mal 3:2–3.

Pentecost: God Shares His Spirit

the age: "His winnowing fork is in his hand, and he will clear his threshing floor, gathering his wheat into the barn and burning up the chaff with unquenchable fire" (Matt 3:12; cf. Luke 3:17). John's language resonates with images of Jesus' final judgment, when he returns at the end of the age to resurrect the just and the unjust and permanently establish his kingdom (Acts 24:15). According to charismatic theologian Larry Hart, John the Baptist is using comprehensive language to summarize the total impact of Jesus' saving mission, a mission of both judgment and blessing, Spirit and fire. The Spirit-and-fire phase of God's kingdom mission was initiated when Jesus came on the scene and will conclude at his second and final appearance, when "his winnowing fork is in his hand" to subdue every last power beneath his supreme reign. Hart remarks that "John is speaking in the broadest terms of how Jesus both inaugurates and consummates the kingdom" through a baptism of Spirit and fire.[14]

Because the prophets before John spoke of an outpouring, John could naturally adapt their fluid metaphor to his own ministry by contrasting his water baptism with Jesus' spiritual one. Similar liquid metaphors would become the standard way of describing the Spirit's activity: e.g., outpouring, filling, being full of the Spirit.[15] Each metaphor illustrates the dynamic movement and flexibility of God's presence in the lives and ministries of his people, a perfect changeability. It is appropriate, therefore, to interpret the baptism of the Spirit as a flexible and open metaphor, recognizing that the Spirit's ministry cannot be restricted to one designation or another. The language of the Spirit's ministry is rather inconsequential. What matters is the dynamic, relational, ever-continual provision and empowerment of the Spirit's presence.

The metaphor of Spirit Baptism is intended to illustrate the believer's immersion into the interpenetrating presence of God *and into the rule of Christ*. Therefore, sharing in God's presence entails the obligation for surrendered obedience to Jesus the Messiah.[16] Because John was tying Spirit

---

14. Hart, "Spirit Baptism," 111.

15. Throughout Acts, the Spirit's activity on the day of Pentecost is described in seven ways by seven different metaphors: the promise of the Father (Acts 1:4; 2:33, 39), a baptism (1:5; 11:16), coming or falling upon (2:3; 8:16; 10:44; 11:15; 19:6), a pouring out (2:17–18, 33; 10:45), a gift (2:38; 10:45), received (2:38; 8:15), and a filling. As a common thread throughout Acts, believers are described as being *filled* with the Spirit. The book of Acts contains a total of six references to believers being filled with the Spirit (πίμπλημι: 2:4; 4:8, 31; 9:17; 13:9; πληρόω: 13:52).

16. Because the kingly rule of the Lord Jesus is such a primary feature of Spirit

Baptism into a summary of how Jesus both establishes and consummates his everlasting kingdom, the baptism of the Spirit is not a *single* pentecostal event in history but includes Jesus' overall ministry of blessing and judgment throughout this age. For the duration of his kingdom program, Jesus' ministry under the new covenant is to continually pour out God's Spirit upon those who are surrendered to him—the age of God's relational and ever-expanding kingdom depends on it!

The church has now been commissioned to unleash the presence of God into the world through the expansion of the kingdom message. One might even say that the divine presence has been restored to the church for the express purpose of empowerment for that mission.

Leading His Kingdom: Messiah's Presence

After Jesus conquered sin and death by experiencing the cruel reality of the cross, he rose victoriously from the grave and ascended to the right hand of the Father's throne. Jesus' first act as reigning King of the universe is visibly manifested and experienced in Acts 2 when the Spirit is climactically poured out: "When the day of Pentecost came, they were all together in one place.... All of them were filled with the Holy Spirit and began to speak in other tongues as the Spirit enabled them" (vv. 1, 4).

Jesus' promise that they would soon be baptized with the Holy Spirit is realized in an all-inclusive, communal *filling* of God's presence, adding another liquid metaphor to the Spirit's end-of-the-age activity. In fulfillment of the Father's promise, not some but *all* believers are filled with God's pervading Spirit.

Messiah Sits on His Throne

Shortly after that dramatic event at Pentecost, under the prophetic unction of the Spirit, Peter proclaims that what the people see and hear is the *outpouring of the Spirit on all people* as prophesied by the prophet Joel (Acts 2:16–17; Joel 2:28). It is appropriate to use the language of a "prophetic" unction because the outpouring of the Spirit upon the church is one of a prophetic nature, even a Spirit of prophecy. Inspired (or prompted)

Baptism, which entails a continual yielding to Christ as King and Master, the injunction to surrender for *fresh* baptisms remains intact as an important doctrine for the church today, even in a decisive crisis-moment experience.

Pentecost: God Shares His Spirit

utterance consistently accompanies the Spirit's filling activity in both Luke (1:41–42, 67) and Acts (2:4; 4:8, 31; 13:9). Any time believers were filled with the Spirit, they immediately spoke up.

The infilling, empowering, enabling life of the Spirit-presence did not originate in a vacuum. When Pentecost arrived, Peter spoke up and made emphatic the connection between the Spirit's outpouring and Christ's enthronement: "Exalted to the right hand of God, [Jesus] has received from the Father the promised Holy Spirit and has poured out what you now see and hear" (Acts 2:33). Through Trinitarian outreach, the last days promises of God were meted out as Jesus took his throne in the heavenlies. The baptism of the Spirit, the very outpouring anticipated by the prophets and now infusing every believer, resulted from and forever remains the reigning provision of the final Davidic King.

The promised Deliverer had come through the line of David (Acts 13:22–32), ratified the new covenant, and brought further development to David's eternal kingdom: Jesus is now forever seated on David's throne (15:16). After Yahweh sought to dramatically reduce the distance between himself and the world through the Abrahamic covenant by extending blessing to every person throughout the world, God's covenant with David ensured that his presence would eventually be experienced in the context of kingdom life. In fulfillment of those covenants of old, it is from David's throne that our King releases an outpouring of God's empowering presence. Those who repent and are baptized come to know both the presence of God and the realized promise of complete forgiveness, which are the twin distinguishing marks of the new covenant message (Acts 2:38–39).[17] Forgiveness renders our rebellion powerless and frees the world to receive the reign of God's presence.

The Lord Jesus is the long-awaited Messiah of Israel and the Deliverer of the world. Not only has he taken his seat on David's throne in fulfillment of the Davidic covenant, but he has also received from the Father a commission related to the divine presence. Although numerous metaphors are attached to the Spirit's work in Acts, Messiah has one very special new covenant obligation: He disseminates the Spirit! In Trinitarian sophistication, Messiah is continually pouring out the Spirit upon every believer in order to enable, empower, and embolden us to declare his victory reign. Among other things, Jesus fulfilled the role of another Prophet like Moses

---

17. Throughout the New Testament, the forgiveness of sin is connected to the new covenant; see Matt 26:28; Mark 14:24; Luke 22:20; 1 Cor 11:25; Heb 9:15; 12:24.

(Acts 3:22–26; Deut 18:15), the ultimate Prophet, Priest, and now, reigning King. Jesus' ministry brings believing men and women everywhere into the actual presence of God!

When people are first introduced to God's presence, the manner in which they are said to receive the Spirit remains dynamically open. In the book of Acts, the Spirit was initially received by 120 believers who waited in an upper room, having given themselves to prayer (Acts 1:14; 2:1–4). At other times, however, the Spirit came through the laying on of hands after belief and baptism (19:5–6) or through the laying on of hands *accompanied with prayer* after belief and baptism (8:15–17). Still at other times, the Spirit was given at the moment of faith before being baptized (9:17–18). In another place, the filling of the Spirit simply followed after belief and baptism (2:38). On another occasion, water baptism followed after receiving an evidentiary filling of the Spirit (10:44–48). So it seems that the Spirit has tremendous freedom in regard to how he moves into people's lives. Such dynamic activity is reminiscent of Jesus' earlier description of the Spirit's initial work in salvation: "The wind blows wherever it pleases. You hear its sound, but you cannot tell where it comes from or where it is going. So it is with everyone born of the Spirit" (John 3:8).

Despite the variety involved in the Spirit's reception, the ministry of the resurrected King is initiated the same way for everyone who believes: a Spirit Baptism into a new kingdom life that's characterized by God's powerful presence. In contrast to the few individuals who were "filled" with the Spirit in Luke's gospel, the precursor to Acts (Luke 1:14, 41, 67; 4:1), after Jesus' ascension it was said that "all of them were filled with the Holy Spirit" (Acts 2:2)—but that was just the beginning! Another open and relational aspect of Christ's kingdom is the limitless potential for every believer to be *freshly* baptized in the Spirit, enjoying a frequent, and even daily, stirring of God's presence: "And the disciples were continually filled with joy and with the Holy Spirit" (Acts 13:52 NASB; cf. Gal 5:22–23).[18] The fact that those disciples were continually *filled* means that there was always an active agent who performed that filling, none other than Jesus himself. Being the ongoing source of the Spirit, our risen Lord remains very closely involved in the daily life of his church.

This open-ended, all-inclusive spiritual outpouring was the divine response to Moses' wish expressed so many centuries before: "I wish that

---

18. In Acts 13:52, the Greek imperfect tense emphasizes the continual nature of the filling that occurred: "They were more and more filled with joy and with the Holy Spirit."

all the LORD's people were prophets and that the LORD would put his Spirit on them!" (Num 11:29). Now that all believers do, in fact, share in the same Spirit, the Spirit has consequently created for us an inseparable link to the King of kings and Lord of lords, immersing us into the kingdom reign of the divine presence. On an individual, personal level, believers experience the King and his Spirit. Throughout the book of Acts, we see such disciples as Peter (Acts 2:4; 4:8, 31) and Paul (9:17; 13:9) repeatedly touched with the Spirit and therefore touched by Jesus. Both of those men were often described as being "filled" and should be understood as representative of the larger following of disciples: Every believer should continually encounter the Spirit!

Messiah Reigns Through the Spirit

The kingly rule of Jesus the Messiah began in a demonstrative way under the new covenant. Jesus announced this covenant at the Last Supper (1 Cor 11:25) and ratified it at Pentecost when key features of that covenant were experienced by his followers, particularly the forgiveness of sin and the outpouring of the Spirit. As Jesus was inaugurating his kingdom, he was also ratifying the covenant.

The focus of Jesus' message had always been the kingdom of God, which continues to be the message of his church in word and action. But even before Pentecost, the Spirit's power was evident in Jesus' ministry and evidenced that his kingdom was already intruding upon this world: "But if it is by the Spirit of God that I drive out demons, then the kingdom of God has come upon you" (Matt 12:28). It is fitting, then, that Jesus' first official act as reigning King, Priest, and Prophet was to share the Spirit's powerful kingdom presence, the equivalent of a spiritual manifestation of the King himself. The evidence of his presence was displayed initially in the miracle of tongues (or languages) and then in every kind of sign and wonder throughout the book of Acts, including the preaching of Peter, Paul, and others.[19]

---

19. Tongues are mentioned on only three occasions in Acts, and on the last occasion, prophecy appears with it (Acts 2:4; 10:36; 19:6). Tongues and prophecy are a common evidence of the Spirit, illustrating that the presence of the kingdom enters human history with credible manifestations of a supernatural nature. That's not to suggest that tongues are always the evidence of the anointing, however. Due to the descriptive rather than prescriptive quality of Acts, we can affirm that tongues are indeed *an* evidence of both salvation and ongoing empowerment, but we cannot affirm that tongues are the *sole* or

Sharing in God's Presence

In Acts 2, the prophetic expression of unlearned tongues and other more general prophetic unction were the immediate evidence that Messiah had initiated fulfillment of new covenant hope (vv. 4, 14).[20] As Peter preached the fulfillment of Old Testament promises, declaring that Messiah Jesus "has received from the Father the promised Holy Spirit" (v. 33) that was predicted centuries beforehand by the prophet Joel (Joel 2:28), Peter's inspired preaching exemplified the profound truth that all Scripture points to Jesus (Acts 2:16–39). When Jesus unleashed the Spirit upon Peter and the others, he fulfilled the Scriptures by giving believing humanity the gift of God's restored presence in their lives—the ultimate gift of sharing in God's presence! The divine presence was immediately experienced as a felt fellowship of the *spoken* word through Peter's bold declaration of kingdom truth and through the supernatural utterance of tongues as people declared in unlearned languages "the wonders of God" revealed in Jesus Christ (Acts 2:11).

Praise be to God that his presence has come to his people in a dynamic, relational fashion! Even though believers throughout Acts are intermittently filled with the Spirit, Luke's emphasis is certainly not that the nature of the Spirit's interpenetrational activity is temporary or fleeting. On the contrary, such regular imbuements demonstrate that the reigning Christ has organized his kingdom in such a way that he remains active and available to the lives and needs of his people, resulting in a relational kingdom because he loves relationship and maintains his relationship to us. Because the dynamic of a relational kingdom requires a continual Spirit-provision, Jesus is always present to pour out a fresh renewing empowerment to accomplish the kingdom mission. Christ Jesus our Lord truly is "with [us]

---

primary evidence of such empowerment. For further elaboration on tongues and prophecy, see chapter six.

20. On the day of Pentecost, tongues were an *expression of prophecy* spoken in fulfillment of Joel 2. Whereas Paul distinguishes between tongues and prophecy (1 Cor 12:8–10; 28–30), Luke presents tongues as a manifestation of prophecy. Tongues are the only result cited in Acts 2 as fulfilling Joel's words regarding the Spirit's connection to the prophetic. Immediately after the believers *began to speak in tongues as the Spirit enabled them* (Acts 2:4), the Apostle Peter explains this phenomenon and favorably quotes the prophet Joel, where Yahweh declares, "I will pour out my Spirit in those days, and they will prophesy" (v. 18; cf. Joel 2:29). The expression of prophecy in the second half of Acts 2:18 ("and they will prophesy") does not appear in the Hebrew text of Joel 2, highlighting Luke's intentional connection between the prophetic and Spirit-evidenced tongues. This indicates that prophecy is open to more than one expression.

Pentecost: God Shares His Spirit

always, to the very end of the age," just as he promised he would be (Matt 28:20).

In Acts, every aspect of the Spirit's work that pertains to the believer fits into this single scenario: Jesus the Messiah is always dynamically involved through the Spirit. The Holy Spirit is inseparably related to the Lord (Yahweh) Jesus and to his reign. Because the Spirit's work is decisively Christ-centered, the Spirit is called both the *Spirit of Yahweh* and the *Spirit of Jesus* (Acts 8:39; 16:7; cf. Rom 8:9; Gal 4:6). Messiah's ministry is the continual dynamic provision of Spirit-motivated mission and Spirit-driven unction for the new community.

Because Jesus desires to remain involved in our lives and to have a reigning ministry through us, he continually pours out his Spirit directly from his heavenly throne. It wouldn't be farfetched to consider that such a ministry has a ubiquitous effect, bringing believers directly into the throne room of the royal Presence and granting us the privilege of living in the presence of the King! Because Jesus has delivered the promised Spirit to the sacred assembly, he has opened the door for a relationship with his creatures that resembles the relationship that exists within the triune Godhead. That relationship is one of unity and peace with God, and by the mystery of divine indwelling, there now exists an interpenetration of his life into the believer. As Paul put it, "Whoever is united with the Lord is one with him in spirit" (1 Cor 6:17). We should consider this a uniquely precious sharing in God's presence, which is profoundly intimate and deeply spiritual.

Now with God in us, believers share the perfect mixture and beautiful blending of divine life with human nature, such that God and his people are filled with each other in an astonishing dance of united, loving life. This life is experienced on the level of a hidden spiritual kingdom presence but remains true nonetheless. Through Spirit-infilling, believers are forever in God and God in them. The church is united in fellowship with God for the sake of intimacy and for the practical purpose of fulfilling its moment-by-moment kingdom mission, which is only possible because we share in the King's presence.

The Acts narrative demonstrates that the provision of the Spirit is not just a onetime event at Pentecost, which was only the beginning, or that God's Spirit permanently lives within us, which is also true, but that Christ is dynamically and vigorously involved in our daily Christian ministry. The permanent indwelling of the Spirit that every believer receives at the moment of salvation guarantees that Christ is reigning *in* us, while the ongoing ministry of fresh Spirit Baptism ("filling") guarantees that Jesus will reign *through* us. Christ the King remains dynamically engaged with his people through continual baptism with the Holy Spirit.

Manifesting His Kingdom: Word and Wonders

Praise be to God for sharing his presence with the people of this world! The church has been anointed to manifest Christ's kingdom both in word and deed (Acts 8:12; 19:8; 20:25; 28:23), made possible through the prophetic Spirit who is still being poured out on everyone who believes.[21] Our Spirit-empowered ministry is for the purpose of mission and to manifest and witness to the kingdom of Christ. The *word* of the kingdom is the emboldened declaration of the good news of the King. The supreme Conqueror over sin, death, and the devil overcame all opposition by one decisive victory blow at the cross, being raised in power because death could not possibly hold him in its clutches (Acts 2:24). The *deeds* of the kingdom include every act of love and forgiveness and every manifestation of the King's presence and power. Early on in Acts, Jesus promised the disciples that they would receive "power" when the Spirit came upon them (Acts 1:8). That power belongs to and flows from the only true Sovereign, our Lord Jesus Christ.

Regarding that power, Craig Keener asks, "What does Luke mean by power? Although not all references involve healing and exorcism, these constitute the most common expressions of that power in Luke's narrative."[22] Following Keener, the term power in Luke and Acts primarily refers to the miraculous. When Peter summarized Jesus being anointed with the Spirit and power, that power was manifested both in *doing good* and in miraculous *healing*: "You know what has happened throughout the province of Judea, ... how God anointed Jesus of Nazareth with the Holy Spirit and power, and how he went around doing good and healing all who were under the power of the devil, because God was with him" (Acts 10:37–38). But Jesus wasn't the only one who walked in power!

---

21. Throughout this book, I take a non-cessationist approach to spiritual gifts, affirming that the supernatural and miraculous gifts of the first-century church continue today (e.g., tongues, prophecy, healing, etc.). Possibly the best defense to date remains Jon Ruthven, *On the Cessation of the Charismata*.

22. Keener, "Power of Pentecost," 49. See Luke 4:26; 5:17; 6:19; 8:46; 9:1; Acts 3:12; 4:7. For Paul's perspective on power and the Spirit, see Fee, *God's Empowering Presence*, 35–36.

Pentecost: God Shares His Spirit

Even though a believer named Stephen was not an apostle and hadn't walked with Jesus, he is one example of a person who, being "full of God's grace *and power*, performed great wonders and signs among the people" (Acts 6:8, emphasis added). Power here is clearly connected to the miracles that accompanied Stephen's ministry, which suggests that a ministry characterized by the miraculous power of God is not restricted to Jesus and his apostles but is accessible to any believer to empower the overthrow of Satan's kingdom.[23] What the Spirit accomplished in Acts in both power and mission is intended for all believers for all time: "God says, I will pour out my Spirit on all people. Your sons and daughters ... your young men ... your old men ... Even on my servants, both men and women" (Acts 2:17–18).

This talk of power, however, should not detract from the truth that Christ's kingdom reign is one of humble meekness. In fact, it is a reign of power *through* weakness! This humility was demonstrated in Christ's obedience to the Father all the way to the cross, where the weakness of the cross was devoured by the power of the resurrection (Phil 2:8–9). Jesus succumbed to violent men who exacted the power of destructive hatred against him, so that in the end, those worldly powers would be shown to be utterly powerless. When Jesus finally rose from the grave, the power of humility and the apparent weakness of divine love had won out.

Now from the highest position of humble authority, Jesus graciously seeks to restore the vice-regency that he initially entrusted to humanity in the garden (Gen 1:26–30). Through vice-regency, God shares his authority over the created world. That responsibility is restored through the church when believers manifest Jesus' kingdom authority in the same ways that he did: through healing, casting out demons, prophesying, and boldly declaring the kingdom of God. Believers truly are kingdom representatives—Christians—who bear the powerful name of Jesus Christ! This was the case when Paul cast out a demon "in the name of Jesus Christ" (Acts 16:16–19), because he was acting as Jesus' representative when he declared his name. We too are Christ's ambassadors ministering in his stead (2 Cor 5:20).[24]

---

23. Throughout Acts, the ministry of the Spirit is characterized by amazing works accomplished by Christ's followers in numerous expressions of signs, wonders, and miracles of every kind. Reading Acts, one never gets the sense that God intended such manifestations merely for a transition from the old to the new but as bindingly characteristic of the new age.

24. In the garden of Eden, a demonized serpent stole that God-given authority, but in the new paradise as God's kingdom is being restored on earth, Christians take authority

Just as the King has made room for the church within the community of the triune identity, he never hoards the Spirit but graciously anoints his followers with this dynamic presence. As the Spirit of God lives in us, Jesus remains involved in the world through the community of faith. In addition to the intimacy of fellowship that this affords to the church, there are two primary reasons for our anointing. First, we're anointed for empowerment to accomplish what we *cannot* do ourselves, and second, we're anointed for enablement to carry out what we *would* not do in our own strength. The church's anointed mission remains the same since the day of Pentecost: to extend the kingdom of God through the gospel of Jesus Christ. While his kingdom advances, the enemy's kingdom is subdued, thus the need for an empowered anointing also implies the presence of a demonic kingdom that must be opposed.

On our own, humanity cannot participate in God's war against the forces of darkness because the ensuing battle occurs in the spiritual, supernatural sphere and then overflows into the seen world (Eph 6:12). Until salvation, people remain in Satan's kingdom of lost souls under the authority of the prince of darkness. Through the Spirit, believers are at once freed and given supernatural weaponry to wage war against supernatural forces of darkness. Paul tells us, "The weapons we fight with are not the weapons of the world. On the contrary, they have divine power to demolish strongholds" (2 Cor 10:4). The kingdom of Satan is therefore overcome by the kingdom of Christ manifest in the church. As we share in God's presence, we become effective spiritual weapons in his hands. As the weapons of God, every believer becomes a spiritual conduit through which the reign of Christ faces off with the kingdom of Satan. Christians manifest Christ's kingdom reign by boldly confronting the dark powers with a gospel far more powerful, "because the Spirit who lives in you is greater than the spirit who lives in the world" (1 John 4:4 NLT).

The gospel message is a claim to reality over and against the kingdom of Satan. Every supernatural act of God that defies the laws of nature functions as an assault against the demonic kingdom. Because Satan had usurped God's rightful authority over the created order all the way back in the garden of Eden, even aspects of nature will experience the wonders of God anew when Jesus reminds nature of his reign. This was evidenced in Jesus' encounters with both people and nature. When confronted by a

over the demonized, and in this way, manifest the reign of Christ and the restoration of our vice-regency.

demoniac, Scripture attests, "Jesus rebuked (*epetimesen*) him, saying, 'Be quiet and come out of him!'" (Luke 4:35 NASB; cf. 4:41). Using the very same language as Luke, Mark's gospel describes Jesus approaching nature with similar nerve when he "rebuked (*epetimesen*) the wind and said to the waves, 'Quiet! Be still!'" (Mark 4:39; cf. Matt 8:26). Jesus approached people *and* nature as forces opposing the Creator and needing to be subdued, and he accepted it as his mission to confront those powers.

When Jesus anointed his disciples to go into the world with the same exorcising, miracle-working power that he displayed, he was also providing the church with a faithful model to do the same (Luke 9:1–2).

Conclusion

Yahweh began to reveal his kingdom to Abraham and Moses and then fleshed it out with King David, until Jesus came on the scene and announced the presence of an encroaching kingdom in his very own person. When Jesus conquered the grave and sat down on David's spiritual throne in the heavenlies, his kingdom was inaugurated, but it will not be fully established until the end of the age. Jesus' resurrection ushered in the glory of Pentecost as God's most sustained expression of the divine presence in society and, without comparison, the believing community's most personal and comprehensive sharing in God's presence yet.

In Jesus' role as Messiah and resurrected "Prince and Savior" (Acts 5:31), he announced the Spirit's presence as characteristic of the new covenant age. The new covenant lays out the kingdom's spiritual architecture, bringing together the promise of the forgiveness of sin and a new ministry of God's presence through Messiah, even a Spirit Baptism. Jesus' baptism of Spirit and fire summarizes his role throughout the age: a special divine agent who brings blessing and judgement, depending upon a person's response. The baptism of the Spirit fulfills the spiritual outpouring anticipated by the prophets, and it now remains the reigning provision of the final Davidic King. Under the new covenant, our risen Lord remains dynamically involved in the daily life of his church as the ongoing source of God's presence, the Holy Spirit.

Christ's spiritual reign manifests throughout this age in an open-ended, relational kingdom. It is yet to be decided who will ultimately constitute the eternal kingdom, but it remains open to Jew and Gentile, slave and free, male and female alike (Acts 10:34–35; Gal 3:8). While there remains incalculable untapped potential for God's glorious kingdom presence to be revealed through the church's message and miraculous exploits, the furtherance of such a mission depends largely upon the believer's obedience but also requires the Messiah's ongoing dynamic of Spirit-provision.

5

Prayer: God Shares His Plans

BECAUSE GOD SHARES HIMSELF, his Son, and his Spirit in fundamentally transformative ways, it shouldn't come as a surprise that his daily influence inspires us to participate in the most natural form of fellowship with him: prayer. Prayer is the most natural expression of a life lived in God's presence and the indispensable driving force behind Christian mission and outreach. Prayer confirms to the church that we have been accepted and privileged to be partakers of the divine nature, because we do not live and minister in word only but by words uttered in the very presence of the triune God!

Through prayer, believers tap into the power behind effective evangelism and a bold witness for Jesus Christ. We move into the nitty-gritty of knowing God personally through conversation that changes the world! Because we've received the Breath of prophecy at Pentecost—the very person and presence of God the Spirit—we are now a community whose utterance is of a supernatural character and quality. Sharing in God's presence means that we share in words and conversation that have supernatural effect. Confession of Christ's lordship is one thing, but participation in the vice-regency of cooperative prayer is quite another. Vice-regency means that God shares his power and influence with us; and in the case of prayer, God gives every believer the opportunity to share in his plans.

We will now turn to the devotional heart of God's presence on a supremely personal level: the intimacy of prayer.

The Best Possible Future

When believers take God's message to the world, they speak with supernatural enablement and with the boldness of Pentecost. And when I speak to the LORD, not even my frail human nature can hinder the dynamic engagement that takes place, for Scripture tells me that "the Spirit helps us in our weakness. We do not know what we ought to pray for, but the Spirit himself intercedes for us through wordless groans" (Rom 8:26). Just as the Spirit hovered over the chaos in the beginning, awaiting God's spoken word (Gen 1:2), so now the Spirit personally broods over our hopeless situations, awaiting our prayers. The Spirit waits in anticipation for us to speak out and pray so that he can create new possibilities, new realities, new inevitabilities, and even a new future! Prayer truly can enlarge future possibilities, much like the prayer of Jabez in the Old Testament: "Jabez cried out to the God of Israel, 'Oh, that you would bless me and enlarge my territory!'" (1 Chr 4:10). Indeed, God did that very thing! Perhaps the church hasn't yet grasped how much power there is in simply talking to God and taking the time to ask him to bring us into the best possible future.

In the book of Genesis, we're first introduced to the "image of God," not through Yahweh's visible presence, but by his breath and through his spoken word: *Let there be . . . and indeed there was!*[1] Just as Scripture's very first impression of the divine image is the spoken word, an image that humanity shares with God (Gen 1:26, 27), his image is restored to people in a special way when we interact with him in the simple act of prayer. Because God's image is being restored in our lives through mere words, we can impart life to others not only by proclaiming the gospel but also through the powerful practice of prayer. Because we were made in the divine image and now possess the prophetic Spirit, God's holy Breath, like never before in history our prayers are intended to be the channel for God's creative life. Our prayers create new future possibilities, including new possibilities for us, new possibilities for the church, and even new possibilities for God. What a privilege, therefore, that God shares his plans *and his planning* with us!

Just as God's own spoken word is creative, he wants to create through us. But our prayers have no creative power in themselves, not even by virtue of faith. Although my faith must cooperate with God, prayers are powerless apart from God's presence and the divine life settling upon them. Uniting

---

1. See Gen 1:3, 6, 9, 11, 14, 15, 20, 24, 26.

Prayer: God Shares His Plans

faith, prayer, and God's faithfulness, he chooses to use my prayer relationship with him to create future reality that would not otherwise be possible. Even though prayers cannot change God's ultimate purpose, the minute details of his plans are subject to revision because he shares his plans with me and considers my input.[2]

Because God's heart is open to my every prayer, he actually listens and takes my request and my perspective into account—which is no small thing! Listen to this remarkable account from the days of Joshua:

> On the day the LORD gave the Amorites over to Israel, Joshua said to the LORD in the presence of Israel: "Sun, stand still over Gibeon, and you, moon, over the Valley of Aijalon." So the sun stood still, and the moon stopped, till the nation avenged itself on its enemies, as it is written in the Book of Jashar. The sun stopped in the middle of the sky and delayed going down about a full day. There has never been a day like it before or since, a day when the LORD listened to a human being. (Josh 10:12–14)

But is that really what the author means, that there's never been another day in all human history that Yahweh actually listened to someone? Of course not! The precedent here is that God truly does listen to people. Joshua's prayer was simple, specific, and full of faith. Despite the fact that Joshua's request bordered on the absurd, the LORD still heard his very special request and answered immediately with precision. *But has there "never been a day like it"?* Surely there has never been another day in which the sun stood still, but the author is also pointing out that Yahweh heard the specifics of an extremely unusual prayer and still answered! The New Living Translation captures the sense: "There has never been a day like this one before or since, when the LORD answered such a prayer." The bottom line is this: God hears our prayers and values what we have to say. He mulls over your perspective and your arguments and takes your requests seriously. He wants us to be specific in our prayers because he plans for the future in light of them, changes course because of them, and delivers, saves, and heals in response to them![3]

To put it another way, prayer not only rearranges the furniture in the room but actually changes the architecture of God's kingdom here on earth. This statement takes seriously Jesus' model prayer when he says to the

---

2. Tiessen, *Providence and Prayer*, 72.

3. Pentecostal scholar Kenneth Archer says it like this: "God encourages us to participate with him in creating the future" (*Gospel Revisited*, 86).

Father, "Your kingdom come, your will be done, on earth as it is in heaven" (Matt 6:10). But we're not yet living in God's kingdom, are we? This world is a war zone filled with violence, hate, evil, and demonic devastation. A massive renovation is underway to transform Satan's earthly kingdom into the kingdom of God, and only believers can move hell and high water to accomplish this as bearers of God's presence. As divine representatives, ambassadors even, his presence is always with us! While the gospel is our world ministry, prayer is the fuel and driving force behind our mission. The church *will* transform this world through gospel and prayer for the sake of the kingdom of God.

The Openness of Prayer

As Almighty God responds to prayer, he also allows himself to be affected by it, and therefore changed, because of our thoughtful conversation with him. God has gone so far as to require prayer as an essential structural component in the success of his kingdom's establishment. John Wesley, the great founder of Methodism, once made the radical statement that "God does nothing but in answer to prayer."[4] As extreme as that may sound, it's only a slight exaggeration! Terrance Tiessen qualifies this idea and provides an excellent summary on what I am calling the *openness* of prayer:

> There are many things that [God] will do for the good of his creatures, whether or not anyone prays, but there are also things that he will not do unless he is asked to do them. There are specific goods that people will not have if they do not ask for them and specific evils that will occur if the prayers of God's people are not offered for their prevention. This does not mean that everyone, even every obedient believer, gets what she asks for. God is free, as his creatures are, and may choose a better course than is suggested by us. But petitionary prayer has a real effect on the way things turn out and even on the actions that God takes to influence those outcomes.[5]

The openness of prayer simply means that God is truly open to our prayers. Because God experiences time and space in some sense at the pace of the world he created, so he remains open to fresh dialogue and often will not move forward with his plans apart from it. Prayer means that we are

4. Wesley, *Christian Perfection*, 157.
5. Tiessen, *Providence and Prayer*, 72.

Prayer: God Shares His Plans

involved with God in a partnership to build his kingdom and push back the forces of darkness, as we prayerfully open up to him about our thoughts, feelings, plans, and perspectives. In the truest sense, we are "God's co-workers" as we prayerfully share in his presence (2 Cor 6:1).

The openness of prayer is evidenced in nearly every communication that occurs between God and people in Scripture. Personal one-on-one communication occurred prior to the fall and after it. Adam's sin could have easily kept him from speaking up in the garden when God sought him out, but it didn't. God had warned Adam in no uncertain terms that he would certainly die if he ate from the tree: "You must not eat from the tree of the knowledge of good and evil, for when you eat from it you will certainly die" (Gen 2:17). Once Adam ate the forbidden fruit, his initial reaction was to flee and hide from God. But when Yahweh searched for him, he came out of hiding and depended upon God's gracious flexibility to meet him where he was. After eating the fruit, one wonders what Adam's initial thought might've been: Is God going to kill me, or will he perhaps be open to forgiveness?[6]

Instead of continuing to hide, Adam responded and entered back into a dialogue with his Maker: "But the LORD God called to the man, 'Where are you?' [Adam] answered, 'I heard you in the garden, and I was afraid because I was naked; so I hid'" (Gen 3:9–10). Adam's response implies the hope that God might help him in his desperate situation. In fact, such hope is heard in the cries and prayerful pleas we find throughout Scripture.[7] We learn here from Adam's own lips that the reason behind his hiding was not fear that God might strike him down, or even some ambiguous conviction over his disobedient act, but the entrance of a foreign never-before-experienced sense of shame: Adam was naked. Although God's response resonated with frustration over what the man and woman had done, he did not immediately kill them as he said he would. Instead, he made the ground more difficult for humans to work (Gen 3:17), promising the man that he would return to that same ground, "for dust you are and to dust you will return" (v. 19).[8] Adam and Eve were then banished as exiles from Eden, just

---

6. On the judgment language that pertains to God "walking in the garden in the cool of the day" (Gen 3:8), see Kline, "Primal Parousia," 244–80.

7. Many such cries appear in Scripture in the form of lament, beseeching God to look upon the believer's situation or the attacks of the wicked and to intervene; see, e.g., Pss 44; 60; 74; 79; 80; 85; 90.

8. The man's curse was to die and return to the ground, but the serpent (Gen 3:14–15), the woman (v. 16), and the earth/ground (vv. 17–18) were also directly cursed.

as we all remain today. But their dialogue continued—not only the dialogue between God and Adam but also with Adam's descendants.

Referring to Adam's grandchildren, Genesis records that after the exile from Eden, there came a time when the "people began to call on the name of the Lord" (Gen 4:26).[9] Prior to this, only Eve had directly referred to God as Lord or Yahweh (Gen 4:1), providing some evidence that this stirring of the social order was connected to Adam and Eve's example. It was the personal name Yahweh that people began to call out to, not some distant, ambiguous pagan deity. Moreover, calling on Yahweh "in Genesis is related to God's self-revelation to Abraham (12:7–8), Hagar (16:13), and Isaac (26:24–25)."[10] Calling on Yahweh is connected to God's initiative to personally reveal himself, something the people were beginning to appreciate. Because God had revealed himself by name, he had opened himself up to personal appeal.

For God to allow Adam and his descendants to call upon his name, he initiated a certain vulnerability and accountability toward human relationship. Knowing that the people who used his name were depending on him for answers, God was covenanting himself to be attentive to their offered prayers. Just as Adam's response to Yahweh implied at least the hope that God might bring man out of hiding and resolve the dilemma of a distance masked in shame, so Adam's descendants were awakening to the faithfulness of God toward those who call upon him, the God who reveals his name and covenant.

Calling on the Lord also involved living in the reality of a person-to-God relationship. By providing his name to the community, Yahweh made himself available, made their appeals personal, and made himself personally responsible to them. The fact that men and women were calling out to Yahweh demonstrated that God does not demand to take all the initiative himself but instead places that responsibility on us! Just as Adam and his children accepted the openness of prayer, believers today are expected to know God as the one who welcomes our prayerful initiative. This is consistent with why he has revealed himself to Adam, Abraham, Israel, and the church of God today, so that we might open up and reveal our hearts to him as well. Desiring our reciprocal response, God's heart is forever open to the prayers of his people.

---

9. The Hebrew literally reads without a stated subject, "It was begun to call . . ."
10. Mathews, *Genesis 1–11:26*, 294.

We're at a time in church history when we can know, possibly more so than ever before, that God not only answers and requires prayer but even *depends* on it. This is not an offense to God but rather a joy for him to involve us so intimately in the plans he has ordained for human history. He wants to establish a grand kingdom, and he needs our involvement.[11] Every believer is called to work alongside him through prayer in order to transform this world for the glory of God. Our prayers are not merely ordained speeches that we utter back to God to accomplish what he already intended to do! They literally change God's mind; they direct the power of God and enhance the ministries of God. Our prayers actually mean something because of the divine presence at work in us. My prayers set captives free!

God Prays Too

If we are going to take seriously this notion of sharing in God's presence and plans, we should consider a certain role reversal that takes place in our relationship with him: God prays too. Did you know that we serve a *praying* God? It might seem like a radical suggestion, but Scripture is clear that in some sense both Jesus and the Spirit make "intercession" for the saints (Rom 8:26–27, 34). More than that, doesn't God ask us for things all the time? God works quite persuasively within our hearts, but not through bully tactics or forcing us to do his will; on the contrary, he gently persuades and influences us. One could even say, he asks nicely. Then he reflects upon our decisions and actions, sometimes praising, and at other times regretting, our choices. Our prayers often look like begging, cajoling, bargaining, coaxing, or sweet-talking, but God's prayer looks more like self-reflection (Gen 6:6; 18:17), influence (Acts 7:51), and hope (Jer 3:19). This is the God who prays.

I want us to focus in this section on the aspect of God's prayers that I'll describe as hope or divine optimism. When God created Adam and his wife, how could we deny that he intended anything less than to share the most personal relationship with them for all time? The loving triune Fellowship created persons outside their circle to share in the beauty and bliss

---

11. There is a most evident "openness" in our opportunity to pursue ministry, while within those ministries there remains the simplicity of prayer that seems to be the driving force behind it all. It's up to each one of us to take advantage of our endless opportunities to serve God, bearing in mind that every step of the way we must be a people continually crying out in dependence upon the Lord. The openness of ministry is the subject of chapters 6–8.

of an intimacy the Trinity alone had enjoyed for an eternity beforehand. God now pursues every human being with the vigilance of a lover who, from the eternal past, had been making preparations for his bride. Scripture describes the Spirit of the triune oneness as yearning "jealously" for us (Jas 4:5). Yahweh will go to the greatest lengths to make a people his very own, to have a bride set apart for him.

Our great God has always enjoyed the fellowship of a community of three distinct, yet united persons, together experiencing the delightful wonder and newness of true love. Scripture declares that "God is love," one of the only statements in Scripture that addresses God's inherent being (1 John 4:16). His love never grows old or becomes commonplace. It always enjoys the heights of bliss and the nostalgia of what we think of as new love. Despite all that, the only way to honor divine love was to create beings who could derive their greatest pleasure from sharing in its supremacy. This was God's good pleasure: that we might share in the supremacy of divine intimacy. He wanted his relationship with people to be so personal that he embodied himself when he appeared to the man in the garden (Gen 2:15, 19; 3:8). When Yahweh took on a body, he not only made his interaction personal, but he also demonstrated that man could derive the greatest benefit from enjoying a person-to-person relationship with a Creator who could appear in human form.

When God created man and woman, he created them innocent and good, but placing them in the Garden of Eden, he also provided them with an ideal environment (Gen 1:26–31). He gave them such a satisfying body-oriented relationship and such fulfilling responsibilities that he foresaw the *unlikelihood* that they would disobey him and fall into sin. Although Yahweh was aware of all the possibilities, he nonetheless remained hopeful for their success. In light of other inspired passages of Scripture, this proposal is not only logical but biblical.

The Creator's sentiment could have been much like his later attitude toward elect Israel. Under circumstances far worse than the nearly perfect conditions of Eden, God's thoughts toward Israel were optimistic: "Surely they are my people, children who will be true to me" (Isa 63:8). The New Living Translation is even more emphatic: "Surely they will not betray me again." The Lord's tone resounds with optimism! Surely, surely, surely because they are my people, they will remain true and faithful. Yet the Lord was of course disappointed because the people did betray him again. In Eden, God planted something pure within Adam and his wife, not unlike the new work he sought to produce in Israel, yet things didn't turn out as he had planned: "Yet I planted you a choice vine, wholly of pure seed. *How then have you turned degenerate and become a wild vine?*" (Jer 2:21 ESV, emphasis added). Notice that Yahweh's tone is one of confusion and frustration. He is genuinely perplexed that the good thing he initiated didn't grow into the beautiful vine he was expecting!

But what else could he have done? We could say that God had made preparations for his bride throughout the eternal past, so it wasn't for lack of trying. Yahweh solemnly declares, "What more was there to do for my vineyard, that I have not done in it? When I looked for it to yield grapes, why did it yield wild grapes?" (Isa 5:4 ESV). This is what we might call divinely perplexed. Why did this happen? How could this have possibly occurred? What else could I have possibly done that I didn't already do? Here, God is saying that he did everything he could for the best possible outcome, but Israel still rebelled.

Working with such flawed creatures, the divine heart was always optimistic, expecting more from Adam and from Israel: "I myself said, 'How gladly would I treat you like my children and give you a pleasant land, the most beautiful inheritance of any nation.' *I thought you would call me 'Father' and not turn away from following me*'" (Jer 3:19, emphasis added). The LORD reflects here upon the unexpected: I thought, I hoped, I was optimistic, but you let me down. If he could expect so much from Israel, surely he expected even more in Eden? Yet tragically, there was not victory for Israel or for Adam. Even though God saw that all of his creation was good, including the man and his freedom, the mysterious fall still occurred (Gen 1:31).

God had embraced such optimism for humanity that he never preplanned a future punishment for potentially rebellious people but rather an "eternal fire prepared for the devil and his angels" (Matt 25:41). The eternal fire is apparently plan B for those who choose that fate by rejecting the love of God. But just as God anticipated humanity's victory, he may have also had good reason to expect victory from his angels as well, so it's likely that it wasn't until after Satan's fall that God had prepared the eternal fire. Notice Gerald Bray's comments on Satan's fall: "Did God know when he created Satan that he would turn out this way? This is a question impossible to answer. By giving his angels freewill, God created the possibility of rebellion, but that can hardly have been his intention. The angels were meant to use their freewill to enjoy eternal fellowship with God."[12] Indeed, it's hard to believe that God ever intended the fall of humans or angels.[13]

After being warned, Adam must have known that death at least meant distance from God. In Adam's power of choice, he wielded the power to distance God! He chose to eat the fruit, he chose to die, and he chose to accept a foreign knowledge that competes with, and even replaces, the knowledge of God: "Did God really say, 'You must not eat from any tree in the garden'?" (Gen 3:5). Although Adam's choice was irrational to say the least, it wasn't unthinkable. God was prepared for the worst, but he expected better things for the man and woman;[14] yet there was still something about sin that led to an unexpected outcome: "When the woman saw that the fruit of the tree was good for food and pleasing to the eye, and also desirable for gaining wisdom, she took some and ate it. She also gave some to her husband, who was with her, and he ate it" (Gen 3:6). In a moment of time it became true that "the heart is deceitful above all things and beyond cure. Who can understand it?" (Jer 17:9).

Sin was a foreign invader into humanity's innocence, adding to the soul a combination of the essentially absurd and irrational, resulting in the arbitrary and unpredictable nature of sin. Sin is an unreasonable, vulgar contradiction that lives within us. Even in their innocence, our first parents committed the first act of sin and acquired a proclivity that is now the common experience of every member of the human race (Rom 5:12).[15] Their

---

12. Bray, *God is Love*, 347.

13. One might argue that my proposal more resembles philosophical speculation than theological reflection. In response, it is only the classical foreknowledge position that would demand that God ordained the fall, based on presuppositions of divine knowledge. Scripture nowhere addresses the matter other than to inform readers that all God had made was in fact *good*. We should be able to assume that God's assessment was a metaphysical absolute—it really was good! The only thing that wasn't good was corrected, and God gave Adam a helpmate to bring about an even more ideal existence. If God is truly good, who himself is the very essence and definition of pure and perfect love, shouldn't our theological assumption be that God would give humans the advantage to remain without sin in an ideal relationship with him?

14. Speaking of being prepared for the worst, Revelation 13:8 records that God's Son was "slain from the foundation of the world" (KJV). This translation is debatable, however. Most translations appear to follow the NASB: ". . . everyone whose name has not been written from the foundation of the world in the book of life of the Lamb who has been slain." Cf. Acts 2:23; 1 Pet 1:19–20.

15. The discrepancies by scholars over the nature of sin go on and on. Some teach that the guilt deserving of eternal punishment is inherent in our nature at the moment of birth, while others teach that guilt is imputed after an age of accountability when the

first sin brought about spiritual and physical death for all people universally because we all inevitably sin. The mortal nature is now forever inclined toward sin and godlessness.

God's Repentance

A person's first encounter with prayer is often a bedtime prayer as a child or a prayer quickly uttered at the dinner table. But when people are at once struck with the conviction of their gaping distance from God and their need for salvation, the prayer of repentance becomes their first genuine approach to a responsive, relational God of love: "Jesus, save me from sin and death and give me a relationship with you!" When we become aware that God is real but at a frightful distance from us, in that moment we also become aware of the longsuffering grace of God. That grace shows up to save us from despair so that we can beseech God to deliver us from an impending judgment, a judgment that we now know our sin deserves.[16] Even though God has warned us in his word that "the wages of sin is death," we should also know that as long as we have breath, it is never too late to change his mind (Rom 6:23).

In the Old Testament prophets, Jonah's message to Nineveh was honest, simple, and straightforward: "Forty more days and Nineveh will be overthrown" (Jonah 3:4). This prophet wasn't speaking from his own perspective but from God's. The LORD himself had determined that in forty days this city and its inhabitants would be destroyed, and his integrity depended upon the trustworthiness and urgency of that message. God

---

first intentional sin is committed. Still others would not use the language of sin-nature, as if sin were an entity, choosing instead to emphasize acts of sin. Some prefer to discuss our fallen state in terms of human nature, and sin being our overall disposition. Still others prefer the language of mortal nature, which is necessarily weak but not inherently sinful. Regardless, in our human or mortal nature, apart from the Holy Spirit, people are inclined to think and act contrary to the heart of their Creator. Pelagianism teaches that people can overcome sin through their own efforts, while the mainstream Christian position has always been that people require the overcoming grace of God's Spirit.

16. Today, the prayer of salvation is a simple one, but most importantly, it's a matter of the heart: Do I believe the words that I'm praying, and will my life begin to reflect that? "Father, thank you for sending Jesus to save me. I believe he died on the cross for me and that I can live because of him. I believe that Jesus rose from the dead, and I trust in him for my forgiveness and my future. I believe that my hope is in the resurrection of the dead. Help me turn away from my sin to follow you with all my heart. I ask this in Jesus' name. Amen."

was not somehow held hostage by a foreknowledge that knew otherwise; instead, he proclaimed the truth as he saw it, thus a forty-day judgment was imminent. The integrity of God ensured the validity of his warning: Nineveh would be overthrown.

Of course, Nineveh was not destroyed! Even Nineveh's pagan king was able to perceive the personal responsiveness of God and remarked, "Who knows? God may yet relent (*nacham*) and with compassion turn from his fierce anger so that we will not perish" (Jonah 3:9; cf. 1:6). In light of the remote possibility that God may change his course of action and decide not to destroy the city, the people repented in hopes of *God's repentance*. The result: "When God saw what they did and how they turned from their evil ways, he relented (*nacham*) and did not bring on them the destruction he had threatened" (3:10). Make no mistake, judgment was threatened because the LORD fully intended to carry it out! But rather than being enslaved to an exhaustive foreknowledge, God is perfectly free and open-minded and therefore able to change his mind and reverse the judgment that he was determined to bring against Nineveh. Rather than death and destruction, the people were saved and blessed! Rather than further distance, the prayers and actions surrounding their repentance brought God close to them. Because of their own willingness and determination to repent and turn from their evil ways, the people changed God's mind. Yahweh's thoughtfulness demonstrated that he is a God of personal relationship who responds to the hearts and actions of those who repent.

This and many other passages make us aware that God repents over matters of people's sin. One Hebrew term for repentance is *nacham*, which basically means a change of mind or direction. When *nacham* is used of God, it means the same thing. There are at least 35 uses of the term *nacham* in connection with God changing his mind, not to mention other passages that use different terms to describe the reversal of a divine decision.[17] Based on King Saul's disobedience, Yahweh regretted and repented (*nacham*) over appointing Saul as King (1 Sam 15:11, 35). Yahweh also repented (*nacham*) over creating humankind because all of the world's population had become

---

17. Regarding some things, God does in fact change his mind, while regarding other things, he does not. Of the numerous passages that utilize נחם (*nacham*) to indicate God's change of mind, there are other passages that use נחם specifically to say he does not. Regarding the former, see Exod 32:12, 14; Deut 32:36; Judg 2:18; 2 Sam 24:16; 1 Chr 21:15; Pss 90:13; 106:45; 135:14; Isa 57:6; Jer 15:6; 18:8, 10; 26:3, 13, 19; Joel 2:13–14; Amos 7:3, 6; Jonah 3:9, 10; 4:2. Regarding the latter, see Num 23:19; 1 Sam 15:29; Ps 110:4; Jer 4:28; Ezek 24:14; Zech 8:14.

wicked (Gen 6:6–7). In those situations, God's hopes were shattered, and he found himself at a distance, which resulted in his utter disappointment and a sorrowful regret. God himself was said to repent over his previous choices, choices he expected to result in better things. Because God changes his mind, we can be hopeful that he is concerned over our repentance and actually cares about what we bring to his attention through prayer.

Faith and Prayer

One important question that often arises within evangelical circles is the place of faith in prayer. When I see my prayers go unanswered, is it because I don't have enough faith? Many believers limit the effectiveness of prayer to an exclusive kind of faith, but what a serious allegation it is to accuse fellow believers of remaining unhealed or undelivered because they simply don't have a strong enough faith! Because the real reason prayers aren't always answered is far more complicated than that single variable, we will look at some of the other reasons prayers seemingly go unanswered and the kind of faith that brings answers.

Prayer is not just a matter of faith. Gregory Boyd offers several variables that impact prayer's effectiveness. He first comments that "while prayer itself is as simple as talking to a friend, the actual mechanics of prayer are remarkably complex."[18] According to Boyd, the variables that impact answers to prayer include: God's will (Matt 26:39; 1 John 5:14; Jas 4:3), the faith of the person being prayed for (Matt 9:29; Luke 7:50; 17:19), the faith of the people praying (Matt 8:13; Mark 9:14–19; Luke 5:20), persistence in prayer (Luke 18:1–8; 1 Thess 5:17), the number of people praying (Matt 18:19–20),[19] human freewill (1 Tim 4:10; 2 Pet 3:9), angelic freewill (Dan 10:12–13; 1 Thess 2:17–18),[20] the number and strength of spirit agents (Dan 10:12–20; 2 Kgs 6:16–17; Luke 11:24–26), and finally, the presence of

---

18. Boyd, *Is God to Blame?*, 135.

19. Regarding the variable of the number of people praying, Boyd makes the point, "When dealing with an important matter, most people of faith instinctively ask others to pray for them. The assumption is that with more people praying, it's more likely that this matter will be resolved in accordance with the prayer. This assumption is reasonable" (ibid., 139). Regarding the number of people praying, see also Neh 9:1; 2 Chr 7:14; Matt 26:36, 41; Acts 1:13–14; 4:24–30; Eph 6:19–20; Col 4:3–4; 1 Thess 5:25; 2 Thess 3:1; Heb 13:18; Jas 5:13–16.

20. Regarding the variable of angelic freewill, see Wink, *Engaging the Powers*, 310–11.

sin (Josh 7:10–11; Ps 66:18; Mark 11:25).[21] As you can see, the issue is far more complicated than simply needing enough faith!

When we pray, we mustn't always be mindful of each one of those factors, but we also shouldn't lose sight of them as they do seem to work in tandem with each other. In every matter of prayer, we should first consider the will of God as revealed in Scripture (1 John 5:14). But even if we discern God's will and it leans in one direction or another, he characteristically won't violate the freewill of human beings or of angels to enact his will. The interplay of soldiers in the spiritual battle involves an entire world of free humans (seven billion and climbing), an innumerable company of free angels, and a remnant of praying saints. If we believe that battles in the physical realm are won or lost based on the size of an army, perhaps this is also the case in the spiritual realm! Jesus said it like this: "Again, truly I tell you that if two of you on earth agree about anything they ask for, it will be done for them by my Father in heaven. For where two or three gather in my name, there am I with them" (Matt 18:19–20). Because this is so, we should muster the Christian troops, as many as we can gather, and make it our practice to join the church on the battlefield as we thoughtfully seek to discern God's will and pray.

Besides God's will and the number of people praying, persistence is also one of the most important factors in the effectiveness of prayer. Jesus told many different stories to encourage us in this:

> Then Jesus said to them, "Suppose you have a friend, and you go to him at midnight and say, 'Friend, lend me three loaves of bread; a friend of mine on a journey has come to me, and I have no food to offer him.' And suppose the one inside answers, 'Don't bother me. The door is already locked, and my children and I are in bed. I can't get up and give you anything.' I tell you, even though he will not get up and give you the bread because of friendship, yet because of your shameless audacity he will surely get up and give you as much as you need." (Luke 11:5–8; cf. 18:1–8)

Jesus describes a certain "audacity" that God accepts and expects in prayer. He commends this attitude and wants us to approach God with the nerve to expect his response. The kind of audacity that we bring to the table is "shameless" because it's very bold and forthcoming with its demands. Because Jesus is teaching us to pray in this way, we can be certain that God

---

21. See Boyd, *Is God to Blame?*, 135–47.

Prayer: God Shares His Plans

is not annoyed with our persistence but welcomes it, ready to "get up and give you as much as you need."

But the question remains: How much faith do I need when I pray? Doesn't the simple act of opening my mouth imply a certain level of faith, possibly even enough to qualify as the "mustard seed" of faith that Jesus refers to? Jesus says, "Truly I tell you, if you have faith as small as a mustard seed, you can say to this mountain, 'Move from here to there,' and it will move. Nothing will be impossible for you" (Matt 17:20). When Jesus said this, the mustard seed was the smallest known seed in the Mediterranean world. Consider then that faith as small as a mustard seed is enough to move mountains—a humanly impossible obstacle! I would argue that someone's faith mustn't be any greater than the mere *existence* of faith that's demonstrated in the simple act of prayer: When I pray, my faith *is* a mustard seed. Because it is the Holy Spirit who makes our prayers effective in the spiritual battles of life, we will see mountains move if we keep seeking, knocking, and asking, especially together with the saints (Luke 11:9). And we'll be the ones telling those mountains where to go![22]

But more than faith, what if the greatest release of answered prayer, and even miraculous works, is not great faith but heartfelt compassion? What if compassion itself is the means *and* the end? Before Jesus prayed or laid hands on the sick, he was often moved with compassion when he ministered to people.[23] Remarkably, Scripture never once says that Jesus was moved by his great faith or confidence, but it frequently says that he was moved with compassion: "When Jesus landed and saw a large crowd, he had compassion on them and healed their sick" (Matt 14:14).[24] Prayer that faithfully persists is prayer that joins thoughtful perseverance with *compassion*. If we can cite any key or formula from Scripture that influences prayer and puts into effect God's transforming presence, it's compassion. In all your getting, get compassion! The greatest release of miraculous works is not great faith but true compassion (with mustard seed faith).

---

22. In addition to faithful persistence in prayer, my primary responsibility also lies in the area of personal holiness. I must also be mindful of any sin in my life that has not been forsaken and left behind. Sin assaults the heart with a vivid reminder (shame) of the guilt that once kept us distant from God. The pain of our shame and guilt is now overcome when we turn away from our sins and fix our eyes on God alone.

23. On Jesus' compassion, see Matt 9:36; 15:32; 20:34; Mark 1:41; 6:34; 8:2; Luke 7:13; 10:33; 15:20.

24. Jesus was of course moved by the great faith of others; see Matt 8:10; 15:28; Luke 7:9.

Conclusion

Sharing in God's presence means that we share in words and conversation that have supernatural effect. Because we were made in God's image and now possess the prophetic Spirit, like never before in history our prayers are intended to be the channel for God's creative life. Our prayers really do create new future possibilities, including new possibilities for us, for the church, and even for God. Through prayer, God shares his plans *and* his planning with us!

God is truly open to our prayers. He remains open to fresh dialogue and often will not move forward with his plans apart from it. God responds to prayer and allows himself to be affected by it, and therefore changed, because of our thoughtful conversation with him. Because of prayer, we are involved with God in an all-important partnership to build his kingdom. I would go so far as to say that God requires prayer for the success of his kingdom's establishment and has ordained prayer, perhaps more so than anything else, to *free* himself to influence freethinking creatures.

Finally, we serve a praying God. His prayers don't look anything like our cajoling or manipulation; his prayers look more like self-reflection, influence, and hope. We focused on hope and the idea that God has always been optimistic for people to choose life in relationship with him, even though humanity has often let him down. God prays but so do we, and our prayers are not just a matter of faith. Instead, they're affected by an assortment of variables, such as the number of people praying, the number of free angels at work, the presence of sin, persistence in prayer, and so on. Although many different variables are at work affecting the impact of our prayers, Jesus assures us that with compassion and a "mustard seed" kind of faith, we can move mountains!

6

Gifts: God Shares His Work (Part One)

SHARING IN GOD'S PRESENCE means that God shares with us the important work of ministry. Even though our focus will be on charismatic gifts, this chapter could easily be titled "Worship" because true worship can only occur when believers are *ministering* to one another in the presence of God. In Paul's first letter to the Corinthians, the chapters addressing the ministry of spiritual gifts also describe the gathering of believers for worship (1 Corinthians 10–14). Paul's letters and the other New Testament books never quite describe what we might call a "worship service," but they do describe a gathering where every gifted believer ministers. In other words, worship *is* ministry. Because worship is service to God and ministry to people, God is worshipped as the church compassionately ministers to the needs around her and allows the divine presence to release through us the liberating power of the cross.

One of the highest blessings in an open and abounding relationship with God is enjoying the privilege of sharing in the vitalizing dynamic of God's presence through the *charismata* (spiritual gifts). Yet for this ministry to become most effective, love needs to be our primary motivation. Because the highest virtues of the Christian life are faith, hope, and love, those virtues should be expressed through the full range of *charismata* (cf. Gal 5:6). This might help us to understand why Paul reassures the church that every spiritual gift is at our disposal: "Now you have every spiritual gift you need as you eagerly wait for the return of our Lord Jesus Christ" (1 Cor 1:7 NLT).

Although there are many different aspects to worship, such as singing, giving thanks and adoration to God, and bowing before him, our focus will remain on the mutual ministry that's intended to occur when believers come together to share God's work.

Introducing the Charismata

At the heart of our worship is the charismatic element of God's presence, the *charismata*. *Charismata* is the plural form of the Greek noun *charisma*, which means gift.[1] Every gifted ministry in the church is charismatic service, i.e., the gracious gift of God.[2] Paul tells us that "there are different kinds of gifts (*charismata*), but the same Spirit distributes them" (1 Cor 12:4). Under the unction of the Spirit, God graciously gifts his church for service, the key word being *gift*. In every instance that the Greek *charismata* or the singular *charisma* is used, gift(s) is an appropriate translation.[3] These gifts are intended to be understood as flowing out from God's gracious presence.

In the New Testament, no single ministry is ever clearly defined. This is evident from the various lists of spiritual gifts, none of which ever really describe their actual function.[4] Most ministries are mentioned only in passing, and even when the function of a gift is described, it's quite brief and never fully explained. The fact that every listing of *charismata* is different implies those lists are not exhaustive but remain open and flexible, which means that God is not restricted in the number or types of gifts that he can bestow at any given moment. God's Spirit, who graciously and often spontaneously gifts the church, is open to meeting any ministry need and

---

1. *Charismata* is the transliteration of the Greek noun χαρίσματα, the plural form of χάρισμα.

2. Throughout the next two chapters, I will be using the language of *gifts* and *ministries* interchangeably. Kenneth Berding argues that the "gifts" of the church are not primarily special abilities but rather functions of *ministry*. Thus, believers should not be overly preoccupied with discovering spiritual abilities but should rather step into edifying service. Berding finds the language of "ministry" most appropriate to the scriptural portrayal of gifts rather than the language of gifts or offices. He also helps us to see just how open the ministries are, encouraging believers to simply live out the new birth incarnationally through ministry service. Berding doesn't deny special abilities, especially when stepping out in the miraculous, but feels they are not the starting point for *charismata*. See *What Are Spiritual Gifts?*

3. See Baumert, "'Charism' and 'Spirit-Baptism,'" 149.

4. The primary Pauline lists of gifts are found in Rom 12:6–8; 1 Cor 12:8–10; 28; Eph 4:11. Gifts are also mentioned in 1 Pet 4:11.

Gifts: God Shares His Work (Part One)

filling any void with whatever manifestation he decides is appropriate. In the Spirit's infinite resourcefulness and wisdom, he provides for the needs of the church in the moment. At times, he even creatively distributes gifts or ministries we've never seen before.[5]

When first-century believers gathered together for worship, it was natural for them to fellowship like a spiritual family, whether in the temple, individual homes, the synagogue, or other public places of prayer. The New Testament is quite limited, however, on descriptions of early church worship, other than a summary of the church's daily worship in Acts 2 and another brief glimpse in Paul's letter to the Corinthians.[6] In the Corinthian church, Christians were misusing their gifts, speaking out of turn, and even segregating the congregation during the Lord's Supper. As Paul addresses those matters, we don't find a formal church service but an organic ministry of one believer to another.

Within the course of correcting the issues at Corinth, Paul provides extensive instruction on the proper use of spiritual gifts and also describes a rather dynamic interaction of believers who are each responsible to use their gifts to build up God's people: "What then shall we say, brothers and sisters? When you come together, each of you has a hymn, or a word of instruction, a revelation, a tongue or an interpretation. Everything must be done so that the church may be built up" (1 Cor 14:26). Paul leaves readers with the impression that it would be foreign to this congregation to merely sit by as spectators, while one or two others lead in teaching and worship, as is often the case today. Rather, every member is gifted and therefore expected to be involved in the mutual exercise of his gifts.

Because the gifts are, by their very nature, open, flexible, and dynamic, it's not necessary for us to review every so-called ministry gift in the New Testament. However, we will briefly review the majority of them, what I am designating the unilateral and bilateral gifts. We'll spend this chapter

---

5. Paul Fiddes suggests that "it is not the *charismata* themselves that display the work of the Holy Spirit, but the dimension *within* them that is always opening situations up to new possibilities" (*Participating in God*, 271, emphasis original).

6. Acts 2 gives us a glimpse into the worship of the early church: "They devoted themselves to the apostles' teaching and to fellowship, to the breaking of bread and to prayer. Everyone was filled with awe at the many wonders and signs performed by the apostles. All the believers were together and had everything in common. They sold property and possessions to give to anyone who had need. Every day they continued to meet together in the temple courts. They broke bread in their homes and ate together with glad and sincere hearts, praising God and enjoying the favor of all the people. And the Lord added to their number daily those who were being saved" (vv. 42–47).

and most of the next looking at the charismatic gifts in relation to God's *unilateral* presence. This terminology places most of the responsibility on God. These are the more extraordinary or "supernatural" gifts that noticeably, even unilaterally, depend upon the divine presence. Those gifts cannot be manufactured or reduced to natural talent, and they refer to prophecy, tongues, healings, miracles, the discerning of spirits, and casting out demons (1 Cor 12:9–10).

Through the unilateral gifts, the believer becomes a channel for *theophany*, a theological term that describes God as visibly manifesting himself. Stepping into these gifts, believers actually manifest God's sovereign presence. For instance, Paul says, "If an unbeliever or an inquirer comes in while everyone is prophesying, . . . they will fall down and worship God, exclaiming, 'God is really among you!'" (1 Cor 14:24–25). For Paul, one dimension of the *charismata* is to reveal more poignantly that God's presence truly is among us, functioning as a channel for manifesting himself.

In contrast, the *bilateral* gifts include serving, teaching, encouraging, giving, administration, and showing mercy, which are comparable to a more practical *incarnation* (Rom 12:6–8). I'm using the term incarnation to refer to God embodying or enfleshing himself by the Spirit to work through people. These gifts don't overtly manifest the divine presence, but they do authorize believers as incarnational representatives of God and are noticeably less dramatic.[7]

Just as Paul gives prophecy and tongues the majority of space in his instruction on the *charismata*, we will begin with those two unilateral gifts and then move on to the others in chapter seven.

God Shares Prophecy

For those who walk in step with the Spirit, there exists a stream of supernatural intuition made possible by the God who speaks to his church with a bold vulnerability. The Apostle Paul calls this gift prophecy (1 Cor 12:10).[8]

---

7. Fiddes comments that "the *charismata* should be seen as the taking up of natural faculties into the perichoretic life of God, into interweaving movements of love and justice" (*Participating in God*, 271, emphasis original). All gifts from God, whether perceived as natural or supernatural, are useful and important in the accomplishment of our kingdom mission because God is sharing his perichoretic life-presence through us.

8. For an introduction to the prophetic in the early church, see Aune, *Prophecy in Early Christianity*; Burgess, *Holy Spirit: Ancient Christian Traditions*; Hill, *New Testament*

Gifts: God Shares His Work (Part One)

Even though we accept a completed written canon consisting of 66 inspired books, it's intuitive to a living relationship with God that his word is not altogether closed.[9] Blessed with the indwelling presence of the Living Word, Jesus Christ, the church enjoys an immediate, and even spontaneous, voice from heaven to meet us in current situations. In our relationship with Jesus, we intuitively get the sense that divine guidance is meant to be fresh and frequent. In the gift of prophecy and other gifts like it, God has dynamically gifted his people with a specific and direct guidance, sharing even his very thoughts with us.[10]

Prophecy: The Gift of an Open Future

Prophecy was among the most prominent gifts in the Corinthian church (1 Cor 14:1–5) and should be highly regarded, especially if the future is, in fact, open and full of possibilities, as we discussed in chapter one. Without a divine blueprint outlining the future, along with every detail of the church's victories and failures, we may be even more dependent upon God's immediate guidance. Divine guidance always requires a certain sensitivity to God's inner voice—that "still small voice"—as he seeks to use his people to apply divine ingenuity to otherwise impossible situations (1 Kgs 19:12 KJV). Such an ongoing dependence certainly doesn't downplay the relevance of the written word but adds an aspect of dynamic application that would otherwise be lacking.

We could, therefore, classify the gift of prophecy as the gift of an open future. Because God shares his knowledge through this gift, prophecy is dependent upon God's dynamic knowledge of the past, present, and future as it's applied to the church's current situation. The practice of prophecy in the New Testament church involves a spontaneous *revelation* from God to the individual, which is then *spoken* to the congregation (1 Cor 14:30–31),[11]

Prophecy; and Kydd, *Charismatic Gifts in the Early Church*.

9. The Protestant Canon consists of 39 Old Testament and 27 New Testament books. The Catholic Bible consists of 73 books, which include seven deuterocanonical books.

10. Rather than addressing the "word of knowledge" and "word of wisdom" (1 Cor 12:8 KJV), these are being considered variations of prophecy, but they could also be considered variations of teaching. Readers can review thorough descriptions of these two gifts in Williams, *Renewal Theology*, 2:349–58; and Grudem, *Systematic Theology*, 1080–82.

11. Based on word order, the following passage may also hint at revelation being the content of prophecy: "How will I benefit you unless I bring you some *revelation* or

making prophecy the dynamic process of receiving revelation and sharing it with the community. Prophecy can be either forth-telling or foretelling. Forth-telling focuses on the past and present, while foretelling includes predictions and warnings related to the future. Specific to foretelling, prophecy is God's word for the church as it relates to what is possible, what is probable, or what is certain to take place.

Beyond God's mere knowledge, predictive prophecy often depends on God's *intentions* to bring something about. If God purposes to bring about an expected future, it moves from the possible to the probable or certain. Take, for example, Isaiah 46. The LORD says, "I make known the end from the beginning, from ancient times, what is still to come. I say, '*My purpose will stand, and I will do all that I please.*' From the east I summon a bird of prey; from a far-off land, a man to fulfill my purpose. *What I have said, that I will bring about; what I have planned, that I will do*" (vv. 10–11, emphasis added). Just a few verses earlier, the LORD distinguishes himself from the weakness and ignorance of human-made idols (vv. 5–7), so in contrast to the inability of those lifeless statues, Yahweh declares that "everything I plan will come to pass" (v. 10 NLT).

The LORD's powerful declaration, however, is nowhere said to be based on exhaustive foreknowledge of future events. In Isaiah 46:11, Yahweh announces that his foresight is based specifically on what he has "planned" and what he will "bring about." The LORD brings about what he has planned by persuading and influencing circumstances and people ("a man to fulfill my purpose") through the wisdom of his power, all the while working with free creatures. In this context, Yahweh also says, "I have made you and I will carry you; I will sustain you and I will rescue you" (Isa 46:4). When people understand that they have a Creator who has been sustaining them and helping them along the path of life, they can increasingly open their hearts to work with him for the consummation of his plans.

Besides God's intentions to bring something about, the fulfillment of prophetic promises also frequently depends upon the believer's faithfulness. For a practical example, consider a situation in which the Spirit shares a revelation with an individual in your congregation, impressing heavily upon that person that God will add 100 people to the church within the next year. Assuming this person has rightly heard the Lord's voice, it may

knowledge or *prophecy* or teaching?" (1 Cor 14:6 ESV, emphasis added). The revelation mentioned here could be the content of prophecy just as knowledge is the content of teaching.

not be enough that God has good intentions toward that congregation and desires to bring it about. This prophecy could potentially fail if the church doesn't follow through with its responsibilities in evangelism, prayer, and outreach toward the real needs around it. Because God's influence is gracious and his persuasion is considerate of freewill, he honors that freedom by stepping back enough to allow for our obedience.

Because the future is somewhat open, prophecy is never cut and dried; it's not a black and white prediction of the future. Its fulfillment could depend on God's knowledge of future possibilities, his promise or intention to bring about a future course, or it could largely depend upon our response and faithfulness. Now that we understand a little better what prophecy is, we'll look at Paul's instructions to the Corinthians on the use of prophecy in local gatherings.

Prophecy: A Potential for Error

The disorder in Corinth required special instruction regarding the order of the prophetic. Even though abuses like this don't occur in every congregation, Paul's instructions hold equal authority for churches today. Paul instructed the Corinthian believers that "two or three prophets should speak, and the others should weigh carefully what is said" (1 Cor 14:29). No two prophets are to speak at the same time, and each one needs to be considerate of the others. The "others" who carefully evaluate what is said are likely the rest of the congregation. Because these prophecies are thoughtfully evaluated, it's evident that the revelation comes through a dynamic impression, rather than a definite dictation. People don't hear an audible voice, but instead, they realize that receiving and interpreting a revelation can be somewhat subjective.

Because the evaluation and critique of prophecy is commendable in new covenant churches, and even required, a strong distinction exists between prophecies today and prophecies under Moses' law. Today, evaluation is not only permitted but required, which implies that we are prepared for there to be inaccuracies in the content of the utterance. But under Moses' law, the general understanding was that a false prophecy would result in the prophet being executed as an imposter (Deut 18:20; cf. Jer 14:15), which is clearly not the consequence today. Perhaps even more significant, Yahweh warned those false prophets that he would exclude them from his presence: "I will banish you and you will perish" (Jer 27:15). Today, we would publicly correct a false prophecy as a learning experience for the prophet and the congregation. We're never told why this contrast exists between the Old and New Testaments, but it does imply that even the accuracy of prophecy remains open today.[12]

Paul encourages the Romans to prophesy "in accordance with your faith," or better, *by the measure of your faith* (Rom 12:6). If "your faith" can exist in one measure or another, then the faith Paul's referring to is not the *content* of prophecy (i.e., the body of faith or the gospel), but rather, the *vehicle* through which it is spoken: the person's own ability. Prophecy is only as reliable as the subjective degree of one's faith. As Bible scholar Ben Witherington notes, "Paul has already suggested that some have more faith and some less, and he will go on to say that some have strong faith and some weak (chs. 14–15). The point here is that, if one prophesies beyond the measure of one's faith, the prophecy will be five-parts inspiration to perhaps three-parts perspiration or mere wishful thinking."[13] Because the potential for error exists when prophesying today, the church must carefully evaluate what's spoken, but how do we do that?

When evaluating prophecy, we may need to depend upon our biblically informed wisdom or discernment, although a more precise method may be suggested from the text. We're told earlier in the book of Corinthians that some have a gift of "distinguishing between spirits" (1 Cor 12:10), which would be particularly helpful in evaluating a prophetic message. In Paul's list of gifts, the *discerning of spirits* follows immediately after prophecy. This may be significant, because in the same list, the interpretation of tongues also follows immediately after tongues-speaking: "And to another prophecy, and to another the distinguishing of spirits, to another various kinds of tongues, and to another the interpretation of tongues" (1 Cor 12:10 NASB). Hence, the discerning of spirits could be an *interpretive* gift intended to accompany and validate prophecy.

---

12. The distinction may be due in part to different audiences under the old and new covenants. Prophetic speech is different when it is directed to a nation versus speaking to a congregation. When the prophets of old spoke to the nations, God was speaking to entire people groups, often declaring either warning or blessing on a national level. Hence, the prophet's responsibility to speak for God had national ramifications. Some passages suggest that prophets were trained in schools of prophets, as in the case of Samuel and Elisha (1 Sam 10:5; 2 Kgs 2:3, 15), but for the most part, we no longer have the benefit of such schools. And rather than speaking to nations, we speak to one another.

13. Witherington and Hyatt, *Paul's Letter to the Romans*, 289. Cf. Chrysostom, *Hom. Rom. 21*: "[Prophecy] does not flow forth freely at random but is given only in proportion to our faith."

Gifts: God Shares His Work (Part One)

Prophecy: The Future Interrupted

Regarding the order of prophecy in the church meeting, Paul tells the Corinthians, "If someone is prophesying and another person receives a revelation from the Lord, the one who is speaking must stop. In this way, all who prophesy will have a turn to speak, one after the other, so that everyone will learn and be encouraged" (1 Cor 14:30–31 NLT).[14] Paul's instruction here is somewhat peculiar. While those who prophesy are sitting by in the congregation, God may suddenly and spontaneously reveal a word to one of them, prompting him to stand up and begin to speak the revealed message. Then quite abruptly, that person would need to stop speaking if someone else receives a revelation. All of this begs the question: Why would God speak a word to one prophet only to interrupt him by giving a word to another? There are many possible reasons for this.

The first possibility is that the initial prophet would prophesy and then elaborate on the revelation he received, providing his own commentary or clarification on what God had impressed upon him.[15] While doing so, he would also apply the content of the prophecy to the current situation in the church. If interrupted, the prophet would conclude his personal commentary to allow another prophet to speak. In this way, the content of the inspired revelation would not be interrupted, only the prophet's elaboration and application of it. Such commentary would not be unheard of for either Old or New Testament prophets (e.g., Isa 20).

A second possibility is that the prophet would enter into discussion with the congregation, perhaps the "others" who were evaluating what was said. In this scenario, the prophet himself becomes involved in the evaluation process as he responds to questions or comments. The prophet would then conclude that conversation if another prophet received a revelation. Hence, it is not the inspired revelation that is interrupted but only the prophet's discussion with those evaluating.

A third possibility is that the prophet is indeed in the middle of declaring what the Spirit has revealed to him. Before arriving at the conclusion, the content of his revelation is interrupted by another prophet, such that

---

14. Another possible translation: "the person speaking should conclude" (NET). The present imperative of σιγάω means to become silent or stop speaking. Despite the wording of the NET translation, the idea is that the speaker is not able to conclude because he is interrupted.

15. Speaking of "he," there were also female prophets; see Acts 2:17–18; 21:9; 1 Cor 11:5. Cf. Luke 2:36.

the first prophet is unable to finish his edifying speech. It's possible that the revelation received by the second prophet is itself a continuation or clarifying revelation that piggybacks on the first prophecy. Because God is not one of disorder or confusion, it would be rather unusual for him to bring a dissimilar word that might detract from the first, hence both prophets' revelations would be in sync with each other.

Rather than speculating *ad nauseam*, a fourth possibility is that the future is, in fact, open and the dynamics of prophecy are such that God keeps his church attentive to the most needful revelation.[16] This option takes the passage most literally—an important revelation has been interrupted. In light of an open future, it is somewhat easier to posit the benefit of an interruption.[17] Notice that the text does not say that another prophet *will* inevitably receive an interrupting revelation, but instead, it says that they *may* ("if") receive an interrupting revelation. In other words, it is within the realm of possibility and could be a rare exception. So if God chooses to interrupt the first revelation, it's best to take heed and be attentive to the next one because of its urgency and high priority. Perhaps the first revelation has caused the church to respond in repentance, so God is changing his mind about her future.

In light of an open future, the very nature of revelation makes the prophetic gift of utmost importance. If a prophecy is uttered, God is confident about that future and our part in it that he reveals it to us. Because God's knowledgeable planning is often conditioned upon the freedom and obedience of his creatures, his knowledge of the future changes as human choices are made for right or wrong and for or against God's love. If the future is open and therefore changeable, God nonetheless knows all future possibilities and is able to effortlessly reveal the most needful truth for the moment. The prophetic word sheds light on the role God expects us to play in bringing it to pass, which should impress upon us the value of the gift.

Consider the value of prophecy in light of a future that's constantly changing due to the response and actions of freewill creatures, due to God's own constant influence upon circumstances and people, and even due to angelic beings entrenched in warfare. Because of all these dramatically

---

16. If the future is open, then it is not set in stone and known by God only in terms of certainties. Instead, there are aspects of the future that are certain but other aspects that are only possible. The future, therefore, is full of infinite possibilities.

17. As mentioned before, not all prophecies relate to the future. Prophecy can pertain to the past or present, though this is much rarer. Throughout Scripture, prophecy tends to be predictive, particularly in the New Testament (e.g., Acts 11:28; 21:10–11).

changing factors, we should take special note if God reveals something about the future. After all, the truth that God has revealed has held up through the rigors of a dynamically changing future! Even so, the future is not so volatile and so drastically changing that God cannot keep up with it or is forced to frantically work to keep the church aware. Instead, the dynamics of prophecy should remind us that God is dynamically and relationally *omniscient* and fully in tune with anything helpful to the church's mission at any given moment. Because God created the flexibility of the future, he uses the gift of prophecy to demonstrate that he is sovereign over the future and never caught off guard by it.[18]

Prophecy: God Speaks in the Present

We've already said that prophecy can be either foretelling of the future or forth-telling of a past or current truth, yet all prophecy always "speaks to people for their strengthening, encouraging and comfort" (1 Cor 14:3). This doesn't mean, however, that the message will always be a positive one. It may be a word of warning or potential doom if repentance or obedience isn't taken seriously. Although prophecy is generally for the benefit of God's people, it can, at times, be directed to the nonbeliever. One such example is worthy of our attention.

There are times when nonbelievers or inquirers come into the assembly and, because they don't know God, they lack the sense that the church worships in his very presence. Sadly, they have no understanding of what it means to share in the presence of God! But when the *charismata* are exercised from one person to another, God occasionally reveals the secret content of the inquirer's heart. In the following situation, prophecy is not predictive but forth-telling and directed to the nonbeliever. Paul says, "If an unbeliever or an inquirer comes in while everyone is prophesying, they are convicted of sin and are brought under judgment by all, as the secrets of

---

18. Because God purposely chooses to inspire interrupting revelation, this gives us a clue to the nature of God's own dynamic knowledge of an open and ever-changing future. Whether the future is open or not, God could certainly wait for the first prophet to conclude before revealing something to another, or he could have instructed the church to have the second prophet wait to speak until the first concludes, but this isn't the case. Instead, God chooses to act in such a way that subtly points to the flexibility of an open future, all the while maintaining control over it. God's own knowledge of what would or might occur is interrupted by a flexible future.

their hearts are laid bare. So they will fall down and worship God, exclaiming, 'God is really among you!'" (1 Cor 14:24–25).

Referring to the inquirer, a literal translation of verse 24 reads, "he is convicted by all, he is examined (*anakrino*) by all." The two phrases make the situation emphatic because they are nearly synonymous: The nonbeliever is being both convicted and examined by all. The emphasis points to the inspired *and inspiring* content of prophecy to bring about such results. The prophetic message inspires the inquirer to such a degree that he is overwhelmed by the word in a very personal way, and he is at once struck with the reality that the divine presence itself is behind this human utterance, having inspired what's been spoken. The term *anakrino* ("examined") is related to the same root word used to describe the careful evaluation of prophetic utterances: "Let two or three people prophesy, and let the others evaluate (*diakrino*) what is said" (1 Cor 14:29 NLT).

Because the inquirer is said to be "examined by all" who prophesy (v. 24), he is actually being examined by the *content* of the prophetic word. The inquirer has no background to evaluate the word of God but is instead evaluated by it. This revelatory gift discloses what only God himself could possibly know. The point is not that the person's sins are publicly exposed, but that they are "laid bare" to the individual, which could simply involve an internal conviction. At the same time, in a most personal encounter, the nonbeliever is struck by the truth that God knows him more personally than anyone else could: "So they will fall down and worship God, exclaiming, 'God is really among you!'" (v. 25). In a most profound way, the nonbeliever's inquiry has inadvertently led him to become aware of God's presence!

This passage demonstrates that God knows the thoughts of the nonbeliever. It also implies that he knows the likelihood that the person will repent in response to a prophetic word. After God confidently reveals the "secrets of their hearts" to his prophet, it then becomes the prophet's responsibility to step out in faithfulness to the revelation, not knowing what the response will be or whether they "will fall down and worship."[19]

---

19. We could call the prophet's role a warfare aspect of the gift of prophecy. Even after God's word convicts the nonbeliever's heart, Satan and the dark powers are relentlessly at work to maintain the blackout of unbelief (Matt 13:19; 2 Cor 4:4). While God graciously waits in anticipation for that person's final decision to repent and turn to him, the prophet remains the instrument of divine presence for making war against the distance: "This charge I entrust to you, Timothy, my child, in accordance with the prophecies previously made about you, that by them you may wage the good warfare" (1 Tim 1:18 ESV).

Gifts: God Shares His Work (Part One)

God Shares Languages

The other notoriously prominent gift in the Corinthian church is the gift of tongues or languages (1 Cor 12:10, 28), a supernatural gifting that allows believers to speak in languages they have never learned. Even though the book of Acts portrays tongues as a subset of prophecy (Acts 2:4, 18), Paul distinguishes between the two: "For anyone who speaks in a tongue does not speak to people but to God.... But the one who prophesies speaks to people" (1 Cor 14:2-3). God has gifted the church with a plurality of "different kinds of tongues" (1 Cor 12:10, 28), and because this gift is the dynamic expression of God's voice through people, God uses this gift to share his voice in a strangely unique way.

The gift of tongues remains among the most controversial topics for Pentecostals because they have long held it to be the qualifying evidence of Spirit-baptized empowerment. But if tongues are so central to our spiritual lives, why does Paul imply that believers can practice tongues without practicing any love at all (1 Cor 13:1)? Rather than the determinative evidence, it seems that speaking in tongues is only one of many possible signs that someone is filled with the power of God's presence (Acts 19:6; 1 Cor 12:30). Without question, the more reliable indicators are the fruit of the Spirit (Gal 5:22-23) and the bold declaration of the gospel (Acts 14:31). Paul reflects on the superior quality and duration of the fruit of the Spirit, particularly love, as evidencing the true Christian life for this age *and* the age to come: "Prophecy and speaking in unknown languages and special knowledge will become useless. But love will last forever" (1 Cor 13:8 NLT). Indeed, tongues are temporary but love is forever.

Languages: Many Different Expressions

Because God has given the church a plurality of "different kinds of tongues," the openness of tongues comes across in its many dynamic expressions. Throughout history, God's voice has creatively spoken *in one way or another* (Job 33:14), so it shouldn't surprise us that the speaking gift that he empowers in the church also includes multiple faces. Although Paul could have been speaking hypothetically, he offers the possibility that tongues involve more than human languages: "If I speak in the tongues of men or of angels, ..." (1 Cor 13:1). Regardless, the true benefit of this gift is that men and women can only speak in the tongues of men (or of angels) as "the Spirit enable[s] them" in a most supernatural display of God's presence (Acts 2:4). The gift of languages is truly a supernatural expression of the divine voice through people.

In the context of the assembly, the gift is directed to God in the hearing of others (1 Cor 14:2). But out in the community, this same voice of praise crosses language barriers and can function evangelistically (Acts 2:4, 7–11). The context and surroundings will determine how the gift is used. If tongues are spoken in public outside of the local congregation, as in Acts when an international audience was present, there's no need for an interpretation: "When they heard this sound, a crowd came together in bewilderment, because each one heard their own language being spoken" (Acts 2:6). No one needed an interpreter! When the gift is used in private there is also no need for interpretation because the believer who prays in tongues will "speak to himself and to God" (1 Cor 14:28; cf. 14:18–19).

When the gift is directed toward others in the context of the assembly, however, it must be interpreted so that the entire congregation can be edified: "If anyone speaks in a tongue, two—or at the most three—should speak, one at a time, and someone must interpret" (1 Cor 14:27). Besides, if nonbelievers or those uninformed on the Christian way are present and they hear believers speaking in uninterpreted tongues, they will conclude that you are "out of your mind" (v. 23), and there's just no benefit to that! If the believer speaks in tongues but cannot interpret, Paul advises that "the one who speaks in a tongue should pray that they may interpret what they say" (v. 13). It's remarkable, here, that believers are encouraged to ask God for gifts that are lacking, which also makes it clear that not all gifts are imparted at the moment of salvation. If tongues are any indication, the *charismata* are open to believers to "eagerly desire" and even request from God (1 Cor 14:1).

Even though one could argue that tongues are a gift intended for believers, it can also have an impact on the nonbeliever, and not in a positive way. Scripture enunciates a negative purpose for tongues in the assembly when nonbelievers are present: "Tongues, then, are a sign, not for believers but for unbelievers" (1 Cor 14:22). The point is that when tongues are spoken without an interpretation, they become a *sign* to nonbelievers, that is, a sign of judgment. To illustrate how this would function as a negative sign, Paul draws from Israel's experience and quotes Isaiah 28:11, saying, "In the Law it is written, 'By people of strange tongues and by the lips of foreigners will I speak to this people, and even then they will not listen to me, says the Lord'" (1 Cor 14:21 ESV). Paul's logic is that nonbelievers would find themselves in like company with Old Testament Israel when they were invaded by foreign peoples with an unfamiliar and unintelligible language. Uninterpreted tongues leave a very wrong impression! Tongues must therefore be interpreted; otherwise, there's room for serious misunderstanding.

Paul's overall concern is that the congregation will not benefit from what they cannot understand and neither will the nonbeliever. But if tongues are interpreted, everyone can benefit. Paul concludes,

> I will *pray* [in tongues] with my spirit, but I will also pray with my understanding [by interpreting the prayer]; I will *sing* [in tongues] with my spirit, but I will also sing with my understanding [by interpreting the song]. Otherwise when you are *praising* God in the Spirit, how can someone else, who is now put in the position of an inquirer, say "Amen" to your *thanksgiving*, since they do not know what you are saying? You are giving thanks well enough, but no one else is edified. (1 Cor 14:15–17, emphasis added)

Paul's logic is straightforward: He wants the congregation to benefit from tongues by understanding what is voiced, so the tongue must be followed by an interpretation. Notice from these verses all the various examples for expressing tongues: *praying, singing, praising, and thanksgiving.* Tongues are open to many different expressions.[20]

Could there be a more dynamic voice than to speak in a Spirit-charged language? The Spirit even commands the church throughout this age to be open and accepting of such a divine voice: "Therefore, my brothers and sisters, . . . do not forbid speaking in tongues" (1 Cor 14:39). But this requires us to consider another question: Are tongues a gift for every Christian?

Languages: Are They Open to Everyone?

Although it would be accurate to say that tongues are open to anyone, we need to qualify this and consider whether every Spirit-filled believer actually

---

20. It's possible that there are even more expressions of tongues than what we've touched on. Paul said, "Now, brothers, if I come to you speaking in tongues, how will I benefit you unless I bring you some revelation or knowledge or prophecy or teaching?" (1 Cor 14:6 ESV). Paul could have meant one of two things: (1) Along with tongues, the person must *also* bring a revelation, knowledge, prophecy, or teaching in order to benefit the church. (2) The tongue itself can express one of those four things (revelation, knowledge, prophecy, or teaching), so the congregation would benefit once the tongue is interpreted.

has the ability to do so. The openness of tongues is important because Paul wishes that "all" the Corinthian believers could speak in tongues—"Now I wish that you all spoke in tongues" (1 Cor 14:5 NASB)—yet we know that not everyone does![21] Paul didn't say that he was expecting everyone to speak in tongues; rather, he wanted to emphasize that tongues are not limited to an elite few. David Garland comments, "This wish that 'all' speak basically democratizes the gift. It need not belong to an 'elitist monopoly.'"[22] There's never a monopoly on gifts by a few "super spiritual" believers, but every gift remains open for any believer to pursue and apply in love.

Although tongues are technically open to anyone, not all will speak in tongues, as we will see. Theological inquiry is often an echo in the halls of ambiguity because we find that the biblical writers aren't typically asking the same questions we are. Because that's the case, they usually don't provide any straightforward answers. Fortunately, due to problems caused by the *charismata* in Corinth, Paul anticipated at least the question of whether all believers would have the ability to function in all the various gifts, including tongues. Using a common rhetorical device, he advises his readers, asking, "Are all apostles? Are all prophets? Are all teachers? Do all work miracles? Do all have gifts of healing? Do all speak in tongues? Do all interpret?" (1 Cor 12:29–30). The construction in the Greek text implies a negative answer—no way! The obvious rhetorical value is included in the New Living Translation at the end of verse 30, which succinctly exclaims, "Of course not!" Paul doesn't want to leave us with any confusion on the matter: Do all speak in tongues? *No way!* Can all speak in tongues? *Of course not.* According to Paul, all gifts are open and available to the church, but no single believer can possess every available gift, including tongues.

A common teaching in pentecostal circles has been that there are not just various expressions of tongues but actually two different gifts of tongues. One category of tongues is a "prayer language" intended for *every* believer who's been baptized in the Holy Spirit, which is something every empowered believer will possess. Pentecostals would add that an altogether different gift is an evangelistic use of tongues, such as what we find in Acts 2, and is only available to some. To arrive at this conclusion, they seemingly pick and choose from the description of tongues found in 1 Corinthians 14 (prayer emphasis) and the book of Acts (evangelistic emphasis), mixing

---

21. This wish is no less serious than other passages in which Paul expresses a desire or wish using the Greek term *thelo* (θέλω); see 1 Cor 7:7, 32; 10:1, 20; 11:3; 12:1; 14:19; 16:7.
22. Garland, *1 Corinthians*, 634.

and matching seemingly random portions of those passages to support their claim. Oddly enough, the context in which tongues are described as a prayer language (1 Cor 14:2, 14–15, 28), which Pentecostals allege every Spirit-baptized person will possess, is the very same context in which Paul emphatically denounces the possibility that all can speak in tongues (1 Cor 12:30). What's more, when Paul addresses tongues in his letter to the Corinthians, he speaks generically, referring only to "tongues," without any further qualification.[23] Because Paul is talking about "tongues" in general, his instructions apply to all expressions of tongues in the church. So can all speak in tongues as a prayer language or an evangelistic gift? Of course not.

Paul never distinguishes one type of tongues from another, but he does instruct the Corinthians on a well-known expression of the Spirit as it was used in the context of the local assembly, rather than out in public as we see in the book of Acts. Although we cannot affirm two separate tongues-gifts in the church, we should understand that the gift is open to various expressions in a variety of contexts (1 Cor 14:15–17).

Conclusion

We spent this chapter looking at the charismatic element of God's presence, the *charismata*, which refer to God's gracious gifts. First, we described the Spirit's ministries in terms of God's unilateral versus bilateral presence. The *bilateral* gifts are not associated with God's overt manifest presence, but they do authorize believers as incarnational representatives. The *unilateral* ministries depend uniquely on God's presence and cannot be manufactured or reduced to natural talent. Through these gifts, the believer becomes a channel for *theophany*, the unique manifestation of the divine presence.

So far, we've looked at the gifts of prophecy and tongues. In each case, we emphasized the dynamic process of divine and human interaction. Prophecy is the dynamic process of receiving revelation and sharing it with people, which is one unique way in which God shares his knowledge. We classified prophecy as a gift of an open future because it is dependent upon

---

23. 1 Cor 12:28, 30; 13:8; 14:2, 4, 5, 6, 13, 14, 18, 19, 22, 23, 27, 39. Paul distinguishes between interpreted and uninterpreted tongues, but never once does he suggest that there are two distinct gifts of tongues. Throughout 1 Corinthians 14, the KJV translates uninterpreted tongues as "unknown tongues," though the term *unknown* is not found in the Greek text. Paul also mentions "the languages of earth and of angels" (13:1 NLT), which are two different expressions of the one gift of tongues, rather than two separate gifts.

God's dynamic knowledge of the future (as well as the past and present) as it is applied to the church's current situation.

The *charisma* of languages is the dynamic voice of a Spirit-charged tongue, a supernatural gifting whereby the Spirit enables believers to speak in languages they've never learned, thus God shares his voice in a uniquely strange way. The openness of tongues comes across quite poignantly in its various expressions: prayer, song, praise, thanksgiving, and perhaps even the tongues of angels. Speaking in tongues is one of many possible evidences of Spirit-empowerment, the most reliable being the fruit of the Spirit and particularly love. Believers are encouraged to pray and ask God for a gift to interpret tongues if they don't already have it, which implies that the other gifts are also open to being received through prayer.

In the next chapter, we'll look at other examples of the unilateral gifts of God's presence as well as a summary of the bilateral gifts.

7

Gifts: God Shares His Work (Part Two)

IN THE LAST CHAPTER, we introduced the *charismata* as gracious gifts that God shares with his church. Every gifted ministry is nothing less than *charismatic* in the sense that it is carried out under the unction of the Spirit as the triune God graciously shares his work with us: "There are different kinds of gifts, but the same Spirit distributes them. There are different kinds of service, but the same Lord. There are different kinds of working, but in all of them and in everyone it is the same God at work" (1 Cor 12:4–6). Through a Trinitarian formula, the Spirit, Lord, and God are shown to be dynamically involved in our ministries in terms of different kinds of gifts, service, and working, all because God is at work in us. Paul then explains, "Now to each one the manifestation of the Spirit is given for the common good" (1 Cor 12:7). Charismatic gifts are not only carried out under the unction of the Spirit but are also quite literally the manifestation of the divine presence expressed for the "common good." Because they are intended for our good, spiritual gifts are empowered to bring about the highest and best of everyone touched by them!

In chapter six, we introduced spiritual ministries in terms of God's unilateral and bilateral presence and looked at the gifts of prophecy and tongues. Here, we will first discuss God's dynamic presence and then turn our attention to the *unilateral* gifts of miracles, casting out demons, healing, the discerning of spirits, and faith. We'll close out the chapter by summarizing the *bilateral* gifts that resemble our natural talents.

God's Dynamic Presence

First Corinthians 14:26 assumes that no individual can have every gift, which means that every believer is dependent upon the gifts of others and should be prepared to freely share his or her gifts. By exploiting God's grace, believers are granted an incredible degree of freedom, ingenuity, and imagination in their pursuit to fulfill kingdom ministry. And because God could never be threatened by the diversity of personalities that he has so graciously gifted, he excels in his role of mixing and matching our gifts to the needs around us, so that we can be a healthy church that experiences unity and growth.

As the Spirit of God works within the congregation, he remains dependent upon the willingness and faithfulness of believers to operate in the gifts that he so graciously shares. But God has also given us true freedom, so the *potential* for operating in any gift is not the same as freely choosing to use it. Ultimately, believers have the choice to neglect their gifts to the detriment of both church and world. Indeed, the *charismata* benefit the church, but they also extend sacrificial service to the world and to the community around us. We show the world what God's kingdom can be!

When we step out by faith and begin to walk in the Spirit's power, not only are lives changed, but there is an historic intrusion of end-times proportion—we bring aspects of the future into the present! Even though the consummation of God's kingdom remains open and "not yet," the *charismata* bring an end-of-the-age experience into the church's present practice. Stephen Barton understands this when he says that "the charismata make possible what would not be possible otherwise in the time prior to the coming of the kingdom of God: anticipatory, partial sharing in the life of heaven."[1] So not only does the church share God's work through the *charismata*, but we also share in the life of heaven! And when Jesus finally returns to the earth, all of these temporary, partial gifts will be done away with because the fullness of what they were anticipating will finally belong to God's people: We will see God and understand his love (1 Cor 13:8–12). For the time being, however, it's as if the future kingdom overflows and spills backward into the present age, sharing waves of God's glorious power with both church and world as believers practice our charismatic ministry.

Although God uses the *charismata* to share his work with us, he gifts us for other important reasons as well. The *charismata* are intended

---

1. Barton, "1 Corinthians," 1343.

Gifts: God Shares His Work (Part Two)

to personally instruct us on the divine life and on the very heart of God. As believers work in unison with one another, the diversely gifted body of Christ actually resembles the dynamic, inner life of God. In other words, this is what God looks like on the inside! God the Trinity works in unison, so we work in unison. The *charismata* are therefore revelatory of God's inner being, but they are also incarnational and manifest the divine life itself. We can describe every spiritual gift as incarnational, because through them God is at work in human vessels so that others can easily encounter him. In this way, the gifts actually reveal the inner social and sacrificial life of God as they manifest characteristics of God's own personality and presence through incarnational ministry. When grace-gifts are at work, we see God and experience him! And because we receive grace when grace-gifts are at work, we can only fully experience the gracious and loving presence of God when we are using our God-given gifts and living out our God-given ministries.

Through the gifts, God shares not only his work but also himself. Kathleen Cahalan remarks that "charisms are incarnational gifts, a graced presence that becomes enfleshed in our lives."[2] Because these gifts are incarnational, we find that the ministry of Christ and the dynamism of God's presence are mediated through the grace-gifts. In fact, God's presence *is* our gift! We share in God's presence in a most profound way by living our lives in the context of spiritual giftedness. His universal presence can and does concentrate locally to find expression through us as charismatic vessels: "[Charisms] are to be embodied actions, lived out and expressed in word and deed."[3] Our bodies, actions, and words become the transforming channel through which the divine presence and the ministry life of Jesus Christ impact the world for the greatest good. Jesus is Emanuel ("God with us") because of the indwelling of the Godhead within us and by the radical testimony of the *charismata* through us.

Because it benefits the church to acquaint herself with gifts that represent a true sharing in God's presence, we will now turn our attention to the *charismata* of miracles, casting out demons, healing, the discerning of spirits, and faith.

---

2. Cahalan, *Introducing the Practice of Ministry*, 35.
3. Ibid., 33.

God Shares Miracles

The gift of miracles or "miraculous powers" is essentially a creative act of God *ex nihilo*—out of nothing (1 Cor 12:10)![4] Being the dynamic interchange between the divine presence and the natural order, miracles interrupt the commonplace with kingdom power. The fullness of God's kingdom may be postponed in this age, but that doesn't stop the church from experiencing the "powers of the age to come" (Heb 6:5 ESV). We mentioned above that all of the gifts function in this way, pulling powers of a future kingdom into the present, but miracles manifest God's power in a uniquely *creative* way.

Even though God's triumphant kingdom is still future, he releases kingdom power into our present experience in order to share his creative power with us! The gift of miracles is divine power at work, power that's available to the church to whatever degree Almighty God is open to exercise his prerogative to act, creatively and spontaneously, through his people. It remains his sovereign prerogative when, where, and how to accomplish the humanly impossible and exhibit purely supernatural demonstrations of the divine presence, putting God's almightiness on display.

However, there is a human side to miraculous powers. The human side remains the same for the church as it was for Jesus, namely, that even miracles at times depend upon human belief and acceptance. The Gospel of Mark reveals a significant limitation in the miracle ministry of Jesus the Nazarene. When Jesus was ministering in a certain place, Scripture says, "He could not do any miracles there, except lay his hands on a few sick people and heal them. He was amazed at their lack of faith" (Mark 6:5–6). Mark emphasizes a powerful hindrance to Jesus' ministry, highlighting the fact that Jesus quite literally *could not do* the miracles he may have wanted to. If God truly shares his power with us, then he also shares both the potential and limitations attached to it, as with everything we share with God.

Referring to the same incident, Matthew 13:58 makes the connection with faith even more explicit, adding that Jesus did not perform many miracles there "because of their lack of faith." It was not due to the *weakness* of the faith of believers but rather to the *nonexistent* faith of those who were unwilling to believe. I'm focusing here on Jesus' ministry of miracles because it is that very ministry that believers inherit in the gift of miraculous powers, just as with healings—we share in Jesus' powerful, creative

---

4. Ludwig Feuerbach describes Jesus' miracle of turning water into wine as a miracle that is "a pure *creatio ex nihilo*" (*Essence of Christianity*, 131).

presence! This gift of miracles is open to an unlimited number of manifestations, yet even when God desires to impact the world with impressive displays of supernatural power, he may not be able to do so when people refuse to believe.

At one significant point in Jesus' ministry, he made a clear connection between freewill and miraculous signs: "And you, Capernaum, will you be lifted to the heavens? No, you will go down to Hades. For if the miracles that were performed in you had been performed in Sodom, it would have remained to this day" (Matt 11:23). Although we may detect some level of hyperbole here, the implications are tragic and reminiscent of other passages that suggest a dark side to the universe: If someone had been in Sodom to minister faithfully in the power of God, then things might have been different (cf. Ezek 22:30). A disturbing reality is the possibility that some will use their freedom and refuse to repent *or refuse to take God's saving message to the lost*, even in the face of God's miraculous presence! For Jesus, the purpose of miracles and other *charismata* is to make God's presence known. Some will respond in a positive way, while others will inevitably reject the message altogether. But whatever the response, Jesus was telling his audience how privileged they were to observe God's presence at work. Jesus' point was not that more overt manifestations would inevitably bring salvation but that we should consider ourselves privileged when we do experience God's miraculous presence.

After Jesus performed wondrous miracles, he shared the same displays of the divine presence through the apostles *and the church*. We know that miracles do not extend only to the apostles because non-apostles like Stephen also performed miracles in the book of Acts (Acts 8:6–7). In another place, the apostle John informed Jesus that he had encountered "someone" casting out demons, so he told the person to stop (Mark 9:38). But Jesus rebuked John: "'Do not stop him,' Jesus said. 'For no one who does a miracle in my name can in the next moment say anything bad about me'" (v. 39). Jesus had no idea who that "someone" was. He knew nothing about that person's faith and doctrine other than his or her success at casting out demons, yet Jesus still gave them his seal of approval. Because of that unnamed disciple, we should be encouraged that Jesus has left open the possibility that God can use any true believer in the ministry of miracles.

God Shares Exorcism

The casting out of demons most likely falls under the umbrella of miracles, which might explain why it isn't included in any New Testament list of spiritual gifts. When Jesus rebuked John regarding that "someone" who was casting out demons, he described this as a miracle when he said, "For no one who does a miracle in my name can in the next moment say anything bad about me" (Mark 9:39). Jesus also said, "If I drive out demons by the finger of God, then the kingdom of God has come upon you" (Luke 11:20). So when Jesus or believers command a demon to exit a human body, they are sharing in the power of God's conquering kingdom! The gift of exorcism, therefore, is the kingdom dynamic to overthrow Satan's demonic kingdom.

The demon-possessed person represents the personification of Satan's kingdom and the sphere from which God's presence has departed. The Gerasene demoniac is a vivid portrayal of divine absence, as he sat lonely and alone in a cemetery among broken chains: "This man lived in the tombs, and no one could bind him anymore, not even with a chain. For he had often been chained hand and foot, but he tore the chains apart and broke the irons on his feet. No one was strong enough to subdue him. Night and day among the tombs and in the hills he would cry out and cut himself with stones" (Mark 5:3–5). That man was isolated from Jesus and the rest of society, but Jesus the Deliverer chose to enter that remote place in order to bring him freedom: "When he saw Jesus from a distance, he ran and fell on his knees in front of him" (v. 6).

Later on in Mark's gospel, the disciples failed to cast out a demon, so in private, they asked Jesus why they couldn't do it. Jesus responded, "This kind can come out only by prayer" (Mark 9:29). The King James Version says a little more, ". . . by prayer and fasting." Although the earliest and best Greek manuscripts do not include the addition from the KJV, the point is clear: The ministry of casting out demons is a miracle that requires a consistent spiritual walk characterized by prayer and spiritual discipline. Otherwise, the Christian could find himself in the same horrifying situation as the seven sons of a Jewish chief priest named Sceva (Acts 19:13–16). Sceva's sons would "invoke the name" of Jesus to cast out demons, but they lacked the most essential ingredient to miraculous deliverance—they didn't have a relationship with Jesus through faith and prayer: "One day the evil spirit answered them, 'Jesus I know, and Paul I know about, but who are you?' Then the man who had the evil spirit jumped on them and overpowered them all. He gave them such a beating that they ran out of the house naked and bleeding" (Acts 19:15–16).

Because the gift of miracles is open to various displays of God's powerful presence in this age, which includes the casting out of demons, believers should remain open-minded and believe along with Jeremiah that "perhaps the LORD will be gracious and do a mighty miracle as he has done in the past" (Jer 21:2 NLT).

God Shares Healing

Another example of miracles, the gift of healing is the remarkable dynamic of God's presence imbuing human flesh (1 Cor 12:9, 28). In these last days, the church is privileged to experience supernatural healings in differing displays of divine power, which allows us to uniquely share in God's presence as we minister to one another. That power is manifested under the new covenant in which God is in the process of gradually healing humanity on the basis of the magnitude of Christ's resurrection (cf. Rom 8:19–21).

The ministry of healing is important today because the church lives under the new covenant and what we might call a covenant of healing.[5] It is because of the new covenant that "by his wounds you have been healed," which is the privilege of *every* child of God (1 Pet 2:24). God shares his brokenness in order to make us whole! Through Jesus' victory over sin and death, believers are not only made spiritually whole but also physically whole. Our wholeness won't be complete until the future resurrection, but in the meantime, healing temporarily reverses sickness and disease as encroachments of death and decay. Anyone who turns to Jesus is one more person made whole for the kingdom of God.

After commenting on the literal rendering of "gifts of healings" in 1 Corinthians 12:9, a double plural in the Greek, Harley Schmitt makes a significant observation about the open and relational nature of the gift. He remarks that what this passage "means to say is God the healer keeps his options open. There is no specific way that God heals. God heals in various ways. . . . He may choose to heal in ways that are completely foreign to us. The Lord needs to be the focus, not the healing or the way the healing is

---

5. Prior to Jesus' ministry, healing was involved in every covenant that God made with people (e.g., Ps 105:37; Exod 15:26). For instance, in God's covenant with David, he promised to heal all their diseases (Ps 103:2–4).

accomplished."[6] Because God is so thoughtfully creative when he heals, the gifts of healings have a variety of applications.

In Jesus' earthly ministry, he used a variety of methods and means for healing. At one moment, he would ask someone to perform an act, such as stretching out a limb, and it was instantly made whole (Matt 12:13). On other occasions, he might simply touch the body (Luke 22:51), or spit on the eyes (Mark 8:23), or spit in the dirt (John 9:6), or even put his fingers into someone's ears and spit on their tongue (Mark 7:33). In fact, Jesus had the power to merely speak the word from a distance to effect the cure (Matt 8:8, 13)! Even today, Jesus speaks the word from a distance when he uses believers to heal.

Jesus Christ is still the Healer who creatively operates in a plurality of "gifts" of various manifestations of "healings" through his church. Schmitt goes on to say that "God is a God of variety and the true working of the Spirit never is limited to one specific method through which people are healed."[7] If healing can be as simple as the laying on of hands, anointing with oil, or speaking a prayer of faith over someone, we should learn the lesson of Naaman's servant from the Old Testament. When the prophet Elisha told Naaman to dip seven times in the Jordan river for his healing, he stubbornly refused: "But Naaman went away angry and said, 'I thought that he would surely come out to me and stand and call on the name of the Lord his God, wave his hand over the spot and cure me of my leprosy'" (2 Kgs 5:11). Rather than being open to God's direction, Naaman had his own preconceived notions on the dynamics of healing. Fortunately, he had a wise servant, and his servant's logic is just as applicable today as it was then: "Sir, if the prophet had told you to do something very difficult, wouldn't you have done it? So you should certainly obey him when he says simply, 'Go and wash and be cured!'" (v. 13 NLT). Healing can often start with obeying God's simple commands, but sometimes, healing begins by simply asking: "You do not have because you do not ask God" (James 4:2).

Because of the infinite depths of God's creativity and resourcefulness to bring about a broad spectrum of healing, it would be a practice in futility for us to spend time here to develop a "handbook" on healing. Instead, the church should step out in bold faith and seek God to heal when circumstances appear more commonplace, and especially, when they seem impossible.

---

6. Schmitt, *Many Gifts One Lord*, 105.
7. Ibid.

Gifts: God Shares His Work (Part Two)

God Shares Discernment

The discerning or "distinguishing between spirits" grants supernatural revelation with regard to the origins of a message, whether that message arose from the source of God's Spirit, the individual, or a demonic spirit (1 Cor 12:10). This is quite literally the gift of discerning the *source* spirit. Because God is sharing his wise discernment, this gift is the dynamic of wisdom to thoughtfully receive the Spirit's critique.

The discerning of spirits has been considered a "companion gift to prophecy," which we introduced earlier.[8] The most direct use of the gift may have been to assist in the assessment of prophecy (1 Cor 14:29), much like the way the gift of interpreting tongues is useful and even necessary to understand tongues (vv. 27–28). Even so, when prophecy is spoken and evaluated by the congregation, its assessment is open to the entire congregation and not limited to those with the gift to discern spirits. Paul simply says to "let the others evaluate what is [prophesied]" (1 Cor 14:29 NLT). As a companion gift, the discerning of spirits requires the same spontaneous revelation as prophecy and could therefore be mistaken for prophecy. The difference between this and prophecy is in the content of the revelation. Whereas the content of prophetic revelation is a message of warning or *edification* (1 Cor 14:3–4, 24–25, 31), the content to discern spirits is a message of *origins* (Acts 16:16–18).

The Apostle Paul is one possible example of someone who functioned in the gift of distinguishing between spirits. When Paul encountered a demon-possessed servant girl in the book of Acts, he wasn't immediately aware of the kind of discernment that would be required to understand what was happening. It's important for believers to ask for wisdom when we lack it, but it is also important to remain open to the Spirit's spontaneous ignition of any gift, including divine discernment. As in Paul's ministry, his first intuition was probably not that the source of this girl's insightful message was actually a powerful demonic spirit. Luke recounts the story:

> Once when we were going to the place of prayer, we were met by a female slave who had a spirit by which she predicted the future. . . . She followed Paul and the rest of us, shouting, "These men are servants of the Most High God, who are telling you the way to be saved." She kept this up for many days. Finally Paul became so annoyed (*diaponetheis*) that he turned around and said to the spirit,

---

8. Thomas, *Understanding Spiritual Gifts*, 178.

"In the name of Jesus Christ I command you to come out of her!"
At that moment the spirit left her. (Acts 16:16–18)

Despite the few days of ignorance leading up to it, the content of Paul's rebuke demonstrates the powerful gift of the Spirit's presence to discern the true source of the girl's information. Oddly enough, the prompting for it was an extreme annoyance or, better still, a physically exhausting irritation. The participle *diaponetheis* indicates that an inner struggle was taking place, which abruptly came to an end by Paul's precise and inspired assessment of the situation. When Paul was finally grieved and well beyond any natural resource to accurately assess and confront the matter, the Spirit opened his heart to what was happening; and it was that dynamic process that led to a confident rebuke.

In a dramatic way, Paul's discerning of spirits reveals that *charismata* are open, dynamic, and contingent upon the Spirit's sovereign prerogative in terms of when, how, and to what degree gifts are effectuated: "It is the one and only Spirit who distributes all these gifts. He alone decides which gift each person should have" (1 Cor 12:11 NLT).[9] Gifts may be given and removed, lasting for a moment, a day, a mission, or a lifetime. At least in Paul's situation, it appears that his special discernment was a momentary gift.[10]

God Shares Faith

Through the gift of faith, we experience a supernatural dynamic of *acceptance,* as God shares his confidence with us (1 Cor 12:9). Among the *charismata,* the gift of faith is the broadest category and the most open of all the gifts because all of the other gifts require some degree of faith to perform. Therefore, faith functions as the "unifying aspect" of all other gifts.[11]

---

9. Writing on spiritual gifts, Harley Schmitt acknowledges that every aspect of their distribution remains open under the Spirit's direction: "The Spirit decides where, when, and at what moment to dispense the gifts" (*Many Gifts One Lord,* 97).

10. Just as many theologically interpret the gift of tongues (languages) to illustrate a reversal of the judgment at Babel (Gen 11:1–9), so the gift to discern the source spirit can function as a reversal of the deception of the serpent in the garden. Despite having Yahweh's immediate presence to warn them against the enemy's schemes, Adam and his wife had failed to discern the source of their temptation. Today, the supernatural discerning of spirits exposes Satan's work, so it is yet another means to fulfill God's abiding presence with his people as it was intended to be experienced in Eden.

11. Thomas, *Understanding Spiritual Gifts,* 30.

For instance, miracles fall under the umbrella of faith, while healings and casting out demons are both considered miracles, but all of them depend on faith. Healing is just one example of a miracle, and miracles are just one consequence of a faith that believes and accepts.

For every believer, faith is the gift that works together with grace and our free acceptance of the gospel to initiate us into the community of faith (Eph 2:8). But even though faith belongs to every saint and every expression of faith is the gift of God, there is still something unique to an exceptional expression of faith among the *charismata*. When this *charism* is at work and my life is so filled with God's Spirit, I can fully accept any dynamic move of the divine presence.

To illustrate the gift of faith, we'll consider Paul's hypothetical scenario. In the course of emphasizing the importance of godly faith, hope, and love, Paul maintains that "if I have a faith that can move mountains, but do not have love, I am nothing" (1 Cor 13:2). How powerful it is that one's trust in God can become so intensified that the greatest of obstacles can be overcome—even mountains! This is a fantastic illustration and one that should give every believer confidence in the kind of faith that's possible: God doesn't abandon us to defeat but provides a means for defeating the fiercest of enemies. On occasion, he does this through the gift of faith, and most importantly, a faith that expresses itself through love (Gal 5:6).

To some degree, the gift of faith is the prerequisite for every other supernatural gift. We must believe God to the point of stepping out to effect what the Spirit has prompted us to do. By faith, Paul discerned the demonic spirit that gave voice to a slave girl, and also by faith, he cast out the demon behind it. Believers are often called upon to step out in faith, accepting with confidence that God will perform the very thing that he's impressed upon our hearts.

God Shares Other Gifts

Having looked at the gifts of unilateral presence that largely depend upon a divinely supernatural intervention, we'll look briefly at the *charismata* that function in combination with our own natural gifts and talents. These gifts also require the presence and power of God to fulfill Jesus' ministry in the world, but in a bilateral fashion, hinging upon the believer's natural abilities and input in a more apparent way than the unilateral gifts. Because we put so much of ourselves into these gifts, it becomes even more clear that God shares the work of ministry with us. We've already looked at Paul's list of gifts in 1 Corinthians 12:9–10, so we can now briefly address a less formal list in Paul's letter to the Romans. This list includes serving, teaching, encouraging, giving, leading, and showing mercy.

Paul introduces the list of ministries in Romans 12 with a positive assertion: "We have different gifts (*charismata*), according to the grace given to each of us" (v. 6). He wants us to be aware that our gifts are based upon God's individualized grace in our lives; God's unmerited and undeserved grace molds each gift to each person individually. Paul goes on to describe how God has poured out grace *in the form of ministry* so that believers can excel in what we do:[12] "If your gift is prophesying, then prophesy in accordance with your faith; if it is serving, then serve; if it is teaching, then teach; if it is to encourage, then give encouragement; if it is giving, then give generously; if it is to lead, do it diligently; if it is to show mercy, do it cheerfully" (Rom 12:6–8).

Because we've already looked at prophecy as a unilateral gift, we'll start with the second item in this list: serving. The Greek word *diakonia* is used here and is interpreted as serving or general ministry, but it literally means to wait on tables. Just as faith is the *principle* unifying aspect of all spiritual ministries, we might say that serving is the *functional* unifying aspect. In other words, by faith we serve. Before each of us, God opens many different doors for service, which we're responsible to walk through. But those who are uniquely gifted to serve don't wait for needs to arrive at their door; instead, they seek out opportunities to serve regardless of personal cost or any attention or praise they might receive. Those who serve always do so at some cost to themselves, following the example of the God who also knows what it means to sacrifice: "For even the Son of Man came not to be served but to serve, and to give his life as a ransom for many" (Mark 10:45 ESV). Although the heart of a servant should permeate all other *charismata*, some believers will be especially gifted to serve.

Moving on in the list, teaching and encouraging are also special graces that God gives to some (Rom 12:7, 8). Those who teach share knowledge and those who encourage share optimism. Paul's reason for such a list is not to exhaust every possible ministry but to prompt every believer to perform wholeheartedly in their area of ministry, knowing that it is only by grace that anyone could reach their full potential. As Paul mentions the next gifts

---

12. In the New Living Translation, Romans 12:6 reads, "In his grace, God has given us different gifts for doing certain things well."

in his list, he qualifies them in such a way to make evident that he wants the church to excel: "If it is giving, then give *generously*; if it is to lead, do it *diligently*; if it is to show mercy, do it *cheerfully*" (v. 8, emphasis added). The grace-empowered opportunity to excel is open to every believer, and Paul is telling us to take advantage of it!

We'll conclude with a word of warning: Although the gifts are open and available for every believer to pursue and excel in, Paul warns that Christians must not breach areas of ministry intended for others. Instead, we should accept the grace and measure of faith apportioned to each one of us individually, and we must choose to excel in those areas: "For by the grace given to me I say to everyone among you not to think of himself more highly than he ought to think, but to think with sober judgment, each according to the measure of faith that God has assigned" (Rom 12:3 ESV; cf. 15:20; 2 Cor 10:13–15). Some are tempted to think too highly of their own gifting, while others can be tempted to think too little and even neglect it. Though we can be tempted to give more weight to certain gifts over others and to certain gifted individuals, those gifts that seem less extraordinary are essential to the successful function of all the rest (1 Cor 12:14–26).

The open-ended potential to possess and not lack any spiritual gift (1 Cor 1:7) is not the same as fully exploiting those gifts through grace. Ministry requires that each of us freely choose to serve in the areas of our gifting. Kathleen Cahalan said it well: "Charisms are a gift to be received, recognized, and acted upon, which means they can be ignored, rejected, and diminished, by either individuals or the community.... Because freedom too is a gift, some persons are free to use and accept charisms or not."[13] Although I am free to minimize my gifting, that doesn't negate my responsibility to fulfill the heavenly calling, a calling which Jesus himself impresses upon my life (Heb 3:1). Ministry is the outworking of that heavenly call, beckoning us to live out the united witness of the one body of Christ, serving one another toward the full maturity of God's people in the world.

Conclusion

Looking at the bilateral and unilateral gifts of God's presence, we saw that the divine presence is dynamically manifest through the church as people freely choose to excel in ministry. By doing so, we share God's work with him. We spent the majority of the chapter looking at the gifts of God's

---

13. Cahalan, *Introducing the Practice of Ministry*, 33, 37.

unilateral presence, those ministries that cannot be reduced to natural talent, such as miracles, casting out demons, healing, discerning the source spirit, and faith.

Along with the theme that God shares his work through the various gifts, we saw that the gifts are an inherently dynamic experience of God's presence. We saw that miracles are the dynamic interchange between the divine presence and the natural order, interrupting the commonplace with kingdom power. The casting out of demons was described as the kingdom dynamic to lay waste to Satan's dominion in the world, and healing is the dynamic of divine presence imbuing human flesh. Through healing, we experience the temporary reversal of sickness and disease as encroachments of death and decay. We also looked at the gift of discerning between spirits, which was explained as the dynamic of wisdom to thoughtfully receive the Spirit's critique regarding whether a message has come from the individual, God's Spirit, or a demonic spirit. And finally, the gift of faith was understood to be the supernatural dynamic of acceptance and the principle unifying aspect of all other *charismata*. In each of those gifts, we saw that sharing in God's presence means that God shares with us his creative power, his kingdom, his work at the cross, his wisdom, and his confidence.

We then summarized the *bilateral* gifts, with special emphasis on serving, which we described as the functional unifying aspect of all other gifts: by faith we serve. The bilateral gifts include, but are by no means limited to, serving, teaching, encouraging, giving, leading, and helping. God uses these gifts and so many others to remind us how very involved he is through the presence of the Spirit.

8

Ministry: God Shares His Power

WE'VE ALREADY LOOKED AT numerous spiritual gifts that are born out of the divine presence. God shares those gifts to keep us engaged and to include us in accomplishing a supernatural mission. In his epistle to the Ephesians, Paul assures us that Jesus takes the lead over his mission: "Now these are the gifts Christ gave to the church" (Eph 4:11 NLT). As chief Shepherd, Jesus gives gifts, but he also takes responsibility for the flock in a rather sobering way: He shares his power with us!

Every ministry is a responsibility of thoughtful dependence upon the Good Shepherd, which we carry out by learning to surrender to God's word and the movement of his presence. Because Jesus is personally involved in our lives as the Shepherd who cares for his people, he has arranged ministries within the church in a manner that exalts his leadership. If God shares his power with us by giving every believer an area of responsibility, then we should seek to understand our potential for various leadership and ministry roles as well as our personal responsibility to serve in a way that depends entirely upon Jesus Christ.

In this chapter, we'll be addressing matters related to what I am calling the openness of ministry, which refers primarily to the freedom and potential to fulfill our ministry. Additionally, charismatic openness means that God is fundamentally relational and closely involved with his church, so he remains open-minded in the many creative and resourceful ways that he uses the *charismata* to reach the world through the gospel of his presence. If God desires to make his presence known throughout the world, much of that mission will depend upon believers to share his power and fulfill their ministry.

Introducing the Fivefold Ministry

Gifted leadership represents Jesus' authority and humility toward his church. In a profoundly humbling way, the Lord has invested his approval and authority into men and women who are now *little shepherds* called to represent the Master Shepherd. As God makes people his vice-regents and graciously shares his authority with mere human beings, divine humility is profoundly exemplified. The heart of God teaches us that every true leader is first a servant. As servants, God's gifted leaders set the tone for depending entirely upon his presence, as they pioneer the way into the glory of a profound intimacy with Jesus Christ.

The Lord Jesus personally sets ministries in place while delegating shepherding responsibilities and other ministry roles to men and women who become qualified through word and Spirit (cf. Acts 6:3, "full of the Spirit and wisdom"). As Chief Shepherd, he installs under-shepherds who share responsibility for the church's daily care. It's notable that the New Testament never outlines the form and function of any ministry role but leaves room for flexibility, which should give us a sense of the potential and opportunity that exist in one's service to God.[1]

With regard to the flexible dynamic of early church ministry, church historian Laurie Guy remarks, "Certainly there was leadership, but no determining template. The boundaries of specific leadership functions were not always clear, and there was a lot of overlap. Much of the shape of ministry was ad hoc response to particular situations. From a systematic perspective, NT leadership looked messy, but it was dynamic."[2] If leadership for the early church was dynamic and flexible, which seems to be the case, then it would be the same today. Perhaps the Spirit, who founded and inspired the early church, left its structure open enough to encourage long-term dependence on him, so that even today, the church can be led

---

1. We might expect Scripture to describe in detail something as important as the form and function of leadership gifts, but that is not the case. Raymond Collins comments that "'overseers' and 'servers' appear together in Phil. 1:1, but apart from the etymological implications of the terms, Paul gives no specific indication of the role of the overseers and servers within the community" (*1 and 2 Timothy*, 78). This lack of specificity isn't limited to Paul's writings but applies throughout the New Testament.

2. Guy, *Introducing Early Christianity*, 85.

by the dynamism of the Chief Shepherd himself through the supernatural gifting of the Spirit!

Guy again observes that "the church's priority on preaching the gospel (2 Tim 4:1–2) meant that although matters of structure and organization were significant, it retained much ad hoc flexibility in its early life."[3] Guy is pointing out that it wasn't only the leadership that was flexible, but it was the whole early church dynamic. We should consider that the ad hoc flexibility and openness of ministry are designed to benefit the church's mission. Leadership and ministry roles are not open for the sake of being open but for the sake of allowing the lively and dynamic nature of God's Spirit to lead his church into thoughtful avenues of ministry, service, and mission. Together we discover creative methods and means for accomplishing our Spirit-filled tasks in order to release God's presence in the world.

Although any detailed instruction is lacking on the exact how and what of performing leadership ministries, Scripture highlights the importance of those roles and the reality that we cannot function without them. The early church's mission of gospel proclamation was carried out under the express command and ongoing authority of Jesus Christ (Matt 28:18–20). It was also carried out within the context of numerous leadership *and other closely related ministries* designed to equip every believer for mission. Because every ministry is important, in this chapter our study won't focus solely on leadership offices but on the fivefold "equipping" ministry. Paul tells us that our Chief Shepherd has given the church a fivefold ministry—"the apostles, the prophets, the evangelists, the pastors and teachers"—for the express purpose of equipping the saints for mutual ministry until we all attain to maturity and the full glorification of God (Eph 4:11–13). Just as the early church thrived under a flexible, multi-faceted plurality of ministries, so can churches today.

First, we will briefly review the openness of the fivefold ministry and the potential that belongs to believers to fulfill those areas of service. God's plan for those gifts can be a useful paradigm for understanding his grace and guidance in all other *charismata*. Whatever openness applies to these ministries can also be applied to the full range of spiritual gifts. After reviewing the openness of the fivefold ministry, we will see how believers can excel in their ministry roles.

---

3. Ibid.

God Shares Apostolic Ministry

The apostle is the first listed among the fivefold ministry in Ephesians 4:11. The ministry of apostle has always been of utmost importance to the church, the *apostolos* being "the one who is sent."[4] Apostles were sent out with a specific purpose: to represent the one who sent them. The church was founded upon this ministry (Eph 2:20), with the initial "Twelve" being the first to make a significant contribution. Known simply as the Twelve, Jesus chose that number out of a much larger following of disciples (Luke 6:13), giving the impression that this number was forever closed and limited to only twelve men.[5]

According to the gospel of Mark, Jesus chose the Twelve for a special purpose: "that they might be with him and that he might send them out (*apostello*) to preach and to have authority to drive out demons" (Mark 3:14–15; cf. 6:7; Matt 10:1, 5; Luke 9:1–2). Mark expresses that Jesus called those men for the purpose of being "with him" as *disciples* and for going out as *apostles* to preach and overcome the demonic kingdom. For such a calling, Jesus clearly placed priority on the fellowship of discipleship. Only after living "with him" in a lifestyle of discipleship were they then sent out to heal the sick and preach repentance as entrance into the approaching kingdom. Because Jesus is the chief "Apostle" and hence the ultimate Messenger from God (Heb 3:1; cf. John 3:17; 17:3), he sent the Twelve out as an extension of his own apostolic ministry (John 20:21), sharing his power with apostolic emissaries.

One needs only to read the first few chapters of the book of Acts to see how important the apostles were to the early church. Jesus chose the Twelve, not only to send them out on mission, but also to prepare them for a larger foundational teaching and leading ministry to the church.[6] Beginning in Jerusalem, the Twelve did not go out with secondhand teaching but as "eyewitnesses" (Acts 1:21–22; 2:32; 3:15; 4:22) of the resurrected Christ who, seated on the Davidic throne at the right hand of glory, manifested the authority of his royal reign through them (Acts 2:43; 4:33; 5:12). The

---

4. Regarding apostleship in the New Testament, Hoke and Taylor observe that "the Greek term *apostello* emerges in two major categories: first, as a broadly used verb, meaning to send in one form or another and by different senders (132 times); and second, as a more specifically used noun connoting the apostolic person (80 times)" (*Global Mission Handbook*, 21–22).

5. Jesus' twelve disciples are listed in Matt 10:2–4; Mark 3:16–19; Luke 6:14–16.

6. See Matt 11:1; 13:10–11; Mark 4:10–11; 8:31; 9:30–31; 10:32; Luke 18:31.

MINISTRY: GOD SHARES HIS POWER

apostles bore powerful witness to the risen Christ, while elaborating on his teaching and showing that Scripture bears witness to him (Acts 2:42; 17:2-3; 18:4). While going out, they established churches and installed local leadership, performing missionary activities while overseeing and ensuring that sound teaching and evangelism were occurring within the churches. There was considerable authority required to fulfill such a task, but that authority extended only as far as it was deemed necessary to facilitate worldwide mission (cf. 2 Cor 10:8; 13:10; 1 Thess 2:6-12).

At the opening of Acts, we quickly learn that the exclusive Twelve was not in fact a closed ministry—they were taking auditions! Because Judas had betrayed Jesus and taken his own life, the other apostles immediately sought to appoint his replacement in a man named Matthias (Acts 1:23, 26). If the Twelve wasn't a closed ministry before, surely it would be now, seeing that it was necessary for Matthias to have been with Jesus and to have personally witnessed the resurrection (vv. 21-22). Even so, not far into the book of Acts, Jesus personally appoints yet another apostle, Saul/Paul of Tarsus, who Jesus was sending (*apostello*) to the Gentiles (26:16, 17; cf. 9:3-16).

Paul clearly recognized himself as an apostle, which demonstrates that even the ministry of apostle was flexible. Paul informed the Galatians, "I did not go up to Jerusalem to see those who were apostles before I was" (Gal 1:17), and to the Corinthians, "I am the least of the apostles and do not even deserve to be called an apostle" (1 Cor 15:9). Not only was he a great leader to the early church, but his apostleship had the support of the Apostle Peter who placed Paul's letters on par with Old Testament Scripture (2 Pet 3:16, "the other Scriptures").[7] There should be no doubt that Paul was an apostle in the strictest sense, even satisfying similar credentials as the Twelve in that he had actually seen Jesus (1 Cor 9:1).[8] Nevertheless, the Twelve were required to be eyewitnesses in an even more restrictive sense than Paul. They needed to have been with Jesus from the very beginning of

---

7. Although such apostles as Paul and Peter wrote inspired Scripture, it wasn't required of the writers of the New Testament to be apostles. Mark and Luke both wrote New Testament books, and neither of them were apostles.

8. Paul said to the Corinthians, "Even though I may not be an apostle to others, surely I am to you!" (1 Cor 9:2). His statement hints at some flexibility or openness related to being an apostle. In other words, my apostolic commission is closed to others but open to you!

his ministry, no doubt "to fulfill their roles as the proclaimers and protectors of the true story of Jesus."[9]

Paul is evidence that there were apostles beyond the Twelve, which implies that this ministry remains open to other believers today. Because we're focusing on the potential and opportunities for believers in ministry, it's important that we consider those who were apostles beyond the strict sense of the Twelve, others like Paul and James, the brother of Jesus (1 Cor 15:7). Examples of other apostles in Scripture include: Andronicus and Junia (Rom 16:7),[10] Apollos (1 Cor 4:6, 9), Barnabas (Acts 14:14), Epaphroditus (Phil 2:25, "your apostle/messenger"), and possibly Silas (Acts 17:10; cf. 15:40–41) and Timothy (1 Thess 1:1; 2:6–7). Donald Dent concludes that the New Testament identifies four different groups of apostles: (1) the Twelve, (2) other commissioned eyewitnesses, such as Paul and James the brother of Jesus, (3) missionary apostles, such as Barnabas (Acts 13:2–5), and (4) envoys of the churches, such as the church in Antioch that sent a financial contribution to Jerusalem (Acts 11:30; cf. 8:14; 11:22).[11] Each of those groups fits the New Testament definition of *apostolos* as one who is sent for a purpose.

Finally, there are two unnamed apostles in the New Testament who are described as "apostles/representatives of the churches" (2 Cor 8:18–23). Just as the apostolic ministry was open to two apostles with unknown identities, their ministry remains open today. Although today's apostles don't produce inspired Scripture, they must nonetheless be sensitive to supernatural revelation. They don't have the same authority as the Twelve, but they do have responsibility over their spheres of ministry, which are often very large ministries. Today, in addition to being commissioned and sent to minister beyond one's local church with a message or gift, the apostolic ministry is fulfilled primarily through *missionary* enterprise, extending the kingdom of Christ throughout the world. A close reading of the New

9. Dent, *Ongoing Role of Apostles*, 36. See also Witherington, *Acts of the Apostles*, 125.

10. Andronicus and Junia are described as "outstanding among the apostles" (Rom 16:7), which can be interpreted two different ways: either they were outstanding *as* apostles or highly esteemed *by* the apostles.

11. Dent, *Ongoing Role of Apostles*, 34. In addition to identifying those four groups to describe the New Testament usage of *apostolos*, Dent briefly summarizes other categorizations that have been suggested: "One traditional view is that only the Twelve and Paul were the only real apostles. Others have noted two groups of apostles, such as the Twelve and others or apostles of Christ and apostles of the church or eyewitnesses and missionaries" (ibid., n. 102).

Testament reveals that there are no clear examples of missionaries other than the apostle.[12] The authority and function that these apostolic missionaries assume remains somewhat open, because the degree of their authority will be determined by the scope and sphere of their discipleship and church planting activity.[13]

Even so, missionary activity does not exhaust the role of apostles today. These men and women will be pioneer visionaries who meet the same requirements as other church leadership (cf. 1 Tim 3:1–7; Titus 1:5–9). They will maintain humility as servant-leaders and assist in establishing other permanent leaders, and they will be examples of sound teaching with a reputation above reproach. Were apostles only men, or was this ministry open to women as well? Current application of the missionary aspect of apostleship can speak to that, and it rarely restricts God's missionary call to men. We should also be aware of the possibility that the first-century believer Junia was a female apostle (Rom 16:7). It seems, therefore, that a man or woman can faithfully fulfill the role of an apostle.

God Shares Prophetic Ministry

The prophet is another gift listed within the fivefold ministry in Ephesians 4:11. At Pentecost, the prophetic Spirit was poured out and indwelt every believer and now inspires each of us to understand and share the full gospel of Jesus Christ. We call this the universal prophethood of believers, because we all possess the same inspiring Spirit: "Even on my servants, both men and women, I will pour out my Spirit in those days, and they will prophesy" (Acts 2:18).[14] As believers "keep in step with the Spirit" (Gal 5:25), the divine presence uses us to share gospel truth under the Spirit's sensitive guidance. This emphasis, however, is not what Paul has in mind in the fivefold list to the believers in Asia Minor. Like every other believer, prophets have the prophetic Spirit, but they also possess the *gift* of prophecy.

Does every saint, then, have the ability to prophesy? Scripture anticipates the question and answers in the negative. Paul asks, "Are all prophets?",

---

12. See Turner, *Biblical Bible Translating*, 16–19; and Hesselgrave, *Paradigms in Conflict*, 215–16.

13. For a charismatic perspective on apostleship that advocates more apostolic authority and less missionary function, see Wagner, *Apostles Today*.

14. This passage presents an *a fortiori* argument: If God's Spirit is poured out on those considered the least (servants), it is certainly poured out on all!

and the implied answer—no (1 Cor 12:29)! We could say the same about any ministry. Even though all believers have the prophetic Spirit, not all believers have the ability to prophesy. When prophets step out to minister, they do so as an extension of the prophethood of believers, but they are uniquely gifted members of the body of Christ. So when Paul mentions prophets, he is referring to those we described earlier in chapter six—those who receive a direct, spontaneous revelation from God.

Although God shares his power with the prophets, those gifted individuals may or may not fill leadership roles.[15] There's no need, then, to imagine that a formal ordination or laying on of hands is required to recognize someone as a prophet.[16] Prophets simply fulfill the role of relaying divine revelation to the church. Although some make a distinction between an *office* of prophet and those who occasionally prophesy, Wayne Grudem observes that "'prophet' appears to be not an office but a designation of function in the New Testament. Those who prophesied frequently or appeared to have the gift of prophecy were called 'prophets.'" Grudem goes on to explain just how open this gift was: "It probably was generally recognized by the believers that 'prophet' simply meant 'someone who prophesies.' Such a non-technical definition fits well with all the New Testament data."[17] Following Grudem's conclusions, the church could recognize anyone as a prophet if God gives him or her a revelation that's meant to be shared with the congregation.[18]

---

15. Although the role of prophets is not primarily to lead, that doesn't keep them from occasionally exercising leadership in the local church (cf. Acts 13:1; 1 Cor 12:28; Eph 2:20; 3:4–5).

16. Grudem observes that "there is no hint in the New Testament about any ceremony of recognizing or installing someone in a prophetic office or to perform some specific prophetic tasks (as with apostles, elders, and deacons in Acts 1:23–26; 6:6; 14:23; 1 Tim. 4:14; 5:22; Titus 1:5; etc.)" (*Gift of Prophecy*, 165).

17. Ibid., 165, 167. Donald Gee of the Assemblies of God expresses similar thoughts as Grudem: "Although there appears to be a distinction between official prophets and those who prophesied, it is arbitrary to claim for the prophets anything more than that they were those who exercised a frequent and proved gift of prophesying" (*Spiritual Gifts*, 43–44).

18. Also with regard to the openness of prophecy in the New Testament, Jack Hayford remarks, "There aren't any restrictions on when, where, or how prophecies may be delivered.... God has been willing to open the door quite wide" ("Despise Not Prophecy," 80). Although prophecy can spontaneously erupt at any moment, we would be remiss to mention that Scripture does place limitations on how and when prophecies can be spoken *to the congregation*: "Two or three prophets should speak, and the others should weigh carefully what is said. And if a revelation comes to someone who is sitting down,

Just as both men and women functioned as prophets in the New Testament, there will also be male and female prophets today. The prophet Agabus had "four unmarried daughters who prophesied" (Acts 21:9). Paul exhorted the believers in Corinth that "every woman who prays or prophesies" should do so with her head covered (1 Cor 11:5), which demonstrates that women were prophets but also suggests that prophesying could be expressed just as regularly and naturally as prayer!

Prophecy can and should have a regular place in our churches today, just as the Spirit commands the church throughout this age to remain open and eager for it: "Therefore, my brothers and sisters, be eager to prophesy" (1 Cor 14:39), and "do not treat prophecies with contempt" (1 Thess 5:20).

God Shares Evangelistic Ministry

Evangelists are next in the list of the fivefold ministry. Whereas Ephesians 4:11 uses the plural *euangelistas* ("evangelists"), the term occurs in only two other places in the New Testament, and both of those uses are singular (Acts 21:8; 2 Tim 4:5). The basic meaning of *euangelistes* is to be a bearer of good tidings, someone who brings good news.

In 2 Timothy 4:5, Paul instructed Timothy to "do the work of an evangelist," and Timothy was obligated to "fulfill" that ministry just as Paul had done (vv. 6–8). In Acts 21:8, Philip was known simply as "the evangelist." He was not an apostle but was indeed a man "full of the Spirit and wisdom" (Acts 6:3). Because Philip was an evangelist, he couldn't keep quiet but boldly "proclaimed the Messiah" (Acts 8:5) and "preached the word wherever [he] went" (8:4; cf. v. 40), faithfully demonstrating what an evangelist is expected to be. Not only had Philip "proclaimed the good news of the kingdom of God and the name of Jesus Christ" as an effective communicator of the gospel (8:12), but he was also quick on his feet and adapted to circumstances as they presented themselves. When he encountered a traveling eunuch who was reading from the scroll of Isaiah, Philip "began with that very passage of Scripture and told him the good news about Jesus" (8:35).

As mentioned earlier, the New Testament likely locates the missionary role with the apostle rather than the evangelist. Evangelistic ministry is much broader in its application than missionary service. Although every believer is expected to evangelize, there will be some who are especially

the first speaker should stop" (1 Cor 14:29–30).

gifted in that area and will have a certain zeal to promote the gospel. Just as God shares his power in so many different ways, he also shares the power of the gospel: "For I am not ashamed of the gospel, because it is the power of God that brings salvation to everyone who believes" (Rom 1:16).

As an equipping ministry, the evangelist will equip other believers to become more effective ministers of the gospel. As with most gifts, the task of equipping others is flexible enough for the evangelist to use his natural talents, creativity, and common sense, while always remaining sensitive to the Spirit's inner voice.

God Shares Pastoral/Teaching Ministry

The fivefold ministry concludes with pastors and teachers. The phrase "pastors and teachers" in Ephesians 4:11 can be understood as "pastors and *other* teachers (*didaskalous*)," which means the pastors are teachers but there are also other teachers besides pastors.[19] Before we discuss pastors, the ministry of teaching extends to anyone who is an able communicator willing to faithfully explain and apply God's word, a ministry that's open to men and women alike. In Titus 2:3, it is specifically the women who are encouraged to be *kalodidaskalous*—teachers of what is good. For simplicity's sake, we will treat teachers under the same heading as pastors.

Turning our attention to pastoral ministry, in Gerald Bray's systematic theology, he offers a helpful abbreviated definition of the practical function of pastor, stating, "The specific duty of a pastor is to shepherd those who have responded to the preaching of the gospel and to guide them along the pathway to spiritual maturity."[20] Through pastoral ministry, God shares the power of his shepherding with his under-shepherds!

---

19. A cursory glance at various Bible commentaries shows that many scholars interpret the ministry of pastor and teacher (*tous poimenas kai didaskalous*) in Ephesians 4 as one gift, the "pastor-teacher." A closer look, however, reveals that this is a misuse of Granville Sharp's Rule. According to the Rule, in the TSKS construction (article-substantive-καὶ-substantive), the second noun refers to the same person mentioned with the first noun *when neither noun is impersonal, plural, or a proper name*. In Ephesians 4:11, the construction *tous poimenas kai didaskalous* is disqualified because it contains plural nouns. According to Daniel Wallace, the plural construction in Ephesians 4 is likely an example of the first group being a subset of the second, "the X and [other] Y" (*Greek Grammar*, 271–72, 278–86). Other examples include Matt 5:20; 9:11; Luke 6:35; 14:3.

20. Bray, *God is Love*, 698.

Ministry: God Shares His Power

Pastoral ministry is rather flexible in terms of its form and function, which is evident even in the titles of early church leaders. Among other things, the scriptural designations include elder (*presbuteros*, James 5:14), shepherd or pastor (*poimen*, Eph 4:11), overseer or bishop (*episkope*, 1 Tim 3:1), and leaders (*egoumenon*, Heb 13:7). Although there's disagreement on the matter, each of those titles likely refers to one and the same role: the pastor. By the end of the second century, extracanonical writings distinguished the bishop/overseer from the other elders, although that distinction is not explicit in the New Testament.[21]

The apostles Peter and Paul both appear to use elder and overseer interchangeably (Titus 1:6–7).[22] Speaking to the elders (*presbuterous*) in Ephesus (Acts 20:17), Paul commands them to "keep watch over yourselves and all the flock of which the Holy Spirit has made you overseers (*episkopous*). Be shepherds (*poimainein*) of the church of God" (Acts 20:28). Likewise, Peter enjoins elders (*presbuterous*) to be shepherds (*poimanate, pastors*) who submit fully to the authority of the Chief Shepherd (*Archipoimenos*), the Lord Jesus Christ (1 Pet 5:1, 2, 4). According to both Paul and Peter, the elders and pastors appear to be one and the same—pastoral elders. Although the ministry of apostle is distinct from the pastor (Acts 20:17), the apostles were often times also teachers, prophets (cf. Acts 13:1; Eph 2:5),[23] and elders (cf. Acts 15:2; Gal 2:9; 1 Pet 5:1). Even Paul described himself as "a preacher, an apostle, and a teacher" (2 Tim 1:11 NLT).

As an equipping ministry, the role and involvement of pastoral elders is open to various applications. The earliest reference to elders in the book of Acts mentions them receiving a relief-gift because of a famine (Acts 11:30). Paul beseeches the elders in Asia Minor to protect the flock of believers and practice church discipline (Acts 20:28–31). In general, church leaders are said to "direct the affairs of the church" and are responsible for "preaching and teaching" (1 Tim 5:17), being people who are "able to teach" (1 Tim

---

21. Ignatius, an early second-century bishop of Antioch, distinguishes between a single bishop and a plurality of elders, likening the elders to the apostles (*Smyrn.* 8; cf. *Pol.* 6; *Trall.* 6). Contrary to Ignatius, other early extra-biblical sources describe only a plurality of elders or bishops (1 *Clem.* 42:4; 44:3; *Did.* 15:1; *Herm. Vis.* 8:3; 13:1; *Herm. Sim.* 104:2).

22. See Merkle, *Elder and Overseer.*

23. As with Ephesians 4:11 above, Wallace argues that "the apostles and prophets" (*ton apostolon kai propheton*) in Ephesians 2:20 and 3:5 are another example of the first group being a subset of the second, "the X and [other] Y." The apostles are prophets, but there are also other prophets besides them: "the apostles and *other* prophets" (*Greek Grammar*, 284–86).

3:2) and lead (Heb 13:7). There is some dispute over whether a teaching elder should be distinguished from an elder who leads (cf. 1 Tim 5:17).

It should come as no surprise that the New Testament is somewhat flexible as to how the church should identify its leadership. Elders were prominent in first-century Jewish synagogues where at least some overlap existed with the role, authority, and character requirements of the church elder. This could explain why that role was easily adapted to the church's organization, but there may have been other reasons as well.[24] Possibly most telling is the first-century Mediterranean conception of an elder as simply a mature man with seasoned judgment. Unlike the official office most churches recognize today, the early church elder/pastor may have been much less formal. In light of the multiple house churches that rose up throughout first-century cities and towns, elders were likely chosen from among the more mature and respected members of a household or community.[25]

On Paul's first missionary journey, he and Barnabas "appointed (*cheirotonesantes*) elders for them" (Acts 14:23).[26] Luke uses the term *cheiroto-*

24. Benjamin Merkle reviews the four most popular views on the origin of the elder in early church government. The office could have originated from (1) Old Testament leaders who were designated "elders" in the Septuagint, (2) the Sanhedrin, (3) the Jewish synagogue, or (4) the culture, as in a senior male within the community or family. Merkle concludes that the Christian office of elder was not directly borrowed from any of these. Instead, the church borrowed the title and "defined for itself the specific duties that those who held this title performed" (*40 Questions About Elders and Deacons*, 72–74).

25. See Campbell, *Elders: Seniority within Earliest Christianity*. Reformed theologian and missionary Harry R. Boer suggests, "It may also be that the older members of the Christian community were automatically looked upon as the leaders" (*Short History of the Early Church*, 28).

26. Most references to leadership in the New Testament are plural. We're told that "elders" were to be appointed "in every town" (Titus 1:5). It isn't entirely clear whether that plurality refers to multiple elders per town or multiple elders per church. We're also told that "Paul and Barnabas appointed elders for them in each church" (Acts 14:23). This seems to suggest that each church was composed of multiple elders. But does that refer to the city church, like Jerusalem, made up of multiple house churches, or something else? Although most denominations acknowledge a plurality of leadership in the early church, others argue for a single elder or pastor based on the sole "angel" of the churches of Revelation (Rev 2:1, 8, 12, 18; 3:1, 7, 14), the singular "overseer" mentioned by Paul (1 Tim 3:2), and the sole "elder" that appears in the Johannine Epistles (2 John 1; 3 John 1). Most see James as a primary leader over other elders in Jerusalem (Acts 12:17; 15:12–13; 21:18; Gal 1:19; 2:9), forecasting the role the bishop would later take on. As important as church government is, the Spirit never directed the early church to formalize a doctrine. Instead, their progress for God's kingdom was rather dynamic and more interested in action and growth than building governing bodies. For an introduction on the representative views

neo, which literally means to stretch out the hand (to vote). But it's unclear whether the elders were chosen and appointed or if they were appointed by voting. Moreover, we're not told what the criteria for selecting leaders might be until Paul provides a brief summary of qualifications in his letters to Titus and Timothy (Titus 1:5–7; 1 Tim 3:1–8). Based on those lists, it should be evident that Paul was primarily concerned with an overall godly lifestyle, rather than checking off a list of character qualities. Those who stood out were recognized as people of wisdom who were able to teach but not necessarily skilled at it.[27] They may not have been to seminary, but they knew God and manifested a godly maturity that others recognized.

Regarding the question of women in pastoral leadership roles, this is somewhat difficult to answer from the New Testament alone. In 1 Timothy 2:12, Paul says that he does not "tolerate" (*epitrepo*)[28] women "to teach or assume authority over (*authentein*) a man." He then grounds his logic not in a cultural sensitivity but in the biblical doctrine of creation, saying, "For Adam was formed first, then Eve. And Adam was not the one deceived" (vv. 13–14). While we consider Paul's intent, it should remain in the back of our minds that the fullest New Testament picture of worship, ministry, and mission seems to emphasize a move toward ever-increasing liberation and freedom, whether for slaves or women's rights. It also appears that the pastorate remains open to women largely due to the meaning of the Greek terms and construction found in 1 Timothy 2:12. Linda Belleville observes that the specific manner of teaching that Paul refers to is not teaching in general but teaching in a domineering way. We follow her lead when she remarks that

> the Greek verb *authentein* . . . is not found elsewhere in Paul's writings or the NT. In the Greek of the day, the word meant "domineer." . . . Furthermore, in the Greek, we see a "neither—nor" construction: "neither teach nor domineer" (NLT, "have authority over"). Such constructions in the NT pair synonyms ("neither despised

---

of church government, see Engle and Cowan, *Who Runs the Church?*; and Brand and Norman, *Perspectives on Church Government*.

27. Newton, *Elders in Congregational Life*, 38. Newton argues that not all elders are called to "pulpit ministry."

28. Through personal email correspondence with Dr. Daniel Wallace, we discussed a nuance of the Greek term ἐπιτρέπω that is not captured in lexicons; namely, *toleration*. For instance, Jesus stated, "Moses permitted (ἐπέτρεψεν) a man to write a certificate of divorce and send her away" (Mark 4:10). The nuance is clearly one of toleration: Moses *tolerated* divorce.

> nor scorned," Gal 4:14), . . . In this context it seems that the Greek correlative "neither—nor" defines a single activity. . . . This means that women here are not prohibited from roles that involve teaching men. The issue is rather the manner in which they teach—that is, they should not teach in a dictatorial or domineering way.[29]

Finally, the elder is a servant ministry intended to equip the saints. The experience of the first-century church was not a clergy-laity distinction but rather numerous complementary roles working together and sharing God's power while bearing not even a hint of *lording it over your faith* (2 Cor 1:24). The leaders were ministers among equals, men and women who recognized that all believers are fulltime ministers called to serve under the headship of Jesus Christ. The church of Corinth never once mentioned an elder or other leader taking over the worship service. Rather, every member ministered one to another through the manifestation of God's presence and gracious gifts (1 Cor 14:26).

As we consider various ministry roles in the church, the manner in which people enter their ministries is another important area that remains open, which is what we will focus on for the remainder of the chapter.

Excelling in Fulltime Ministry

Every believer commits to fulltime Christian service the moment we're saved, making each of us fulltime ministers who are responsible to fulfill our spiritual gifting. Much of what's expected in ministry will first be recognized by other believers instead of by our own self-identification as an apostle, prophet, or some other gifting. In the 1996 feature film *The Apostle*, Robert Duvall baptizes himself and thereby appoints himself as an apostle, but this is by no means the norm for our churches! In fact, the person who claims a title for himself should be approached with caution.

Although certain ministries like prophecy and evangelism do not necessarily require recognition and appointment by other believers, others will look at how an individual uses those gifts and will respectfully evaluate his faithfulness to God's word as well as the benefit to the body of Christ. God desires that we take an active interest in pursuing service that will most build up his church, but he also wants us to pursue ministries of personal interest that will ignite a fire of passion to reach out to the lost and turn this world upside down for Jesus. To accomplish this, you should know that

---

29. Belleville et al., *Cornerstone Biblical Commentary*, 55.

Ministry: God Shares His Power

God has gone so far as to call *you* his partner or "co-worker" (1 Cor 3:9; 2 Cor 6:1) and intends to consider your desires.

Because believers are a Spirit-led people, it should be taken for granted that much of where we serve will be based on God-given motivation and desire. However, that doesn't diminish the freedom we have to seek out ministries and ministry needs. It should encourage you to know that you are not ordained for one particular ministry or locked into one area of service but can prayerfully pursue your passion and burdens. Of course, once a person commits to a given ministry, she or he is responsible within that sphere of influence to abide and "fulfill your ministry" (2 Tim 4:5 ESV).

As we consider the believer's potential to excel in ministry, we will see that leadership and other ministry roles are open to us through divine and human appointment and on the basis of desire and availability.

God Appoints Ministers

Even when God calls the minister of his choice into a specific area of service, it doesn't always turn out for the best. We know from Scripture and from experience that God's will is not always done; otherwise, a prayer like "thy will be done in earth" would be in pretense only (Matt 6:10 KJV). This is the risk of being Creator and Lord over a world in which God honors choices that are truly free.

God may initially choose a person for a specific ministry that ultimately turns out for good *or bad*, even though he was basing that choice on an already proven character and faith. This was the case with men like Moses, David, and King Saul. God chose Saul not for just any position but to be the first king of Israel! No doubt Yahweh had plans for Saul that were meant to bring about great blessing for Israel from generation to generation. Yet in the end, Saul's disobedience led to God's grim change of mind. Yahweh told the prophet Samuel, "I regret that I have made Saul king, because he has turned away from me and has not carried out my instructions" (1 Sam 15:11a). Although Samuel had always been a faithful prophet to Yahweh, he didn't take Yahweh's regret lightly: "Samuel was angry, and he cried out to the Lord all that night" (v. 11b). Here, Scripture suggests that Samuel wasn't happy with God's decision or perhaps with Saul himself, so by crying out throughout the night, it appears that Samuel was attempting to change God's mind just as Moses and others had done.

In Jesus' ministry, he had personally selected each of his twelve apostles, those who would be sent out to fulfill the foundational post-resurrection ministry of establishing his church in the new age. Even so, Jesus' personal call didn't stop Judas Iscariot from being influenced by Satan and using his freedom to pursue a path of destruction (Luke 22:3–4; Matt 27:3–5). But despite Judas's failure, the Lord didn't become apprehensive about his choices but later chose the Apostle Paul whose obsession had been to destroy the church (Acts 8:3). Even with a background of religious, murderous piety, Paul went on to serve Christ's kingdom as a true representative of the heart of God, sharing even the "affection of Christ Jesus" for God's people (Phil 1:8). In God's infinite grace, he can call even the very *worst* of sinners to his service (1 Cor 15:9). If you have only ever seen yourself in a negative light and still struggle to accept that God would call you to minister, be certain that he truly is calling you, because every believer is called to fulltime Christian service.

God can call anyone at any time into any ministry in his church, but his "call" is not required. Many assume that leadership roles are settled in God's mind and that all leaders must sense "the call" or experience some confirming event in their lives. Of course, that could be the case, as with men like Abraham, Samuel, and the Twelve, but surely it is the exception rather than the rule. Absent from Paul's instructions to Titus (1:5–9) for appointing elders "is any reference to appointing those who are, in modern jargon, 'called to preach.'"[30]

People Appoint Ministers

Throughout Acts and Paul's letters, people are appointed by Spirit-led leadership into positions of authority and other ministry responsibility. This appointment can occur through election or by direct commission. Such a task requires a great deal of discernment but also rests upon the approval of a plurality of gifted individuals, whether that be a plurality of elders or the whole congregation. Many of the leaders of first-century churches were appointed by apostles, but as the churches matured, that responsibility necessarily fell into the hands of local churches.

The authority of the first apostles did not continue indefinitely. As an apostle, Paul had a unique gift and calling as well as a unique responsibility and authority over the churches. He was, in large part, responsible for

---

30. Newton, *Elders in Congregational Life*, 38.

all the churches (2 Cor 11:28). But the apostles of the first century had a unique authority that cannot be duplicated today. For example, in order to replace Judas's position among the Twelve, they looked at men who had walked with Jesus since the time of John's baptism and who had also witnessed Jesus' resurrection firsthand (Acts 1:21–22). This, of course, was not the case with all first-century apostles, as even the Apostle Paul did not meet that criteria. Nevertheless, there was something unique about their role and sphere of authority.

Because we no longer have the original apostles around today, local churches now bear the burden to prayerfully and thoughtfully consider who meets the qualifications of leadership (1 Tim 3:1–7). It is of utmost importance to select men and women of high moral character without ignoring other important qualities, such as the ability to teach and correct and to have sufficient leadership skills. It's often the case that those gifted for leadership are already present in any seasoned congregation and can be discovered without having to search outside the local church. It can also be the case that some churches are young and immature and would therefore benefit from outside leadership (cf. Titus 1:5–9).[31]

Whether churches appoint, elect, or even "cast lots" after selecting a person of character and ability, there is something awe-inspiring about God's desire for believers to participate with him in the high calling and extreme responsibility of leading and ministering to his people.[32] As Chief Shepherd, Jesus demonstrates that he shares his own power and authority through delegation. Instead of sovereignly appointing leaders, he prefers to give his church a voice in the process. He takes into account our identification of gifted individuals and allows our choices to have real consequences as we experience a living church.

---

31. Regarding Paul's instructions to Titus, Samuel Ngewa provides a helpful observation: "In instructing Titus to appoint elders, Paul is not making a theological statement governing all situations. It was simply the case that the church in Crete was young, and the best approach there was to appoint the elders. In some churches today elders are still appointed, while in others they are elected by the members. The method does not matter; what is important is that those who lead the church have the right qualities to be leaders" (*1 and 2 Timothy*, 338).

32. In Acts 1:23–26, in order to fill Judas's empty position, the apostles cast lots to decide between two equally qualified men.

People Pursue Ministry

If God shares his power but also desires to see human freedom played out in every area of church life, the implications are profound and demonstrate a church more alive and more involved than many may realize. God is heavily invested in our free choices, but he still reserves the right to call some people into ministry more specifically than he calls others. The church must then identify those individuals for leadership by whatever thoughtful means necessary.

There are few passages in the New Testament that address leadership selection. When someone is identified as a gifted person of high character, even before being appointed or elected, there must be some indicator to help us discern God's will. The Pastoral Epistles suggest that a most revealing sign is the burden or passion that a person has to pursue the pastorate: "Here is a trustworthy saying: Whoever aspires (*oregetai*) to be an overseer desires a noble task" (1 Tim 3:1). Regarding the Greek root word *orego*, Raymond Collins comments that such aspirations "would connote striving after something good, even the kingship (see, e.g., Plutarch, *Solon* 29.3; *Phocion* 17.1; Josephus, Life 13 § 70, a passage that uses both aspire and desire)."[33] The believer's personal striving is viewed in the best possible light: not as a greedy or selfish endeavor but one that arises out of good intent. It is a positive thing to want to serve God in an area that interests you, and this isn't limited to leadership gifts. Paul tells us to "eagerly desire [all] gifts of the Spirit" (1 Cor 14:1).

One of the most precious aspects in the way God provides leadership and other important ministries is that he desires to involve us in the process. He wants us to thoughtfully consider the areas of ministry that interest us, but we should also adopt an attitude of availability, so that we will be available when the need arises. Because God hasn't ordained every detail of human existence, including the details of leadership and other roles in the church, believers are expected to prepare themselves for the opportunity to serve. God may be calling you into unexpected situations to accomplish unexpected exploits for his kingdom! "And who knows whether you have not come to the kingdom for such a time as this?" (Esth 4:14 ESV).

Deborah, a prophet and judge in Old Testament times, is one example of a woman who had the right character and temperament to take on a significant leadership role in a culture dominated by men, and God used

---

33. Collins, *1 and 2 Timothy*, 79.

her mightily (Jud 4–5)! Deborah knew how important it is to be available and open to the needs of the work God has for us. She even compiled a song and sang of the availability of God's people to be used by him. She sang, "My heart is with Israel's princes, with the willing volunteers among the people. Praise the LORD!" (Jud 5:9). For Deborah, it was praiseworthy that those "volunteers" were eager to serve the LORD and had willingly prepared and offered themselves to the need of God's work.

By being available, believers can pursue areas of ministry that they're passionate about even without sensing an inward calling, because in many cases, *the desire is the inward call*. Although each of us should be aware of our personal ambitions, we're also expected to remain open and available to serve the needs around us. God calls us to minister whether it's convenient or not because the needs are always right in front of us. Paul exhorts Timothy and everyone else who reads his letter, "Be prepared, whether the time is favorable or not" (2 Tim 4:2 NLT).

Conclusion

We first looked at the fivefold ministry: apostles, prophets, evangelists, pastors, and teachers. Our broad survey of the biblical material revealed that there is no detailed outline for leadership in God's church or for other closely related ministries. What we see is a theological portrait of godly men and women living out the flexibility of church life with the help of God's presence and the inspiring leadership of the Holy Spirit; the church is never without the Spirit of Jesus to guide us. And because present-day pastors and other ministers are without a strict pattern to follow, we're all the more dependent on God's daily word and fellowship to lead us. As it is with the rest of the spiritual gifts in the church, the form and function of the fivefold ministry remain largely open.

We then turned our attention to the dynamics of getting involved in ministry. Believers enter various gifted roles through divine or human appointment and on the basis of desire and availability. Ministry is an area in which God occasionally takes the sovereign prerogative to handpick his man or woman, but in the majority of cases, it is the church's responsibility to recognize leaders without neglecting the full spectrum of *charismata*. God is delighted for us to pursue areas of service that we are passionate about as we prepare ourselves for the needs before us.

9

Revival: God Shares His Glory

SHARING IN GOD'S PRESENCE should be a life-changing revelation for each of us, if we begin to grasp the depths of belonging to God. In fact, we are *meant* to belong to him. The sense of belonging that our humanity gropes for is found in the one who shares everything with us. The divine being is so perfectly compatible with our humanness that he became one of us, sharing in our humanhood so that we can share in him. This implies that God's presence is actually made available to us through the vehicle of our humanity. Rather than hindering us and keeping us from knowing him, he uses our humanness to make his presence known, because in Jesus Christ, he is now the human God.

The presence of God should become so personal to our sense of being that we won't settle for anything less than full ignition into an awareness of him. But this requires revival, the awakening of the heart to the realization that our belonging is in God and we are his children—we know him and must become like him. Salvation itself is the microcosmic display of revival, and if taken seriously and brought to its ultimate conclusion, the church will live in the spirit of revival. As individual hearts are awakened, the slumbering church becomes awakened to a fresh zeal for the coming reign of God and to a renewed solidarity with those who are broken and hurting.

Paul tells us that the purpose for the saving presence of God in our lives is "that you might share in the glory of our Lord Jesus Christ" (2 Thess 2:14). So to conclude our journey into sharing in God's presence, we'll focus on the glory of the divine presence—the *value* of the divine being—as it is best displayed in the Spirit of Jesus Christ. We'll first see how Jesus and the

Spirit are the most reliable means for understanding the divine presence in the world, and we'll conclude in a devotional atmosphere of revival as we consider the potential for God's powerful presence to once again touch his church throughout the world.[1]

Jesus Reveals God

The top priority of any theology should be to know God and to know him intimately. The most direct and conveniently packaged revelation of God is found in the person Jesus Christ. Jesus is the true and reliable "image of the invisible God" (Col 1:15), and because the essence of God hasn't always included human nature, Jesus' appearance should lead us to no other conclusion than to affirm that God does in fact change: "Who, being in very nature God, did not consider equality with God something to be used to his own advantage; rather, he made himself nothing by taking the very nature of a servant, being made in human likeness. And being found in appearance as a man, he humbled himself . . ." (Phil 2:6–8). There is a mysterious tone here that immediately betrays any notion that God doesn't change. Significant change took place in God when the second person of the Trinity "humbled himself" and "made himself nothing."

We touched on this theme in chapter one and will conclude the book on this theme, because *sharing in God* can only happen by knowing him through the humanness of Jesus Christ. One of the most profound revelations of the divine being is the humility of the Almighty God to assume the humble role of a servant. By becoming a man, the Godhead experienced not merely a change in appearance but an undeniable change in essence. The internal makeup of the Trinity became something it previously was not! At least to our knowledge, the incarnation is the most radical change that has occurred with God, yet there also remains a changeability related to God's knowledge and experience. God's practical changeability occurs frequently in relation to his creatures as he seeks out, interacts with, responds to, and even blesses and judges people. But such change never implies that the *character* of God in any way changes, because "God is faithful" (1 Cor

---

1. As Michael Hundley remarks, "Divine Presence, like divinity itself, is difficult to explain, much less envision, as one must describe in human terms what by definition transcends them. Such a quest remains an effort to grasp the ungraspable" (*Keeping Heaven on Earth*, 39).

1:9; 2 Cor 1:18) and will always remain true to his ultimate standard of love. While some aspects of God will always change, other aspects cannot.

Divine changeability is best understood in the context of love, because love is experiential and always longs to share in reciprocal love with free creatures. In Jesus Christ, believers "do not have a high priest who is unable to empathize with our weaknesses" (Heb 4:15), which is a very human experience. This is a profound statement about the ability of Jesus, and therefore of God, to be affected by and to enter into our individual experiences. Through Jesus Christ, God truly does embrace us with human compassion because he is "really related" to us. We never have to doubt that our loving God "is really related to his creatures, where 'really related' means that it makes a difference to God how things are with the creatures."[2]

God is *most moved* by the experiences of a world full of the people he has chosen to relate to. Not only are his actions appropriate in response to what happens to humanity throughout history, but he also feels, experiences, and reacts to our pain and struggles, as well as to our joys and pleasures. Yet somehow, God is not bipolar in his simultaneous experience of every human being on earth. There is an effortless perfection in God's all-powerful knowledge, so he is more than capable of feeling and experiencing a divine empathy for billions of different human emotions and experiences all occurring at any given instant throughout the world. The psalmist affirms, "Great is our Lord, and abundant in power; his understanding is beyond measure" (Ps 147:5 ESV). Indeed, God understands us and loves us still.

The epitome of the vulnerable love of God is Jesus Christ crucified, a reality of God's experience that cannot be avoided. Jesus Christ, while suffering at the hands of his own creatures, thereby experienced change that involved God's own pain and suffering. When Jesus died a physical death, he experienced change in his humanity, then another kind of change in resurrection when he was exalted to the right hand of the Father. Jesus reveals that God does change and is not at all insecure or threatened by his perfect changeability.[3]

---

2. Hasker, "An Adequate God," 216.

3. Related to changeability, Jesus exemplifies the humility of the Godhead to refuse to be defined in terms of our common misunderstandings of what it means to be an all-powerful and all-knowing God. Regarding the timing of the end of this present age, Jesus declares, "But about that day or hour no one knows, not even the angels in heaven, nor the Son, but only the Father" (Mark 13:32). Perhaps even more telling are the questions that Jesus poses to the Father before and during the crucifixion. Leading up to the cross,

Revival: God Shares His Glory

To better understand God's word, and therefore, God's heart, we use exegetical methods, such as the study of cultural background or the original languages, but there is no greater exegetical rule than Jesus Christ himself. He is the most reliable *exegesis* of the eternal Godhead, the one who explains God: "No one has ever seen God, but the one and only Son, who is himself God and is in closest relationship with the Father, has made him known (*exegesato*)" (John 1:18).[4] Because Jesus is the unique one, closest to the Father's heart, "himself God," there is no other more reliable interpreter or exegete (from *exegesato*) to reveal God to us. And because Jesus Christ changed in birth, in life, in death, and in resurrection, God has also changed and is worthy of our praise because of it.

"And Jesus grew in wisdom and stature, and in favor with God and man" (Luke 2:52). As a human being, Jesus grew older and wiser. His changeability as a person doesn't in any way diminish the accuracy of his representation of the Godhead. God could not have become human if the human template did not match God's eternal nature based upon a special predesigned compatibility. One of the highest truths to embrace is that people have truly been made in God's image. If we're going to begin to know what it means to be human, we must reflect upon God himself and his ultimate revelation to us in the person of Jesus Christ.

Jesus is the exact representation and perfect expression of the Godhead, which proportionately includes his humanity as a necessary component in our comprehending God. Although God is uncreated, the best way to know him is through his creation and, particularly, through Jesus' human experience. God is everlasting, yet his temporal expression in Christ is the most accurate representation of him. Moreover, Jesus is what humanity was intended to be before the fall! It was never human nature that was offensive to our representation of God, but rather death and mortality that were later

---

Jesus inquires of God, "Father, *if* you are willing, take this cup from me; yet not my will, but yours be done" (Luke 22:42, emphasis added). Later, from the cross, Jesus cries out, "My God, my God, *why* have you forsaken me?" (Mark 15:34, emphasis added). None of those statements can be reconciled with a God of exhaustive foreknowledge. Because Jesus Christ is the epitome of divine changeableness, through him we have a better frame of reference for interpreting and understanding God's perfect changeability throughout Scripture.

4. Our theological method begins with Jesus Christ as the lens through which we arrive at any systematic presentation of Scripture. However, not all biblical interpreters will agree on how to apply this, just as Migliore remarks, "Differences in theological method reflect fundamental differences in understandings of revelation and the mode of God's presence in the world" (*Faith Seeking Understanding*, 14).

added to our nature when humans sinned in the garden. At that point, human nature became mortal nature and the odor of death became offensive.

We couldn't be more emphatic that the humanity of Christ is essential revelation for us to know God and share in his presence. If we want to share in God, it will be by getting to know his presence through the person of Christ. God's unknowable and transcendent glory is not ultimately what makes him divine, but his loving, relational, self-sacrificial nature as it is revealed in the person of Christ. Jesus' entire ministry focused on the priority of relationship and self-giving. He sought relationship within every socio-economic stratum of society, with the poor and the rich alike. Relationship is everything to Jesus, so even in his death, he maintained the divine relationship by his dependence upon the Father and the Spirit (Heb 9:14). Jesus is the final revelation to humanity to sufficiently disclose the nature and presence of God.

Jesus Reveals God's Presence

If we're going to better understand the mode of God's presence in the world, we must look to Jesus. The ultimate disclosure of the internal life of God comes to us through the *activities* of the divine persons in salvation history, what theologians call the triune economy. In other words, God's actions reveal who he is. Therefore, if God's actions in salvation history (Father Creator, Son Redeemer, Spirit Renewer) are an accurate depiction of God's everlasting internal existence, then we should also be able to discern God's internal nature through its unique expression in the person of Christ.

Once and for all, the incarnation reveals to the world that it is eternally within God's ability *and nature* to locate himself spatially in one place and not another, if he so chooses. We must confess, however, that we don't fully understand the nature of his movement, whether his presence changes only by intensification or by an actual coming and going.[5] What we do know is that God is perfectly capable of limiting his own presence in one manner or another, because that was precisely the decision made with regard to the incarnation when God became a human being. The Apostle Paul recognized that the incarnation was an event of time and place for the Godhead: "But when the set time had fully come, God sent his Son, born of a woman,

---

5. In *God's Absence and the Charismatic Presence*, I argue for the latter: that an unmitigated divine absence is a real scriptural possibility. This was presented, however, in the form of a proposal rather than a theological conclusion.

born under the law" (Gal 4:4). The Son, begotten and not created, eternally generating from the Father, was born.

It was within *time* that Jesus arrived locally—that God was localized—and *born* into a world *under the law*. Jesus never once acted independently but always in sync with both the Father (John 5:30) and the Spirit (Matt 12:28), revealing the cooperation of the Trinity even in the self-limited sphere of Jesus' personal existence. The incarnation boldly asserts that God may remove the impression of an unlimited spatial occupation by replacing it with a direct and personal presence. In other words, God's omnipresence can become focused in one place and not another through the presence of Jesus.

Until the incarnation, God limited himself to the sphere of a temporary epiphany (e.g., burning bush, gushing rock, pillar of fire, ark of the covenant, etc.) or an angelic presence that, throughout history, had been far removed from people's experiences. One day Yahweh might appear in a cloud or rock or fiery bush, but the next day he might appear over the ark of the covenant or on a mountain. So through the incarnation, God was actually shedding the *limitation* of his heretofore hidden and elusive presence. We could even say that the former limited sphere of God's presence was finally set free!

The incarnation reveals a much less limited God, if we can possibly conceive of that. Not only was Yahweh once limited by the hiddenness of his broad presence and the elusiveness of his special temporary presences, but until the incarnation, God was also limited by the absolute inability of people to see or experience him, or they would die![6] To a significant degree, the preincarnate limitations had negatively affected God's priority for community and obscured the image of God as relational.[7] Yet in Christ Jesus, that barrier was removed in a way never before experienced by God or

---

6. Exodus 33:20 says, "No one may see me and live." Surely *seeing* is not the sole concern here but stands as a metonym of presence; more literally, no one may come into contact with my presence and live! See also Gen 32:30; Judg 6:22–23; John 1:18.

7. Prior to the incarnation, the Hebrew proverbial tradition described God as transcending our spatial frame of reference: "'Do not I fill heaven and earth?' declares the Lord" (Jer 23:24). Such proverbial traditions instill in us an awe for divine transcendence but propel the immanence, closeness, and relatability of God into a vacuum that's difficult to escape from—until Jesus! In other words, we never quite understood the deity until the incarnation. In Christ Jesus, the elusive and transcendent presence is realized as an immanent and relational presence. In the practice of theology, the language of *transcendence* refers to God's distance from people due to his almightiness and unique standing as deity. *Immanence* refers to God's closeness to people.

people. Until Jesus, the divine encounters experienced by every king, priest, prophet, and believer had been a secondary encounter at best. But because God mediates his presence through the *creation* (cloud, angel, fire, etc.), the Father uniquely *created* a divine Son to grant us firsthand contact with deity! "No one has ever seen God, but the one and only Son, who is himself God and is in closest relationship with the Father, has made him known" (John 1:18). No one has come into contact with Yahweh, until now. Jesus knows Yahweh and makes him known to us, so that we learn most about God and his presence through the person Jesus Christ.

The truth cannot be overstated that Jesus not only defines God's presence in the world but also reveals to us the divine presence *par excellence*.[8] Through the incarnation, God's presence has been permanently set free from its limited expression throughout the old covenant. The barriers under the old covenant that kept people at a distance were forever destroyed when Jesus split open the way into the Holy of Holies, which was represented at his death when the temple veil was torn in two (Matt 27:51; cf. 2 Cor 3:15–17). As the perfect image of God, Jesus Christ is the final word on the divine presence in the world. Jesus' new covenant ministry of dispensing the Spirit is Scripture's progressive record (in the vein of progressive revelation) of how the incarnation definitively broadcasts God's presence until the end of the age. This latest revelation should, therefore, replace any prior knowledge or assumption regarding the divine presence.

Jesus Sends His Presence

The Son will always be the most reliable indicator of God's presence in the world and the primary source of the divine presence to the world. This truth was brought to light at Pentecost when Jesus poured out the Spirit, the very presence of God.[9] By virtue of Jesus' victory over death, in his trifold office of Priest, Prophet, and King, Jesus demonstrates that no one else enjoys the prerogative and privilege of dispensing God's presence into the world. At Pentecost, Peter emphasized the victory of the new resurrection

---

8. Regarding the incarnation, Samuel Terrien remarks that "it was the Hebraic theology of presence which dominated all the interpretations of the person of Jesus, from Mark to Revelation" (*Elusive Presence*, 30).

9. Regarding the Spirit as God's presence, in his thorough treatment of the Spirit in Paul's writings, pentecostal scholar Gordon Fee says that the Holy Spirit is "the personal presence of God himself" (*God's Empowering Presence*, 6).

Revival: God Shares His Glory

presence of King Jesus, declaring, "Exalted to the right hand of God, [Jesus] has received from the Father the promised Holy Spirit and has poured out what you now see and hear" (Acts 2:33). Consequently, the Father doesn't just release his presence to anyone in any place but has entrusted that ministry to the Son.

But as Jesus pours out the Spirit upon those who believe, how do we experience God's presence in the world? To begin with, the divine person of the Spirit—the third person of the Trinity—*is* the presence of God in the world (cf. Gen 6:3).[10] In common Hebrew parallelism, David petitioned the LORD, "Do not cast me from your presence (*panim*) or take your Holy Spirit (*ruach*) from me" (Ps 51:11; cf. 104:29–30). In the Hebrew, David beseeched God not to expel him from before his "face" (*panim*), a figure of speech representing God's overall presence. Through a synonymous parallel, David therefore equated an expulsion from God's presence with a removal of God's Spirit (*ruach*).

The same kind of synonymous parallelism is found in Psalm 139: "Where can I go from your Spirit (*ruach*)? Where can I flee from your presence (*panim*)?" (v. 7). Again, the psalmist has no quibble with equating God's Spirit with his presence. Commenting on this verse, one writer says, "In the psalmist's mind the spirit of Yahweh is concomitant with his universal presence throughout all of the created order."[11] Through the words of the prophet Ezekiel, God anticipated the outpouring of his presence upon his people, saying, "I will no longer hide my face (*panim*) from them, for I will pour out my Spirit (*ruach*) on the people of Israel, declares the Sovereign LORD" (Ezek 39:29). It's evident, here, that Yahweh longed for the day that his people would experience his Spirit—namely, his presence—in a profoundly personal way, which would ultimately be fulfilled through the Lord Jesus Christ.[12]

---

10. Moltmann's Trinitarian pneumatology describes the Spirit as "the name given to the experienced presence of God" (*Spirit of Life*, 120). I should clarify, however, that because the Spirit is more than his functions, he is not solely the *experiential* presence of God in the world. He is one person among three who eternally co-exist as the triune Godhead.

11. Grant, "Spirit and Presence in Psalm 139," 145. Also commenting on Psalm 139:7, Christopher Wright states that "Jesus knew that . . . God is everywhere present through his Spirit" (*Knowing the Holy Spirit*, 22).

12. Anthony Thiselton, while describing the Holy Spirit as an agent or extension of God, also concludes that "he is often understood as more than the Agent of God; *he represents God's presence*." Thiselton points out that, after the exile, God reassured his people of his presence by specifically using the language of his Spirit: "'And my Spirit remains

Sharing in God's Presence

Moving on to Jesus' role in this, in highly symbolic language, the book of Revelation describes the unique reigning position of Jesus the Lamb as the dispatch center for God's spiritual presence: "Then I saw a Lamb, looking as if it had been slain, standing at the center of the throne, encircled by the four living creatures and the elders. The Lamb had seven horns and seven eyes, which are the seven spirits of God sent out (*apostello*) into all the earth" (Rev 5:6; cf. Zech 4:10). The Greek term *apostello* emphasizes the sender and draws attention to the enthroned Lamb as the one from whom the generating Spirit is sent. Because the seven spirits are equated with the Lamb's own eyes, it is evident that he's sending out a part of himself! Those sevenfold "spirits of God" sound much like the "Spirit of God" that's first mentioned in Genesis 1:2 when "the Spirit of God was hovering over the waters." Just as God's Spirit hovered over the face of those dark waters, is it possible that the divine presence is much like a roving presence throughout the world, sent by Jesus to ensure that his touch reaches everyone?

Given such unusual imagery as the "hovering" Spirit of God in Genesis and the "seven spirits of God" in Revelation, what would be a helpful illustration to better understand God's presence in the world? Although no perfect analogy exists, let's consider the wind. Even before God spoke a single word at the creation, the Old Testament introduces the creative presence as God's Spirit: "In the beginning God created the heavens and the earth. Now the earth was formless and empty, darkness was over the surface of the deep, and the Spirit (*ruach*) of God was hovering over the waters" (Gen 1:1–2). Seeing that the Hebrew word *ruach* can be translated as breath, wind, or spirit, the context suggests that God was manifesting himself like a powerful *wind* that was hovering over the chaos of the world.[13] Hence, we can easily liken the divine presence to the winds that blow throughout the world (Exod 10:13; Num 11:31; Jer 49:36). As the wind blows, its presence can extend throughout the whole earth and even reach unexpected places.[14]

Focusing on the analogy of wind, breath, and spirit may help us to grasp the manner in which God's presence works in the world. While depicting the revival of the nation of Israel after exile, the prophet Ezekiel

among you. Do not fear' (Hag 2:5)" (*Holy Spirit*, 4, 13, emphasis original).

13. The NRSV translates Genesis 1:2b as "a wind from God." For variations on how to interpret *ruach* in Genesis 1:2, see Westermann, *Genesis 1–11: A Commentary*, 106–8; and Young, "The Interpretation of Gen. 1:2," 174–78.

14. There are some parts of the world, however, that have different intensifications of wind and other areas where wind is totally absent, such as under the dark waters of the sea, under the earth, in a deep cave, or in a valley at night.

offers a unique prophetic picture of where the Spirit-presence of God comes from:

> So I prophesied as I was commanded. And as I was prophesying, there was a noise, a rattling sound, and the bones came together, bone to bone. I looked, and tendons and flesh appeared on them and skin covered them, but there was no breath (*ruach*) in them. Then he said to me, "Prophesy to the breath (*ruach*); prophesy, son of man, and say to it, 'This is what the Sovereign LORD says: Come, breath (*ruach*), from the four winds (*ruach*) and breathe (*ruach*) into these slain, that they may live.'" (Ezek 37:7–9)

According to Ezekiel, the spirit/breath blows in from the four winds—namely, from every corner of the inhabited creation—which indicates something of how God's presence is generally at work in the world (cf. Rev 7:1). The wind is called upon by the prophet, and the wind is sent to revive the fallen so that they may live. Just as this prophet can *call* forth the four winds, so can the ultimate Prophet, Jesus, *send* forth the four winds.

If the Spirit can be pictured as the wind, then perhaps our analogy can adopt an image for Jesus as well, such as a single Mountain that powerfully stands out in the world (cf. Dan 2:35, 44). The presence of God would then be represented by *Wind* (Spirit) that surrounds and goes out from that single *Mountain* (Christ): "Now a wind went out from the LORD" (Num 11:31; cf. Gen 8:1). As that wind is blown over every valley, it is occasionally disrupted by watery places, such as seas and oceans, which represent chaos and the enemies of God (e.g., Job 38:8–11). So in those places, God's windy presence can be drastically disturbed. But this is where our analogy ends, because even Jesus taught that there will always be an element of mystery that surrounds the divine presence: "The wind blows wherever it pleases" (John 3:8).

Although Jesus is the custodian of God's presence, one of the most ancient decisions of the church, the Niceno-Constantinopolitan Creed (AD 381), included language that the Holy Spirit proceeded from the Father (cf. John 14:26; 15:26). The Son wasn't ignored, but this pointed to the Father as the source and the Son as the intermediate agency of the Spirit's presence in the world. To this the church later added the phrase, *and the Son*, known as the *filioque* clause (Latin, *and the son*), which intended to clarify that the Spirit proceeded from *both* the Father and the Son. A concern of Eastern Orthodox theologians has been that this clause haphazardly restricts the activity of the Holy Spirit to where the incarnate Christ is explicitly proclaimed and believed upon.[15] Their concern helps to make our point—namely, that people receive the Spirit through the second person of the Trinity. But Scripture never restricts the Spirit's activity to Gospel proclamation. Even though the embodied message is the norm for God's outbreaking presence in the world, the Spirit has been active throughout the creation (Gen 1:2; Ps 104:30), even if he does remain dependent upon the one who sends him.

Just as the roving and investigating "eyes of the LORD" are said to "move to and fro throughout the earth" (2 Chr 16:9 NASB), so God's presence is not limited to the spoken message. The Spirit is free to move about in the world, but the burden to direct him into people's lives belongs to Jesus.

Jesus Sends Revival

As Jesus shares his Spirit, revival is never far behind. Revival tends to break from the systematic approaches that we're familiar with and brings us back to a simple dialogue with our ever-present Savior. But because prayer is often not as easy as it sounds, it's important that each of us find our own personal language of dialogue with God. The traditional methods of folding hands and getting on your knees don't always fit, so find your own language of prayer and devotion. It may help you to draw or doodle, paint or pace, lie down or journal, sing or yell, but take time to find the language that best suits you and will support your frequent return to the secret place of God's presence—because our revival depends on it! And because prayer can be expressed in any number of ways, the writer of Lamentations reminds us that simply pouring out our hearts can keep us in the presence of God: "Pour out your heart like water before the presence of the Lord!" (Lam 2:19 ESV).

It is no exaggeration that compassionate prayer is essential if the church is going to once again enjoy the privileges and impact of revival. Prayer is the only choice for a Spirit-filled remnant! The prophet Isaiah once said, "The fortress will be abandoned, the noisy city deserted; citadel and watchtower will become a wasteland forever, the delight of donkeys, a pasture for flocks, till the Spirit is poured on us from on high, and the desert becomes a fertile field, and the fertile field seems like a forest" (Isa 32:14–15). This vivid language should resonate with us because it offers a

---

15. Migliore, *Faith Seeking Understanding*, 170.

timely reminder of just how radically the Spirit can change things when he shows up. Isn't it a fresh movement of the Spirit that we've all been waiting for? And why shouldn't we expect the "fertile field" of revival to be ushered in by a fresh outpouring of God's Spirit *in this generation?* It may come as a surprise to you, but we could be just one prayer away from a worldwide revival. And because God can wake us up, revival should be our painstaking and unrelenting prayer.

Revival and Conviction

Historically, revival is known for the intense conviction of sin that comes over believers and nonbelievers alike. David Lloyd-Jones summarizes revival as bringing "a sense of the majesty of God, a personal sinfulness, [a sense] of the wonder of salvation through Jesus Christ and a desire that others might know it."[16] It seems to be the general consensus among historians and those who have observed or experienced revival that there is a heightened awareness and sensitivity to personal responsibility over one's sin, especially in the way it impacts and impedes the church at large. Revival brings a profound conviction over any fault or failure to respond to God in the daily Christian walk. That conviction can be so overwhelming because sin is the one thing that can defeat, and even expel, God's presence from a person's life.

Lloyd-Jones goes on to describe the purpose for revival: "God does this thing from time to time, God sends revival, blessing, upon the church, in order that he may do something with respect to those who are outside him. He is doing something that is going to arrest the attention of all the people of the earth.... This is the reason—the glory of God."[17] The reason for revival is clear, and it's not for the church to enjoy the personal excitement and ecstatics of God's presence among us, though that is surely a glorious byproduct. The reason is that Almighty God might "arrest the attention" of those distant from him, those "outside him." In Scripture, when God brought his presence near to the people to perform miraculous wonders, it was to benefit all the nations. Under the leadership of Joshua, after Yahweh had split the Jordan River just as he had split the Red Sea, Scripture attests, "He did this so that all the peoples of the earth might know that the

---

16. Lloyd-Jones, *Revival*, 105.
17. Ibid., 119.

hand of the LORD is powerful and so that you might always fear the LORD your God" (Josh 4:24).

Revival is God's attempt to grab the attention of those who have so distanced themselves that nothing else could possibly reach them. Nothing, that is, except for the radical expression of his loving presence that comes to his people in the life-shaking, foundation-trembling experience of revival. The ultimate expression of love from the divine presence was the crucifixion of Jesus Christ, but the present expression is God's life within his people because of the victory of Christ's resurrection. The purpose of revival is to reach the lost while the motive is to glorify God and exalt the Victor of human history, the Lord Jesus Christ. God is glorified as people experience the realization that he has not abandoned the lost who have so totally distanced him. Even as he continues to reach out to those who utterly reject and neglect him, in a very real way, he wants and needs the church's help.

Here is my definition of revival: *Revival is the awakening of the corporate heart to accept personal responsibility over sin. This conviction emboldens the Christian community to battle against sin's distance by drawing near to God and wielding his loving presence as our greatest weapon.* Revival helps us to accept that we belong to God and he belongs to us. When people are lost, they are lost to God's loving presence. So during revival, as God draws near to his church and manifests his glory in dramatic and tangible ways, a healthy conviction of sin reminds us not only that Holy God has drawn near but that we are on mission to bring deliverance to those who live outside God's glorious, convicting presence.

Conviction in the Christian life should be embraced as a gift of God's presence. Conviction is always a sign that God is near, bridging the gap, breaking the distance between us, and offering his hand of fellowship. Hosea said it like this: "Come, let us return to the LORD. He has torn us to pieces but he will heal us; he has injured us but he will bind up our wounds. After two days he will revive us; on the third day he will restore us, that we may live in his presence" (Hos 6:1–3). Hosea's chief concern is for the people of God to "live in his presence" so that we can experience true healing, revival, and restoration.

Even though believers can no longer experience any real distance from God, our personal sin can become an occasion that opens our minds to Satan's kingdom. Satan uses the sins of believers to deceive us into sensing that a distance remains between us and our heavenly Father, despite the victory of the cross. Rather than leading us into *conviction* that results in freedom and closeness, deception brings *guilt* and shame, resulting in psychological and emotional distance from God that feels quite real in our experience. Because of this, believers can often live at an illusory distance from God, a distance of self-deception that doesn't really exist. But Jesus says to his followers, "I am with you always," and he means it (Matt 28:20). Revival shakes away the lies of distance propagated by "the accuser of our brethren" while bringing both believer and nonbeliever to their knees in a life-changing repentance and acceptance of the forgiving love of God (Rev 12:10 KJV).

Because revival is continually within the church's grasp, it remains our responsibility to take the initiative. The openness of revival means that the opportunity is ever-present and open before us to ignite the wildfire of awakening. God longs to grant the church an intensification of his presence if we will pay the price and continually draw near to him through prayer *and fasting* to release the fullness that's available to every generation (Isa 58:6–8). Although fasting can be painstaking, it is a necessary discipline to add to prayer. When we fast, we set apart time to deny our flesh of its needs or privileges in order to focus our reliance upon a feast of spiritual sustenance and the nourishment of divine presence. In many ways, while we fast and pray, the church still behaves as if God is so close-minded that we must wait upon some sovereign timetable before we can experience true awakening. But even the psalmist says, "You who seek God, let your hearts revive" (Ps 69:32 ESV). While it's true that revival is dependent upon God, the opportunity is always available to God's people to *let our hearts revive* by surrendering and seeking him with all that we are.

God is waiting for you! "If my people, who are called by my name, will humble themselves and pray and seek my face and turn from their wicked ways, then I will hear from heaven, and I will forgive their sin and will heal their land" (2 Chr 7:14). God says—I will, I will, I will! God desires thoughtful, time-consuming *prayer* as we seek his face, and he commands us to turn from our wicked ways to embrace a profound *holiness*, which is the rebuttal and rebuke of the distance produced by sin. "Heal[ing] their land" means that renewal can become so widespread that it begins in the individual heart, spreads to the local church, and is then unreservedly unleashed into the community and every sphere of social, religious, and political life, so that it finally branches out into *all* the land, because genuine revival can affect the entirety of creation!

Revival and God's Presence

The Old Testament portrays revival in terms of God bringing to life: "This is what the Sovereign Lord says to these bones: I will make breath enter you, and you will come to life. I will attach tendons to you and make flesh come upon you and cover you with skin; I will put breath in you, and you will come to life. Then you will know that I am the Lord" (Ezek 37:5–6). Even for dead and dried out bones, the divine breath makes alive! But long before Ezekiel prophesied those words for Israel's renewal, Adam was the first to experience the kind of creation-revival that God is capable of. In the garden, the Creator breathed his own sacred breath into Adam's nostrils, commanding that lifeless body—*Be alive! Live!* (Gen 2:7).

Today, revival comes when the breath of God enters his church in a fresh, new way, reminding us of the paradise of Eden, as if to tell us that he's been here all along. But just as God gave Adam the greatest gift of divine breath and Adam soon rebelled against his Maker, we too can easily allow the truth of God's breath within us to slip away from our minds and ministries. Through revival, God reminds us that we are called to draw upon the sacred breath, even his Holy Presence, moment by moment. As Christians, we live with *Sacred Breath* within us, which is another way to translate the phrase *Holy Spirit*. So "let us keep in step with the Spirit" as he walks us back to Eden to once again draw upon the breath of God and the Edenic presence (Gal 5:25).

Now I must ask you, dear Christian, *Do you know that the breath of God lives in you?* His breath is holy and sacred; he is the Holy Breath, the Holy Wind, the Holy Spirit! It's time for the church to declare once again that we possess more than mere flesh and dust, not unlike Adam's body before God breathed in and commanded life. We must remind ourselves that we are the sacred representation of God, holy and set apart unto eternal life in the very presence of our Maker. As the people of God, we breathe in and release his Sacred Breath to a lost and dying world (cf. John 6:63). When we open our eyes to the reality that God is restoring the Edenic fellowship to us, we can walk in the reality of Eden once again and expect the visible manifestations of the life of God who conquers all of the distance of sin and death.

I'm not suggesting that we should elevate the person of the Spirit above the Father and Son, but we must apprehend the reality that we are forever indwelt and infilled with divine breath—even the triune fellowship of God! The first requirement of revival is knowing confidently that the distance is gone and God is in us: interpenetrating, infilling, intertwined, and embedded within and throughout our new nature. Because God shares his presence with us, we belong to him and he belongs to us. Paul asks the question, "Do you not know that your bodies are temples of the Holy Spirit, who is in you, whom you have received from God?" (1 Cor 6:19). If we aren't living in that knowledge, Paul also exhorts, "Examine yourselves to see whether you are in the faith; test yourselves. Do you not realize that Christ Jesus is in you—unless, of course, you fail the test?" (2 Cor 13:5).

In Eden, God's presence was with people, and he entrusted them with the responsibility to represent his presence throughout the creation. In Eden, the earth was not cursed but had to yield to the commands of human beings as God's vice-regents; even nature was under man's control in the garden. But after the garden, people never again enjoyed such divine blessing until Jesus Christ restored humanity's Edenic power in his own earthly flesh. Jesus rebuked the wind and rain and it obeyed him; he commanded nature and it fell into submission! Because Jesus remained under God's authority and power, he manifested that original human-given power of vice-regency that was granted in Eden. Jesus knew that he lived in the supernatural—not mere flesh but endued with the sacred breath that was first breathed into humankind in the garden. Jesus now reserves the right to transfer that reminder of Edenic power to the church on certain occasions: on occasions of revival and renewal.

We can proudly acknowledge that God calls believers his true church, the people of God redeemed for an inheritance of a new paradise with him, a new heaven and earth being prepared for the end of the age. The exceptional and extraordinary miracles and signs that we experience during revival remind us that the triune God truly is present with his church and that he's restoring to us a reflection of Eden and "thy kingdom come." The miracles of revival are powers of the coming age, the experience of the church living in the "already but not yet" foretaste of an imminent kingdom.

During seasons of revival when we anticipate greater works and powers of the age to come, Jesus speaks to the human spirit and says, *Wake up! Live!* Remember that you are no longer mere flesh but have been baptized in the Sacred Ghost, the Holy Breath of God for new life. Revival comes to the church, not when we enter into something new, but when we surrender to Jesus and the word he's been speaking since the church's inception: "And surely I am with you always, to the very end of the age" (Matt 28:20). Jesus was declaring that he had restored the Edenic presence of God to his people once and for all, such that the church now forever bears a new breath—revival breath—even the revival presence of God!

Revival heightens our awareness of the manifest presence of God in our midst, but, along with that presence, comes boldness to declare that God truly is with us. Revival is not a new work of God but a refresher. Revival bestows a willingness and obedience to clothe ourselves with God's power for boldness to declare the good news. We are bold because he is near! During revival, he reminds us of what has always been true: that divine presence is in our midst both to enjoy and to accomplish his earthly mission. We might even say that the divine mission is ultimately the reason that the church bears his presence.[18]

God has removed the distance that preceded those dreadful words that he spoke to Adam in the garden, "Where are you?" (Gen 3:9). In principle, Jesus Christ has defeated the serpent and every enemy, even death. Every metaphor of the New Testament, from redemption to ransom, from propitiation to salvation, all point to the reality that the distance between God and his church is overcome. Now it's time for the church to live in that reality! We can be a bold witness because the testimony of Scripture is true: God is with us and is forever open to giving us increasingly more of his experiential, and even manifest, presence. Jesus promised that believers, as incarnational representatives, would be the vehicles for a powerful divine ministry: "Very truly I tell you, whoever believes in me will do the works I have been doing, and they will do even greater things than these, because I am going to the Father" (John 14:12). Because Jesus has ascended to his throne and poured out God's presence for all time, we will experience those "greater works" even in the context of miraculous revival.

For the believer, God will never again ask the question, *Where are you?* We can now reckon dead this body of dust and declare that we are no

---

18. One scholar, writing on pentecostal experience in Singapore, captures the sober reality that God's presence is with us to continue the mission. Tan-chow remarks, "Spirit-capacitated participation in the life of the triune God is polyphonic. It involves not just indwelling divine presence, but also continuing the divine mission begun by Jesus. The enabling operation of the Spirit is two-directional: witness and edification. Unlike the intermittent presence and activity of the Spirit in the OT, the coming of the outpoured Spirit-Paraclete will rest upon and indwell the disciples permanently ([John] 14:6f.). The sending of the Spirit-Paraclete to the disciples is for them to continue his work, even 'greater works,...' (14:12)" (May Ling, *Pentecostal Theology*, 107). Right now, in this generation, the opportunity is open before us to say yes to God's presence with us, knowing that our ministries and gifts are two-directional: for the charismatic *edification* of God's people, and to incarnationally *witness* the life of God's presence to a dying world.

longer the fleshly body that was cast out of an Eden guarded by "cherubim and a flaming sword" (Gen 3:24). Instead, we are a new creation, new in spirit, now living in the presence of divine life without distance. Armed with God's presence, we are his flaming sword to this generation, battling victoriously against sin and death. When the church becomes aware of this in any generation, we can experience the first-fruits of Eden and the fullness of divine life as revival is released upon the land.

Revival and Tribulation

Although pockets of revival exist everywhere in the world, the worldwide church may yet experience together another great revival before Jesus returns to establish his kingdom. In both Mark 13 and Matthew 24, after the disciples ask Jesus when the temple would be destroyed, he begins to describe great tribulation. But Jesus also prepares his disciples for this by assuring them that "whenever you are arrested and brought to trial, do not worry beforehand about what to say. Just say whatever is given you at the time, for it is not you speaking, but the Holy Spirit" (Mark 13:11; cf. Matt 10:19–20). Jesus expressly warns his twelve disciples—not a future generation—to prepare themselves for the tribulation that they will experience. But because tribulation is repeated throughout the history of the church until Jesus returns, every generation can rely upon the faithful breath of the Holy Spirit that Jesus promises here.

This passage assures us that even in the midst of a degree of tribulation, even *great* tribulation, the potential for revival always exists—namely, sharing in the presence of the Holy Spirit. Jesus was essentially promising his disciples that there will be periods of tribulation in which they will have a heightened awareness of God's holy presence. In their suffering, they will experience an elevated sensitivity to the fact that they are not alone but dwell in the divine presence, such that they will not need to resort to the flesh for a defense. Instead, God himself will testify on their behalf! The Sacred Breath will anoint their breath to speak, and the Lord will speak to them and through them—to us and through us!

It is in the face of suffering for the sake of Jesus' name that we can be most assured that the Spirit will be at work. Perhaps one of the tragedies of Western Christianity is the comfort and convenience of being free from much persecution. That comfort can relieve us of the need for power to persevere, but it can also steal from us God's glorious presence in revival, that gentle shower that comes after the storm. Whatever tribulation lies ahead for the church, there might yet be another great revival for us to experience in the midst of it.

At last, after the great revival of God's Edenic presence, he will soon return to establish a new heaven and a new earth, the true Eden forever restored to God and his community. The presence of God will never again be under assault! But until then, we hold fast to the words that the divine presence still speaks: Ἀμήν. ἔρχου, κύριε Ἰησοῦ. "Amen. Come, Lord Jesus" (Rev 22:20).

Conclusion

The presence of God should become so personal to our sense of being that we won't settle for anything less than a full awareness of his presence in our lives. But this commitment requires a revival of sorts and the awakening of the heart to the realization that our belonging is in God and we are his children: "And they shall be my people, and I will be their God" (Ezek 37:23). And because we belong to him, he shares everything with us: his heart, his world, himself, his Son, his Spirit, his plans, his work, his power, and his glory. After we realize that life is about sharing ourselves with God, the only thing left is to know him more intimately every day. Simply put, to know Jesus Christ is to know God, because he is the precise image and perfect representation of the Godhead, especially in his humanity.

Jesus reveals to us a God who is not so far away or unlike us that he cannot relate to us as other people do. In fact, God made human nature compatible with the divine nature so that he could become one of us and share himself in the most profound way. God could not have shared the divine nature any more personally than he did when he became one of us; indeed, he became one of us in order to share himself most fully with us. Yet even after Jesus came, the church still didn't fully understand God's presence in the world, but we do know that Jesus gives a face to it and makes it possible for us to truly know God. Jesus reveals our God to us, Jesus sends the precious gift of the Spirit, and Jesus gives his people new and abundant life in the presence of our God.

Sharing in God's Presence means that we can experience God just as Moses did when his face glowed brightly after he came down off the mountain. What a revival that would be—and very much within our reach! Rather than something unattainable, Moses' glory manifested the reality of being in relationship with God. God was simply sharing his glory with his friend Moses, as we would open up and share aspects of our lives with our friends. That kind of revival can begin when a single heart allows itself to be awakened to the glorious intimacy of knowing Jesus Christ and sharing in his presence.

Bibliography

Aland, Kurt. *Did the Early Church Baptize Infants?* Translated by G.R. Beasley-Murray. London: SCM, 1963.
Alexander, T. D. *From Paradise to Promised Land: An Introduction to the Pentateuch.* 2nd ed. Grand Rapids: Baker Academic, 2002.
Archer, Kenneth J. *The Gospel Revisited: Towards a Pentecostal Theology of Worship and Witness.* Eugene, OR: Pickwick, 2011.
Aune, D. E. *Prophecy in Early Christianity and the Ancient Mediterranean World.* Grand Rapids: Eerdmans, 1983.
Barth, Karl. *Church Dogmatics.* 2/1: *The Doctrine of God.* Translated by T. H. L. Parker et al. New York: T & T Clark, 1940.
Barton, Stephen C. "1 Corinthians." In *Eerdmans Commentary on the Bible,* edited by James D.G. Dunn and James W. Rogerson, 1314–52. Grand Rapids: Eerdmans, 2003.
Basinger, David. *The Case for Freewill Theism: A Philosophical Assessment.* Downers Grove: InterVarsity, 1996.
Bauer, Walter, Frederick W. Danker, W. F. Arndt, and F. W. Gingrich. Greek-English Lexicon of the New Testament and Other Early Christian Literature. 3rd ed. Chicago: University of Chicago Press, 2000.
Baumert, Norbert. "'Charism' and 'Spirit-Baptism': Presentation of an Analysis." *Journal of Pentecostal Theology* 12:2 (2004) 147–79.
Beilby, James, and Paul R. Eddy, eds. *The Nature of the Atonement: Four Views.* Downers Grove: IVP Academic, 2006.
Belleville, Linda. "1 Timothy." In *Cornerstone Biblical Commentary,* edited by Philip W. Comfort, 25–123. Carol Streams: Tyndale, 2009.
Berding, Kenneth. *What Are Spiritual Gifts? Rethinking the Conventional View.* Grand Rapids: Kregel, 2006.
Boadt, Lawrence. *Reading the Old Testament: An Introduction.* Mahwah, NJ: Paulist, 1984.
Boer, Harry R. *A Short History of the Early Church.* Grand Rapids: Eerdmans, 1976.
Bonhoeffer, Dietrich. *Creation and Fall: A Theological Exposition of Genesis 1–3.* Minneapolis: Fortress, 2004.
Boyd, Gregory A. *God of the Possible: A Biblical Introduction to the Open View of God.* Grand Rapids: Baker, 2000.
———. *Is God to Blame? Beyond Pat Answers to the Problem of Evil.* Downers Grove: InterVarsity, 2003.
Brand, Chad Owen, and R. Stanton Norman, eds. *Perspectives on Church Government: Five Views of Church Polity.* Nashville: B&H Academic, 2004.

Bibliography

Bray, Gerald. *God is Love: A Biblical and Systematic Theology*. Wheaton: Crossway, 2012.

Brueggemann, Walter. *An Introduction to the Old Testament: The Canon and Christian Imagination*. Louisville: Westminster John Knox, 2003.

Bruner, Frederick Dale. *The Gospel of John: A Commentary*. Grand Rapids: Eerdmans, 2012.

Burgess, S. M. *The Holy Spirit: Ancient Christian Traditions*. Peabody: Hendrickson, 1984.

Cahalan, Kathleen A. *Introducing the Practice of Ministry*. Collegeville, MN: Order of Saint Benedict, 2010.

Calvin, John. *Institutes of the Christian Religion: 1536 Edition*. Translated by Ford Lewis Battles. Grand Rapids: Eerdmans, 1986.

Campbell, R. Alastair. *The Elders: Seniority within Earliest Christianity*. Studies of the New Testament and Its World. Edinburgh: T & T Clark, 1994.

Campbell, Ted A. *Methodist Doctrine: The Essentials*. Nashville: Abingdon, 1999.

Collins, Raymond F. *1 and 2 Timothy and Titus: A Commentary*. The New Testament Library. Louisville: Westminster John Knox, 2002.

Curnock, Nehemiah, ed. *The Journal of Rev. John Wesley, A.M.* Vol. 2. London: Epworth, 1938.

Dent, Donald T. *The Ongoing Role of Apostles in Missions: The Forgotten Foundation*. Bloomington, IN: CrossBooks, 2011.

Dunn, James D. G. *The Acts of the Apostles*. Valley Forge: Trinity, 1996.

Duvall, Robert, Farrah Fawcett, John Beasley, and June Carter Cash. *The Apostle*. DVD. Written and directed by Robert Duvall. United States: October Films, 1997.

Engle, Paul E., and Steven B. Cowan, eds. *Who Runs the Church? 4 Views on Church Government*. Grand Rapids: Zondervan, 2004.

Fee, Gordon D. *God's Empowering Presence: The Holy Spirit in the Letters of Paul*. Peabody, MA: Hendrickson, 1994.

Feuerbach, Ludwig. *The Essence of Christianity*. Translated by George Eliot. Amherst, NY: Prometheus, 1989.

Fiddes, Paul S. *Participating in God: A Pastoral Doctrine of the Trinity*. Louisville: Westminster John Knox, 2000.

Flood, Derek. "A Relational Understanding of Atonement." In *Relational Theology: A Contemporary Introduction*, edited by Brint Montgomery et al., 40–42. Eugene, OR: Wipf & Stock, 2012.

Gabriel, Andrew K. *The Lord is the Spirit: The Holy Spirit and Divine Attributes*. Eugene, OR: Pickwick, 2011.

Garland, David E. *1 Corinthians: Baker Exegetical Commentary on the New Testament*. Grand Rapids: Baker Academic, 2003.

Gee, Donald. *Spiritual Gifts in the Work of Ministry Today*. Springfield: Gospel, 1963.

Grant, Jamie A. "Spirit and Presence in Psalm 139." In *Presence, Power, and Promise: The Role of the Spirit of God in the Old Testament*, edited by David G. Firth and Paul D. Wegner, 135–46. Downers Grove: IVP Academic, 2011.

Grudem, Wayne. *The Gift of Prophecy in the New Testament and Today*. Rev. ed. Wheaton: Crossway, 2000.

———. *Systematic Theology: An Introduction to Biblical Theology*. Grand Rapids: Zondervan, 1994.

Guy, Laurie. *Introducing Early Christianity: A Topical Survey of Its Life, Beliefs, and Practice*. Downers Grove: InterVarsity, 2004.

Bibliography

Hart, Larry. "Spirit Baptism: A Dimensional Charismatic Perspective." In *Perspectives on Spirit Baptism: Five Views*, edited by Chad Owen Brand, 105–80. Nashville: Broadman & Holman, 2004.

Harvey, Dean H. *Ransom: The High Cost of Sin*. United States: Xulon Press, 2010.

Hasker, William. "An Adequate God." In *Searching for an Adequate God: A Dialogue Between Process and Free Will Theists*, edited by John B. Cobb Jr. and Clark H. Pinnock, 215–45. Grand Rapids: Eerdmans, 2000.

———. *God in an Open Universe: Science, Metaphysics, and Open Theism*. Eugene, OR: Pickwick, 2011.

Hayford, Jack. "Despise Not Prophecy." In *Understanding the Fivefold Ministry*, edited by Matthew D. Green, 79–84. Lake Mary, FL: Charisma, 2005.

Hesselgrave, David. *Paradigms in Conflict: 10 Key Questions in Christian Missions Today*. Grand Rapids: Kregel, 2005.

Hill, David. *New Testament Prophecy*. New Foundations Theological Library. Atlanta: John Knox, 1979.

Hoke, Steve, and Bill Taylor. *Global Mission Handbook: A Guide for Crosscultural Service*. Downers Grove: InterVarsity, 2009.

Humphreys, W. Lee. *The Character of God in the Book of Genesis: A Narrative Appraisal*. Louisville: Westminster John Knox, 2001.

Hundley, Michael B. *Keeping Heaven on Earth: Safeguarding the Divine Presence in the Priestly Tabernacle*. Tübingen, Germany: Mohr Siebeck, 2011.

Jersak, Brad, and Michael Hardin, eds. *Stricken by God?: Nonviolent Identification and the Victory of Christ*. Abbotsford, B.C.: Fresh Wind, 2007.

Keener, Craig S. *The Gospel of Matthew: A Socio-rhetorical Commentary*. Grand Rapids: Eerdmans, 2009.

———. "Power of Pentecost: Luke's Missiology in Acts 1–2." *Asian Journal of Pentecostal Studies* 12:1 (2009) 47–74.

Kindelberger, Roy D. *God's Absence and the Charismatic Presence: Inquiries in Openness Theology*. Eugene, OR: Wipf & Stock, 2017.

Kline, Meredith. "Primal Parousia." *Westminster Theological Journal* 40.2 (1978) 244–80.

Kydd, R. A. N. *Charismatic Gifts in the Early Church*. Peabody: Hendrickson, 1984.

Lewis, J. "Baptismal Practices of the Second and Third Century Church." *Restoration Quarterly* 26:1 (1983) 1–17.

Lloyd-Jones, David Martyn. *Revival*. Wheaton: Crossway, 1987.

Louth, Andrew. *Introducing Eastern Orthodox Theology*. Downers Grove: InterVarsity, 2013.

Marguerat, Daniel. *The First Christian Historian: Writing the 'Acts of the Apostles.'* Translated by Ken McKinney et al. Society for New Testament Studies Monograph Series 121. Cambridge: Cambridge University Press, 2002.

Mathews, Kenneth A. *Genesis 1–11:26*. The New American Commentary: An Exegetical and Theological Exposition of Holy Scripture 1A. Nashville: Broadman & Holman, 1996.

May Ling, Tan-Chow. *Pentecostal Theology for the Twenty-First Century: Engaging with Multi-Faith Singapore*. Burlington, VT: Ashgate, 2007.

Menzies, Robert P. *Empowered for Witness: The Spirit in Luke-Acts*. Sheffield, England: Sheffield Academic, 2001.

Merkle, Benjamin L. *40 Questions About Elders and Deacons*. Grand Rapids: Kregel, 2008.

Bibliography

———. *The Elder and Overseer: One Office in the Early Church.* New York: Peter Lang, 2003.

Migliore, Daniel L. *Faith Seeking Understanding: An Introduction to Christian Theology.* Grand Rapids: Eerdmans, 1991.

Moltmann, Jürgen. *The Spirit of Life: A Universal Affirmation.* Translated by Margaret Kohl. Minneapolis: Fortress, 2001.

Newton, Phil A. *Elders in Congregational Life: Rediscovering the Biblical Model for Church Leadership.* Grand Rapids: Kregel, 2005.

Ngewa, Samuel M. *1 and 2 Timothy and Titus.* Africa Bible and Commentary Series. Grand Rapids: HippoBooks, 2009.

Outler, Albert C., ed. *The Works of John Wesley.* Bicentennial ed. Vol. 1, *Sermons I (1–30).* Nashville: Abingdon Press, 1984.

Pannenberg, Wolfhart. *Systematic Theology.* Translated by Geoffrey W. Bromiley. Vol. 1. New York: T. and T. Clark, 2004.

Payton Jr., James R. *Light from the Christian East: An Introduction to the Orthodox Tradition.* Downers Grove: InterVarsity, 2007.

Pinnock, Clark H. *Most Moved Mover: A Theology of God's Openness.* Carlisle: Paternoster, 2002.

———, et al. *The Openness of God: A Biblical Challenge to the Traditional Understanding of God.* Downers Grove: InterVarsity, 1994.

Pool, Jeff B. *God's Wounds: Hermeneutic of the Christian Symbol of Divine Suffering.* Vol. 1, *Divine Vulnerability and Creation.* Eugene, OR: Pickwick, 2009.

Ruthven, Jon. *On the Cessation of the Charismata: The Protestant Polemic on Postbiblical Miracles.* Sheffield, England: Sheffield Academic, 1993.

Sanders, John. *The God Who Risks: A Theology of Divine Providence.* Downers Grove: InterVarsity, 1998.

Schmitt, Harley H. *Many Gifts One Lord: A Biblical Understanding of the Variety of Spiritual Gifts Among Early Christians and in the Church Today.* Fairfax: Xulon Press, 2002.

Schreiner, Thomas R. *New Testament Theology: Magnifying God in Christ.* Grand Rapids: Baker Academic, 2008.

Stein, Robert H. "Baptism in Luke-Acts." In *Believer's Baptism: Sign of the New Covenant in Christ,* edited by Thomas D. Schreiner and Shawn D. Wright, 35–66. NAC Studies in Bible and Theology. Nashville: B&H Academic, 2006.

Stronstad, Roger. *The Prophethood of All Believers: A Study in Luke's Charismatic Theology.* New York: Sheffield Academic, 2004.

Swinburne, Richard. *The Coherence of Theism.* Oxford: Clarendon, 1977.

Terrien, Samuel. *The Elusive Presence: The Heart of Biblical Theology.* Religious Perspectives 26. San Francisco: Harper & Row, 1983.

Thiselton, Anthony C. *The Holy Spirit—In Biblical Teaching, Through the Centuries, and Today.* Grand Rapids: Eerdmans, 2013.

Thomas, Robert L. *Understanding Spiritual Gifts: A Verse-by-verse Study of 1 Corinthians 12–14.* Rev. ed. Grand Rapids: Kregel, 1999.

Tiessen, Terrance. *Providence and Prayer: How Does God Work in the World?* Downers Grove: InterVarsity, 2000.

Turner, Charles V. *Biblical Bible Translating.* United States: Lightning Source, 2001.

Wagner, C. Peter. *Apostles Today: Biblical Government for Biblical Power.* Ventura, CA: Regal, 2006.

Bibliography

Wallace, Daniel B. *Greek Grammar beyond the Basics: An Exegetical Syntax of the New Testament*. Grand Rapids: Zondervan, 1996.

Wesley, John. *A Plain Account of Christian Perfection, As Believed and Taught by the Rev. John Wesley, From the Year 1725, To the Year 1727*. New York: Lane and Scott, 1850.

Westermann, Claus. *Genesis 1–11: A Commentary*. Translated by John J. Scullion. Minneapolis: Fortress, 1984.

Williams, J. Rodman. *Renewal Theology: Systematic Theology from a Charismatic Perspective*. Grand Rapids: Zondervan, 1996.

Wink, Walter. *Engaging the Powers: Discernment and Resistance in a World of Domination*. Minneapolis: Fortress, 1992.

Witherington III, Ben. *The Acts of the Apostles: A Socio-Rhetorical Commentary*. Grand Rapids: Eerdmans, 1998.

———, and Darlene Hyatt. *Paul's Letter to the Romans: A Socio-Rhetorical Commentary*. Grand Rapids: Eerdmans, 2004.

Wright, Christopher J. H. *Knowing the Holy Spirit through the Old Testament*. Downers Grove: InterVarsity, 2006.

Yong, Amos. "Relational Theology and the Holy Spirit." In *Relational Theology: A Contemporary Introduction*, edited by Brint Montgomery et al., 18–20. Eugene, OR: Wipf & Stock, 2012.

Young, Edward J. "The Interpretation of Gen. 1:2." *Westminster Theological Journal* 23:2 (1961) 151–78.

www.ingramcontent.com/pod-product-compliance
Lightning Source LLC
Chambersburg PA
CBHW071453150426
43191CB00008B/1335